PROJECT MANAGEMENT
QuickStart Guide®

PROJECT MANAGEMENT

QuickStart Guide®

The Simplified Beginner's Guide to Precise Planning, Strategic Resource Management, and Delivering World-Class Results

Chris Croft

Editors: Bryan Basamanowicz, Jesse Hassenger, Marilyn Burkley
Cover Illustration and Design: Katie Donnachie, Nicole Daberkow, Copyright © 2022 by ClydeBank Media LLC
Interior Design & Illustrations: Katie Donnachie, Brittney Duquette, Copyright © 2022 by ClydeBank Media LLC

First Edition - Last Updated: July 4, 2023

ISBN: 9781636100586 (paperback) | 9781636100609 (hardcover) | 9781636100593 (ebook) | 9781636100623 (audiobook) | 9781636100616 (spiral bound)

Publisher's Cataloging-In-Publication Data
(Prepared by The Donohue Group, Inc.)
Names: Croft, Chris, author.
Title: Project management QuickStart guide : the simplified beginner's guide to precise planning, strategic resource management, and delivering world-class results / Chris Croft.
Other Titles: Project management Quick Start guide
Description: [Albany, New York] : ClydeBank Business, [2022] | Series: QuickStart Guide | Includes bibliographical references and index.
Identifiers: ISBN 9781636100586 (paperback) | ISBN 9781636100609 (hardcover) | ISBN 9781636100616 (spiral bound) | ISBN 9781636100593 (ebook)
Subjects: LCSH: Project management. | Strategic planning. | Conflict management.
Classification: LCC HD69.P75 C76 2022 (print) | LCC HD69.P75 (ebook) | DDC 658.404--dc23

Library of Congress Control Number: 2022933400

Author ISNI: 0000 0000 3547 0767

For bulk sales inquiries, please visit www.go.quickstartguides.com/wholesale, email us at orders@clydebankmedia.com, or call 800-340-3069. Special discounts are available on quantity purchases by corporations, associations, and others.

OVER
850,000

READERS **LOVE** *QuickStart Guides.*

Really well written with lots of practical information. These books have a very concise way of presenting each topic and everything inside is very actionable!

— ALAN F.

The book was a great resource, every page is packed with information, but [the book] never felt overly-wordy or repetitive. Every chapter was filled with very useful information.

— CURTIS W.

I appreciated how accessible and how insightful the material was and look forward to sharing the knowledge that I've learned [from this book].

— SCOTT B.

After reading this book, I must say that it has been one of the best decisions of my life!

— ROHIT R.

This book is one-thousand percent worth every single dollar!

— HUGO C.

The read itself was worth the cost of the book, but the additional tools and materials make this purchase a better value than most books.

— JAMES D.

I finally understand this topic ... this book has really opened doors for me!

— MISTY A.

Contents

PART V – SUPERCHARGE YOUR PROJECT MANAGEMENT SKILLS

BEFORE YOU START READING, DOWNLOAD YOUR FREE DIGITAL ASSETS!

 Project Brief Template

 Monthly Monitoring Form

 Six Cost Performance Scenarios

 Risk Assessment Template

TWO WAYS TO ACCESS YOUR FREE DIGITAL ASSETS

Use the camera app on your mobile phone to scan the QR code
or visit the link below and instantly access your digital assets.

or

go.quickstartguides.com/project

 SCAN ME

💻 VISIT URL

Introduction

They say necessity is the mother of invention.

I wrote this book because when I started out in project management, nothing like this existed. If you are like I was, a busy professional who doesn't necessarily have "project manager" in your job title but who is still asked to manage projects from time to time, then it's really hard to know where to begin. How on earth are you supposed to pull the project off in time and on budget when you have all your other day-to-day work to stay on top of? It's stressful. But it's also not as if you can say no—right?

Maybe you decided to have a cursory look at some of the books and online courses devoted to the topic. If so, then you already know that project management is notoriously complex. At least, teaching it can be. So much to learn, so many moving parts, complex math, and mind-numbing terminology—all those TLAs! (that's short for three-letter abbreviations).

And yet it really doesn't have to be.

When I started reading about project management, I wasn't satisfied with the books I encountered. They were either too complex—almost as if the author was intentionally overcomplicating the subject—or addressing project management theory without speaking much to real work experience from the field.

Don't get me wrong, some of the books were amazing, some had some great ideas and information. They just all seemed to be directed toward people who were doing projects all the time. But I was a busy manager doing the stuff I was employed to do for my day job, with a few projects thrown in each year to keep it interesting! I couldn't locate the book that spoke to me. I wasn't interested in gaining a PhD in project management but instead wanted a simple, proven system that would work all the time.

My mission ever since has been focused not so much on adding to my project management knowledge, but on gathering it all up and cutting it back, leaving only the stuff that matters most. Only the stuff that works.

I began assembling this material in online courses. In fact, I'm proud to note that I have the most-viewed online project management course in the world, called *Project Management Simplified* (2021). Last time I checked, I had over ten million students. I'm stunned by those numbers every time I look—and while I'm proud of my work in the field, my success mostly tells me that the approach of cutting back and paring down project management knowledge is something lots of people want and need.

So when I was approached to write a book on project management, I was thrilled. It has been on my bucket list for years, but I am so busy running training programs or visiting clients and helping them to master project management that taking the time out to write a book has always gotten bumped off the priority list. Until now.

This is the book I wish I could have read when I began my career in project management. It's the boiled-down essence of what you need to know about the subject that will allow you to manage any project, of any size, with any budget, and without the angst. *Project Management QuickStart Guide* isn't a magic wand, but it's as close as you will get without abducting Harry Potter.

It doesn't cover the mathematics or the theories or complex algorithms. It just focuses on what works. Simple, easy-to-do processes that can transform any project brief into a detailed project plan and Gantt chart (a type of horizontal bar chart that visualizes the project schedule). No fancy software required, just a packet of Post-its and good old Excel.

Imagine that you are asked by your boss to lead a new project. Instead of pretending you know what you're doing and stressing about it until it's done, you have a clear road map. And you have the tools and understanding to push back with confidence if your planning finds problems. It's very hard to argue with a well-constructed, logical plan. Planning always makes you stronger.

So relax your project management fears: by the time you've finished this book, you will know exactly where to start and how to progress through a clear 12-step project management process without any unnecessary complexity or jargon. The process I'm going to show you is a process that works, regardless of whether you're set to begin your first project or your hundredth.

Let's get started!

Chapter by Chapter

The book is divided into five parts. Part I is an overview of project management, what projects are, and the various methodologies. Part I also covers step 1 of the 12-step process: define the project. Part II is about itemizing all the tasks involved and finding the optimal path for their execution (steps 2–4). Part III is where your carefully laid plans must adapt and conform to the realities at hand (steps 5–8). Part IV covers what to do once the project starts (steps 9–12). And finally, part V explores how to supercharge your project management skills by taking on bigger projects, avoiding common mistakes, paying attention to the people involved, and, for those who want to do project management full time, reviewing the qualifications available.

» **PART I: Project Management Overview**

» Chapter 1, "What Is a Project?" is intended to give the reader a clearer understanding of exactly what a project is, making the distinction between projects and processes. All projects share three characteristics: they have a finish line, they aim to deliver change or something new, and they contain benefits that are reaped in the future. Chapter 1 clarifies when project management is essential: when there are more than ten tasks, when the project involves more than three people, or when the project will take longer than three weeks to complete. If any of these three is true, a proven project management process is essential.

» Chapter 2, "Overview of Project Management Methodologies," is exactly that, looking at the main options that include the Project Management Institute's (PMI) body of knowledge known as the *PMBOK Guide*, and also PRINCE2 and Agile. Of the three, PMBOK is the best, but it is extensive and sometimes overly complicated. This book is therefore focused on a slimmed-down version of PMBOK, which I'm calling PMBOK Lite. Chapter 2 also briefly explores the various software platforms that are available to assist project managers. But don't worry, all you need is Excel.

» Chapter 3, "Define the Project (Step 1)," is the start of my 12-step project management process. Projects are usually defined in the first kick-off meeting, where stakeholders (usually customer or boss) will explain what they want, by when, and for what budget.

» **PART II: Mapping Out the Ideal Plan**

» Chapter 4, "List the Tasks (Step 2)," explores the various methods for ensuring that you create a complete list of tasks for your project. This is a critical step because any missed tasks have the capacity to alter the timeline and the budget. It's also important to get the granularity right. In other words, the task must be broken down far enough so that one person or one team can be responsible for each task but not so far as to unnecessarily complicate the project plan.

This chapter also explores the difference between bottom-up and top-down planning and the pros and cons of each.

» Chapter 5, "Set the Running Order (Step 3)," introduces you to the idea of network diagrams as a way to visualize the project. This can be done using Post-it notes, a super-simple way to set the running order for the tasks in your project so you can see what follows what and which tasks can be done at the same time. This chapter also explains the two major network diagram methodologies, critical path method (CPM) and project evaluation and review technique (PERT), and explores why I believe CPM is better and easier to use than PERT.

» Chapter 6, "Put Estimates on the Tasks (Step 4)," explains how to add time estimates to a network diagram using the smart estimating technique I've developed, which in turn helps you work out the critical path for your project. I'll also explain the whats, hows, and whys of the critical path, which lets you know the minimum amount of time it will take to complete a project.

» **Part III: Adjusting the Plan for Reality**

» Chapter 7, "Crash the Plan (Step 5)," explores your options if the timeline and/or costs you arrive at after step 4 are more than the stakeholders were hoping for. If you need to speed up the project, then you will need to focus on crashing—or speeding up—the tasks on the critical path.

» Chapter 8, "Gantt Charts (Step 6)," is the heart of the book and outlines why the organizational tools called Gantt charts are so useful for project managers. Not only do they take project visualization to a whole new level, but they also improve communication and allow for better resource planning, efficient progress monitoring, and improved financial management. This chapter shows you how to make quick and easy Gantt charts that will then direct your plan.

» Chapter 9, "Resource Planning (Step 7)," examines how to add resource allocations to your Gantt chart, drilling down into the resources you will need to make sure you have access to what you need when you need it. Chapter 9 gives you options for what to do if you have a shortfall of resources on one project and what to do if you have a shortfall across multiple projects. It also introduces you to the Gantt of Gantts—a Gantt chart that allows you to see all your projects on one page or screen. It's unique to this book, and I know you'll love it.

» Chapter 10, "Risk Planning (Step 8)," covers how to assess your plan for risk. First you need to identify as many of the project's risks as possible. Look at past projects or brainstorm with the project team. By scoring those risks based on likelihood and severity, you can arrive at a weighted risk factor that can be communicated to stakeholders.

» **PART IV: Managing the Implementation of Your Project**

» Chapter 11, "Monitor Progress (Step 9)," takes you back to your Gantt chart. Steps 1 through 8 have been about planning the project. If you reach Step 9, then you have been given the green light from the stakeholder and will have to deliver the project. Keeping the Gantt chart up to date and colored-in to indicate progress allows you to know exactly where the project is at any given moment. If the communications plan has not been agreed on prior to step 9, then now is the time to confirm how the stakeholders want to be informed of progress and how often.

» Chapter 12, "Monitor Costs (Step 10)," ensures that you as the project manager are looking at complete data on the project. "Spend so far" is important, but to get a full picture of the project, that spend must be married with progress so far. Only by looking at the progress on the Gantt chart and the required resources (also on the Gantt chart) will you be able to appreciate how the project is really going. First you need to know what's happening now, and based on that you can estimate what is likely to happen next. To do this effectively, you need to calculate the cost performance index (CPI) and the schedule performance index (SPI). I will show you a simpler and better way to measure SPI, unique to this book.

» Chapter 13, "Modify the Plan (Step 11)," explores what to do when you need to modify or adjust your plan. There are some golden rules to consider if you want to stay on the right side of the project owner: don't modify the plan too often; if you need to modify the plan, do so in the middle third of the project; and ask for more than you need. Use change request forms for any change that the stakeholder asks for—these are *their* modifications, not yours. Remember, all projects are challenging and almost none come in on time and on budget. There are always unforeseen issues that can force a recalibration. This chapter also covers options to consider if your project is running late or over budget.

» Chapter 14, "Review (Step 12)," covers the last but often forgotten final step. It is imperative that you review the project once it's over. This is rarely done, for seven understandable but ultimately incorrect reasons. The review should be done in a spirit of thanks and celebration—no finger pointing but simply a look at what went well and what could be improved upon. Documenting these reviews and keeping them in a central location allows everyone in the business to learn from every project.

» **PART V: Supercharge Your Project Management Skills**

» Chapter 15, "Planning of Larger Projects," looks at what happens when the projects you manage start to get bigger. Project management is a highly sought-after skill, and once you've mastered this 12-step process and have a few wins under your belt, it's inevitable that you will be asked to manage progressively larger projects; this chapter explores ways to feel more comfortable with that task.

» Chapter 16, "Top 10 Mistakes You'll Now Avoid," reviews the common mistakes, first introduced in other chapters, that you will be able to avoid now that you understand the 12-step process. Being aware of the mistakes ahead of time and having a process to ensure you avoid them will fast-track your progress and your career progression.

» Chapter 17, "Remember the People Side of Project Management," explores the thorny issue of people. The single most challenging part of any project is the people: having enough of them, getting them to do what they've committed to do at the right time, and holding them accountable is tough. This chapter explores the aspects of people management that make the biggest difference to project management success. It looks at communication skills, control, delegation, monitoring, motivation, and stretching others so that everyone benefits from the project and the experience.

» Chapter 18, "Managing a Project Manager," looks at what happens when you become so great at project management that you are asked to manage other project managers. The most important four words you can utter are "bring me the plan." By asking for the plan, you can immediately gauge where that project manager is and therefore the likely outcome of the project. More important, you still have the time to support or coach that project manager should the plan be nonexistent or not up to scratch. This chapter also explores some other great questions to ask your project manager.

» Finally, chapter 19, "Careers in Project Management," explores the options should you want to take project management further. This book is dedicated to those who are called on to manage projects from time to time as part of their everyday workload. More than likely, "project manager" is not part of your job title. But the 12-step process may inspire you to change that! This chapter covers the various project management qualifications, helping you to decide which ones are worth the effort.

PROJECT MANAGEMENT OVERVIEW

| 1 |
What Is a Project?

Chapter Overview
- » The basics
- » What constitutes a project
- » When is project management useful?

> *Expect the best, plan for the worst, and prepare to be surprised.*
> — DENIS WAITLEY

The evidence of successful projects is all around us. The car you drive was once a project. The airplane you board on your summer vacation was a project. Iconic buildings like the Eiffel Tower, the Sydney Opera House, the Empire State Building, and so many in between were, at one point, simply an idea or an aspiration. Each one was brought to life and made real by successful project management. But not all projects are high-flying examples of human ingenuity and creativity. Some are much more mundane and functional: the supermarket we visit for our weekly shopping, the street we walk down every day, and the gym we wish we visited a little more often are also examples of the projects that populate our lives. For the most part, we're not even aware of them. Our opinion of the finished result may be positive, negative, or indifferent, but the project itself is more neutral: a structured way of facilitating the delivery of change.

The speed and pace of those changes can be exhausting, particularly in businesses. We live in a VUCA world—one that is volatile, uncertain, complex, and ambiguous. And yet good project management can help to minimize those four VUCA components, allowing change to be delivered with a lot less angst. Change capability is an increasingly important part of any career, especially in the C-suite. After all, if nothing changed, we would hardly need management—especially not creative managers.

Because projects are such a vital part of life in general, they're certainly an especially vital part of any management job. It's impossible for a manager in any profession or industry, at any level, to avoid projects. If you're serious about developing your career, and you want to grow and improve the organization where you work, project management is essential. It is also a transferable skill, so once you master it you will be able to use it anywhere, in any business, at any level. It won't matter what you are tasked with creating or what change you are asked to bring about; your project management skills will ensure that you'll know what to do.

> *Operations keeps the lights on, strategy provides a light at the end of the tunnel, but project management is the train engine that moves the organization forward.*
>
> –JOY GUMZ

This *QuickStart Guide* is going to teach you everything you need to know to be able to run any project of any size in any industry, so that you can deliver all your projects on time and on budget.

Three Characteristics of a Project

If you think about what you do in the course of your daily working life, most of your activity will fall into the category of being either a project or a process. How do you tell the difference between the two? There are three characteristics that differentiate a project from a process (figure 1).

WHAT SEPARATES A PROJECT FROM A PROCESS?

fig. 1

A PROJECT HAS A FINISH LINE

A PROJECT INVOLVES SOMETHING NEW

A PROJECT DELIVERS A BENEFIT, BUT NOT STRAIGHT AWAY

A Project Has a Finish Line

Perhaps the most defining characteristic of a project is that it has an ending—in other words, there is a finish line. There will be a point in time when the hospital is built, or the office has relocated successfully into its new premises, or the vacation is over and your family is back home. This is not true for processes. Most of the activities that go on in a factory, call center, or hospital, for example, are endless. Those operating the machines in the factory do the same things over and over again, without the expectation that the daily work will no longer need to get done. Similarly, a call center has no finish line: inbound calls are answered and outbound calls are made, forever. That's the process. The activity ends only when an individual employee's shift is over or the center is closed for the evening; they start over again at the next shift, or the next morning. In a hospital there may be different patients and many more processes, but the same applies. There is no definitive halt in the supply of patients who need care. A hospital may engage in projects, like the building of a new radiology department, but the vast bulk of daily activity is focused on processes: checking in patients, examining patients, discharging patients.

Projects always have a conclusion. It can be either a completion date or a desired outcome. Of course, there are activities that muddy the waters slightly. For example, research may have a desired outcome; the finish line for cancer research may be to cure cancer. But the research, at least for the time being, is a process. A lot of research seems to go on indefinitely, like the exploring of a maze. Those involved never really know what they are going to find, so even the desired outcome or finish line may change.

But for the most part, projects have a very specific life span. They come into existence to deliver a specific outcome within a certain budget, ideally by a particular date. This is the exciting part of projects. The fact that there is a deadline with set deliverables that must be achieved means that projects, while challenging, can be the most interesting and engaging part of any management career.

There is always variety: new problems to solve and new wins to celebrate with the team. No two days are ever the same in project management. It's like having a new job every few weeks, or every time a new project comes around. And you get a feeling of achievement as each project is finished.

A Project Involves Something New

Change of any type, personal or professional, always involves creating or doing something new. This is part of the reason we often find change so challenging. It can feel uncomfortable and disorienting, and we will often want to retreat to our comfort zone.

Life begins at the end of your comfort zone.

– PETER HENDRICK SHARP

Because a project is a collection of tasks designed to bring about change, it can also cause discomfort, because we are asking ourselves or others to do or learn something new in order to bring about that change. Say you are tasked with installing a new customer relationship management (CRM) software system in your business; the software is going live on a set date and your job is to make sure the installation goes well, to ensure that everyone who will use it is given the necessary training, and to monitor the transition from the old system to the new. The people currently using the old system are probably quite happy with the process they have already learned and are using on a daily basis. They might not be thrilled about the new system because it calls for a change in their behavior. And that often feels like hard work.

Projects always involve making something new. It may be new to the world, like the 1969 Apollo 11 moon landing, or, more likely, it will be new to the team charged with delivering the project and the people on the receiving end of it.

When you move to a new house for the first time, it's a project. There are many things to consider. You need to pack up your belongings in a way that will make the move easier on the other side. This might include marking each box with the destination room so that the "kitchen" box is taken to the kitchen in your new home, rather than the bathroom. You need to set up a forwarding address for your mail, arrange to have the utilities turned off, and schedule the moving company for the right day. You need to make sure that you can move out of your old place and into your new home on the same day—or else you'll need to rent storage space. You need to say goodbye to the neighbors and do a final check in which you give the whole house one last sweep to make sure nothing has been left behind. Did you remember to check the loft or the garden shed? Moving is difficult and complicated, and you need to plan it.

But what if you move frequently? If you are in the military, or if you are a manager in a company that sends you overseas every few years, then moving no longer involves something new, and this usually entails a process. It has shifted from being a project, when you did it the first time, to a process, when you are packing up your tenth house in ten years. Even by your second move, you know what to do and what to expect. If you're frugal or environmentally conscious, you might even reuse the same boxes and bubble wrap. You call the same company to arrange the move, and you don't lose much sleep over the moving process anymore. It's still complicated, and there are still many moving parts, but your experience of moving means there are rarely any surprises and it's relatively straightforward.

You could think of the transition from project to process as a continuum (figure 2) in which a group of tasks that are all new, comprising a project, gets a score of 1 and a group of tasks that are all familiar, comprising a process, gets a score of 4.

PROJECT/PROCESS CONTINUUM

fig. 2

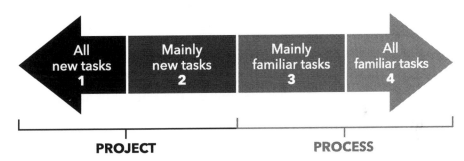

We are engaged in a project when we are seeking to deliver something that is completely or primarily new. It may be that we have experience with some aspects of the project, some familiarity with what's involved, but there are likely to be variations. Processes, on the other hand, are made up of the opposite: standard tasks and activities that we are already very familiar with. When we are engaged in processes, it's likely that we hardly have to think; our activity and effort are almost habitual.

Depending on the experience level of the contractor involved, building a highway bridge is probably three or four on the continuum. That's often why a particular contractor has won the bid—they've built many highway bridges before! All the tasks, or at least most of them, are already familiar;

they know what they're doing. If I'm booked for triple-bypass heart surgery, I really want it to be a process, almost routine. I want the doctor to be almost *bored* by the procedure because of the number of times they have successfully performed it. I certainly don't want my heart surgery to be a *project* for the doctor, the nurses, or the anesthesiologist. Sometimes novelty is not what's needed!

It's the novelty that can make projects feel daunting, but on the other hand, variety really is the spice of life. Although it can be more challenging to try new activities and learn new skills, life would be very boring if we only did what we've already done. Plus, there is something genuinely liberating and exciting when we realize that we can tackle something new and succeed.

As soon as you trust yourself, you will know how to live.

– GOETHE

Imagine how great it will feel when you have a proven way to plan and deliver *any* project on time and on budget. Whether setting up an overseas office, launching a new website, or simply organizing the family vacation, you've got this project management thing tackled. Whatever anyone asks, you can reply, "Sure, I can do that."

A Project Delivers a Benefit—But Not Right Away

In business, processes tend to equal money or results *now*. They are often the day-to-day core activities of a business that generate ongoing revenue, through either delivery of products or services or attention to costs. There would be no business without the processes the business is built on.

For projects, the money or benefit is rarely immediate. Instead, projects usually bring pain and disruption now, with the promise of a greater reward, either financial or in the form of greater efficiency, later on. Projects change the world and can often improve it, whereas processes facilitate business as usual.

Projects are where real value is added to a business, because they promise change for the better (even though that may not always be fully delivered!). In five years' time, looking back, you'll likely see that all the progress you made in your organization or your career came from the projects you are doing now.

When Do We Need Project Management?

Some projects are short and simple—but even then, it's worthwhile to engage in project management. When we start anything, especially something we've never done before, there are always going to be challenges and obstacles. It's likely to feel overwhelming and uncomfortable at times. Project management is no different, so starting with small projects can help you to fully understand the nuts and bolts of project management, how everything fits together and why it works. It also allows you to gain confidence in your ability to manage projects successfully, even if the first one you are involved in is delivering a PowerPoint presentation to four senior managers. Looking at the project through the lens of project management, rather than simply a task to get over with as soon as possible, allows you to break it down into parts that will impact the final outcome, thus ensuring that the outcome is as good as it can be.

Beyond those early projects to gain valuable experience using the project management methodology I'll outline in this book, it's also definitely worth using project management for any project that passes the Project Management Test, as illustrated in figure 3. If the work in question involves more than ten tasks or more than two people or takes more than three weeks to complete, it has passed the threshold of requiring project management. Even if it's a mix of factors—for example, if the project has only eight tasks but involves five people over five weeks, or eighteen tasks but only two people for eight weeks—project management is worth doing.

PROJECT MANAGEMENT TEST

fig. 3

> 10 Tasks

> 2 People

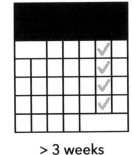

> 3 weeks

- **Does your project have more than ten tasks?**
- **Does your project involve more than two people?**
- **Does your project need more than three weeks to complete?**

> *Project management can be defined as a way of developing structure in a complex project, where the independent variables of time, cost, resources and human behavior come together.*
>
> – RORY BURKE

Using a proven project management process helps you to avoid the ten biggest project management mistakes. I'll cover these in more detail in chapter 16, but it's useful to know what they are now:

> » **Having the plan in your head**: It's not possible to keep everything in your head, especially when you have more than one project in progress and an already hectic work schedule.

> » **Saying "maybe" or "I'll try"**: You need to go away and figure out whether what's being asked for is going to be possible. It has nothing to do with determination or a can-do attitude.

> » **Answering the question, "What's the best we can do if all goes really well?"**: Projects are challenging and always throw up unexpected issues, so it's incredibly rare for things to go according to plan.

> » **Not involving the team enough**: Projects require a team effort. It spreads the load and ensures that you get the very best inputs from the start.

> » **Having a list of tasks and dates**: This is marginally better than keeping the project in your head, but it's not robust enough for most projects.

> » **Not planning for enough resources for all the projects**: Too often there is no coordination in a business across all the projects to make sure there are enough resources to do them all.

> » **Using stories rather than colored-in Gantt charts**: Projects can be entertaining, so it's easy to get caught up in the latest story, but nothing beats a colored-in Gantt chart for showing real progress.

> » **Thinking underspending is OK**: It's not just about the budget; you need to compare work progress with cost to get the full picture.

» **Rescheduling too late:** It can be tempting, especially in your early days as a project manager, to imagine that it will all come good in the end. This is almost always a recipe for disaster.

» **Not reviewing:** In the rush to get to the next project, it can be easy to forget about reviewing the just-finished one, but reviews give vital insight to the whole team that will always improve the next project.

Having a process right from the start makes project management (and your life) easier from the outset.

Projects, regardless of size or how many you need to juggle, will always be less stressful and more successful if you have a plan at the start, agreed on by all. As this book continues, I'll show you how planning a project can be super quick and easy—so that it's worth doing even for small or semi-routine projects.

Project management capability is a highly sought-after and transferable skill. Practice on the small projects so you can master it for the large ones.

Chapter Recap

» Projects are all around us. They turn the invisible into the visible and the intangible into the tangible. Projects make ideas come to life.

» Projects have three characteristics: they have a finish line; they involve doing or creating something new (either new to the world or new to the team charged with the delivery), and they provide a benefit—but not necessarily right away.

» Everything is either a process or a project. Only projects involve doing something new.

» When the characteristics of endpoint, novelty, and benefit are present, it is always wise to use project management. But when the project has more than ten tasks, involves more than two people, or will take more than three weeks, using project management will always make the project less stressful and more successful.

| 2 |
Project Management Methodologies

Chapter Overview
» Explanation of the three main methodologies
» Advantages and disadvantages of each methodology
» Why the method in this book is the best!

Those who plan do better than those who do not plan, even though they rarely stick to their plan.

— WINSTON CHURCHILL

Imagine the scene: You've been called into your manager's office. It turns out the business is looking to open another office in a different location. There needs to be better parking, easier transport links for staff, and more room for some new hires the business hopes to make in the next few weeks and months. And your manager would like *you* to find the premises and coordinate the project to get the new location ready. There will be ten people recruited to the new office. It's definitely a project, because it needs to happen before a specific date.

The project is going to be inconvenient and cause some upheaval before the benefits of the new office are evident to everyone in the company. But it will also bring extra work for you and several of your existing team members. People tend not to like change. Projects always bring change, and you are now officially in charge of your first project.

After making all the right noises to your boss and assuring them that you're thrilled about the opportunity and won't let them down, you go back to your desk. What now? Where do you even start? You definitely need help, because even off the top of your head you can list twenty pretty significant tasks, it's going to involve many more people than two, and you've got three months to pull it off. So a vague plan and a couple of lists, together with a dollop of good intentions and a large chunk of luck, is not going to cut it. You decide to have a cursory glance online at the various project management tools and methodologies you could use. And that's when things get really interesting.

MAIN METHODOLOGIES PMI PMBOK, PRINCE2, and Agile	
Some of the tools included in PMBOK	**Some of the Agile methodology terms** (and there are many more than this!)
• Gantt charts • Critical Path Method (CPM) • Program Evaluation and Review Technique (PERT) • Project initiation document (PID) • Work breakdown structure (WBS) • Product breakdown structure (PBS) • Critical tasks • Floating tasks and float • End-to-start dependencies (also start-to-start, end-to-end, and start-to-end)	• Acceptance Test-Driven Development (ATDD) • Adaptive Project Framework (APF) • Anti-pattern • Backlog • Burndown chart • Cadence • Definition of Done (DoD) • Extreme Programming (XP) • Kanban • New Product Introduction (NPI) • Outcome mapping • Package Enabled Reengineering (PER) • Planning Poker • Product backlog • Product owner • Rapid Application Development (RAD) • Release train • Scaled Agile Framework (SAFe) • Scrum • Scrumban • Sprint • Story mapping • T-shirt sizing • Test-Driven Development (TDD) • Timebox • User story • Velocity • Waterfall
Methodologies related to Project Management	
• **LEAN**: Associated more with processes than projects, but very useful and important • **CRITICAL CHAIN PROJECT MANAGEMENT**: A variation of the critical path method, suggested by Eliyahu Goldratt • **SIX SIGMA**: Associated more with quality management than project management	

fig. 4

This table displays the daunting array of approaches.

And that doesn't even include the software platforms! (More on them later.) But don't panic. Although many have quite impressive-sounding names, when you scrape the surface, they are often essentially the same thing or offshoots of the three main approaches, which are

1. PMBOK
2. PRINCE2
3. Agile

I use and teach a skinny version of PMBOK, and you can forget all about the software—this book will teach you the easiest method for managing any project of any size, using software you probably already have: *Excel*.

PMI's PMBOK

Most of what we will cover in this book comes from the Project Management Institute's (PMI) *A Guide to the Project Management Body of Knowledge*, or **PMBOK**. It is also sometimes called the PMI recommended process.

The Project Management Institute is a US-based not-for-profit professional membership association. It's generally viewed as the global governing body for project management. Started in Philadelphia, Pennsylvania, in 1969 by founders James Snyder, Eric Jenett, Gordon Davis, E. A. "Ned" Engman, and Susan C. Gallagher, the PMI now has close to three million members and is considered a leading authority on project management. Through global advocacy, networking, collaboration, research, and education, the PMI supports, trains, and prepares organizations and individuals to work more effectively in a constantly changing world. There are local chapters all over the world where members can get together and discuss all things project management.

Prior to the formation of the PMI and the *Association for Project Management (APM)* in the UK (more on APM in a moment), project management was practiced informally. People needed to get things done or needed to implement change, and everyone had their own ideas about what worked and what didn't. Therefore, those tasked with delivering projects tended to muddle through as best as they could. There was no hard-and-fast science and certainly no proven methodologies to help the bewildered. In fact, this is exactly why both the PMI and the APM were founded—to bring greater understanding, rigor, and a set of proven, predictable procedures that would vastly improve project success rates.

Who knows where project management really began—possibly as far back as the pyramids? Certainly the Industrial Revolution saw huge change that could only come about through what we would call project management (figure 5).

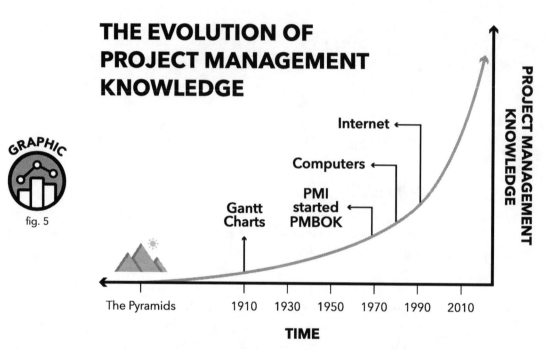

THE EVOLUTION OF PROJECT MANAGEMENT KNOWLEDGE

fig. 5

But from the mid-twentieth century onward, project management began to emerge as a distinct profession and career path. The first version of *A Guide to the Project Management Body of Knowledge*, known as PMBOK, was published in 1987 by the PMI. It contained sections A through H, with five to six pages per section. Forty-eight pages doesn't necessarily warrant the title "Body of Knowledge," but the newer editions certainly do. By 2012, the fifth edition was 589 pages long; the seventh edition, published in 2021, was thankfully reduced to 365 pages, possibly as a nod to the need for greater corporate environmental responsibility and sustainability.

As "body of knowledge" implies, this is the collective accumulation of knowledge around project management that has been gathered together, tested, used, and adapted over the last one hundred years. Though the PMI was founded in 1969, it reached further back in history to collect various techniques and tools that had proven useful in project management over the years. (For example, **Gantt charts** were invented in 1910.) No one person developed PMBOK. Rather, it's a collection of the recurring elements, tools, and techniques present in successful project management. It includes proven practices that are widely applied, and it outlines innovative emerging practices, as long as there is widespread consensus about their value and usefulness.

PMBOK is essentially the project management bible. This is both a blessing and a curse. The blessing is that it outlines everything you need to know to potentially make your project successful. It offers comprehensive, detailed, and documented best practices regarding project management. The curse is that it is so extensive that people use parts of it and give those parts different names, thinking they are referring to something else or something new.

Common PMBOK Confusions

If you have ever been in a meeting and someone is waxing lyrical about the project management system they use—perhaps they refer to "APM," "waterfall," or "Gantt"—you will be relieved to know that they are simply different names for the same approach. Life in business can sometimes be a little egocentric, with people trying to look more informed than they are. So let's run through the misconceptions.

APM stands for Association for Project Management and is essentially the UK-based equivalent of the PMI. It started in 1972 and today is a chartered body and educational charity dedicated to promoting the value of project management through membership, qualifications, publications, and events. The APM, like the PMI, is a very extensive and useful source of information about how project management should be done, and both organizations take essentially the same overall approach.

You might hear people talk of "doing waterfall." Often those who adhere to the Agile methodology (more on that in a moment) will use "waterfall" in a derogatory way: "Wow, you're not doing waterfall, are you?" The implication is that the person adopting this approach is somehow a bit misguided or behind the times. But waterfall is also just another name for PMBOK, or the **project management process**. It focuses on tasks and phases that are to be completed in a linear, sequential way, and each stage needs to be finished before the next stage starts.

Finally, claiming to use Gantt is a reference to using to Gantt charts, which we will unpack in more detail in chapter 8. Gantt charts are also part of the PMBOK.

The confusion arises largely because PMBOK is not a methodology—but many methodologies, like Gantt and waterfall, are *based* on PMBOK. PMBOK covers all the important areas of projects and provides detailed guidance on each of the activities in those areas. It's therefore hardly surprising that PMBOK so often becomes the base for "new" project management methodologies and has become the de facto standard.

What Is PMBOK Lite?

I believe that a slimmed-down version of PMBOK—what we'll call **PMBOK Lite**—is the most effective, especially for busy professionals who don't have the time for lots of form filling or approval meetings, let alone the inclination to learn complicated software or dedicate their scarce time to learning a complex project management methodology.

Project management is about getting stuff done on time and on budget to deliver an agreed-upon objective or outcome. The methodology is only meant to support the successful completion of tasks, not to become a project in its own right!

PMBOK Lite is my super-simple, practical, and highly effective approach that utilizes the best of PMBOK without the complexity. When you're selecting bits and pieces of PMBOK, it's hard to know which parts give the most bang for their buck. With PMBOK Lite, I've done the work for you. It's the outcome of over twenty-five years of working in and teaching project management. It focuses on the bits that really work. I've simplified PMBOK, gotten rid of a lot of the math you really don't need in real life, and also included some great techniques most people don't know about. The key is to decide on a simple, practical system and then stick to it. There are no shortcuts in project management, but PMBOK Lite will give your project structure and can certainly make your life easier and less stressful.

Advantages of PMI PMBOK Lite

» PMBOK has a solid track record of success. The body of knowledge has been growing for a hundred years and contains a hundred years' worth of insight, knowledge, and expertise.

» Everyone agrees to the plan at the start, so you have backup if the customer complains afterward about what you've delivered.

» Changes can be made at any time, and the cost and extra time will be known and agreed on at that point.

» PMBOK minimizes client time, as everything is agreed on up front—meaning there is minimal need for project meetings involving the client.

» Clear responsibilities and accountabilities mean that everyone knows what they are doing and when those tasks must be finished. Again, this keeps the meetings and ongoing negotiations to a minimum.

» PMBOK accounts for dependencies, which makes the management easier and smoother. When team members fully appreciate who is dependent on their deliverables and when they are due, this can help to hold everyone's feet to the fire and keep the project on track.

» It is very easy to create a critical path, even in a very large project. This allows you to correctly forecast the project delivery date, monitor progress, and, if necessary, speed up the plan or rejig resources around the critical path.

» Resources (people or equipment) can be booked in advance so you can be sure you get them when you need them. As a result, if there is going to be a problem, you can see it coming a long time in advance, which enables you to plan around it or make other arrangements.

» It's far easier to plan for risk and make informed judgments about what can be mitigated and what needs greater attention.

» It is very easy to monitor progress, especially if you use Gantt charts. Gantts offer a fast visual overview of even the largest projects, which allows the manager to immediately see what's on track and what needs attention.

» Review is also much easier because it is possible to go through each stage of the process to establish how well it was done. It allows you to drill into the review and fully extract the nuggets of wisdom that lie in all projects, regardless of whether they're successful or not.

Disadvantages of PMI PMBOK

» Full PMBOK is very big and complicated. If you have several projects, and maybe family and friends you'd like to see occasionally, it's too much. This is especially true if project management is just part of your job. You need PMBOK Lite, which is what this book is all about.

» A common complaint about PMBOK is that it is inflexible. Once you've got a plan, everyone has to stick to it. However, I would contest that; every project changes as it goes along. As Prussian Field Marshal Helmuth von Moltke once said, "No battle plan withstands contact with the enemy." In other words, all plans change when faced with reality, but we should still always go into battle with the best plan we can. PMBOK simply forces people to engage with the project early on to collectively come up with that best plan.

» You need to know what you want at the start. The project owner or customer will therefore have to do some thinking about this, which they don't always want to do. Again, I would deny that this is a disadvantage. Every project manager worth their salt should insist on knowing where they are heading. Customers or project owners may urge you to "start anyway," but it's usually because they've not thought about it deeply enough. There is always going to be trouble ahead if the target destination or deliverable is unclear.

» A subset of the previous "disadvantages" would be that PMBOK is time-consuming up front. And this is true, especially when compared with Agile. But when I hear this complaint, I am always reminded of Abraham Lincoln, who said, "Give me six hours to chop down a tree and I will spend the first four sharpening the axe." PMBOK does demand up-front thought and effort to create the plan and get sign-off—but not as much as you might think, as you will soon discover. And yes, that time could have been used to jump into the tasks, but preparation before action will always reduce effort, outlay, and angst down the road. The question, as Lincoln clearly understood, is whether it's worth planning and preparing in order to get better performance later when you implement the project.

» PMBOK demands that you be able to list and estimate everything before you start, and this is not always easy. Some tasks are more creative and very hard to estimate. Some things depend on what happens at previous steps. If the project needs to be changed because you as the project manager got your estimates wrong, it's going to be a bit embarrassing! But a best guess is still better than nothing. And this uncertainty can also be easily dealt with in PMBOK through the addition of contingency (more on that in chapter 6).

» Full PMBOK has a high failure rate, although estimates vary on exactly what it is, and it depends on how you define failure. Is delivering 1 percent over budget a failure? Is delivering late when the customer changed the specification a failure? Of course, it's not just projects using PMBOK that have this disadvantage; the statistics on project delivery are woefully consistent. In 1990, Harvard professor John P. Kotter stated that up to 70 percent of change initiatives fail; a decade later, Malcolm Higgs and Deborah Rowland concurred. In 2005 the same authors went further, reporting that "only one in four or five change programs actually succeeds." A year later, after surveying 1,546 business executives, McKinsey & Company confirmed that only 30 percent of change initiatives were considered successful. Projects are difficult because change, or creating something new, is bound to be difficult, but it's not always the project management that's at fault. Sometimes the government, politics, company culture, or other stakeholders can cause the failure. Most would have been worse without a plan.

PRINCE2

The original PRINCE was slightly less interesting than princes are often made out to be in fairy tales. It was derived from an earlier project management methodology called PROMPT II (Project Resource Organisation Management and Planning Techniques). The Central Computer and Telecommunications Agency (CCTA) adopted a version of PROMPT II in 1989 as the UK government standard for managing projects that were based on information systems (IT). In a feat of impressive (if highly creative and contorted) acronym construction, this new standard was named PRINCE, which originally stood for "PROMPT II IN the CCTA Environment." PRINCE2, released in 1996, expanded its scope beyond IT projects—but stuck with the questionable acronym. *PRINCE2* stands for PRojects IN Controlled Environments.

PRINCE2 is a highly structured project management methodology designed to cover all types of projects, although it does still have a distinct IT flavor. It is popular all over the world and, perhaps unsurprisingly considering its origins, it's the go-to methodology for project management in many UK government departments and within the United Nations. However, there are signs of its popularity waning in recent years.

In 2013, ownership of the rights to PRINCE2 were transferred from the HM Cabinet Office to AXELOS Ltd in a joint venture. According to AXELOS, PRINCE2 is made up of principles, themes, and processes within the project environment. Figure 6 gives a brief overview of PRINCE2.

COMPONENT PARTS OF PRINCE2

fig. 6

Source: www.axelos.com

Seven Principles

These principles determine whether a project is being managed using PRINCE2 or not. All must be present for a project to qualify.

1. **Continued Business Justification**: There must be clear justification for running and managing the project.

2. **Learn from Experience**: PRINCE2 project teams always seek to learn from experience and draw on past lessons.

3. **Defined Roles and Responsibilities**: PRINCE2 project teams involve the right people at the right time for the right tasks.

4. **Manage by Stages**: PRINCE2 projects are planned, assessed, and controlled on a stage-by-stage basis.

5. **Manage by Exception**: Those working on the project should be given the authority to work effectively within the project environment.

6. **Focus on Products**: PRINCE2 projects focus on product specifications, quality requirements, and delivery.

7. **Tailor to Suit Project Environment**: PRINCE2 projects are tailored to suit the project environment, paying particular attention to size, scope, complexity, capability, importance, and risk.

Seven Themes

These themes are aspects of project management that must be addressed throughout the project. The idea is that these themes help people stay on track by stating the minimum requirement needed for each theme.

1. **Business Case**: A thorough and documented business case as clear justification for the project

2. **Organization**: Defined roles and responsibilities of each member of the project team

3. **Quality**: Quality requirements and how they will be assessed and delivered

4. **Plans**: Outline of how the plan will be developed and what PRINCE2 techniques to use

5. **Risk**: Identification of any and all risks and opportunities that may influence the project

6. **Change**: Determination of how the project manager will assess, monitor, and potentially make changes to the project

7. **Progress**: Ongoing assessment of performance and progress against the plan and next steps

Seven Processes

The processes outline the steps in the project life cycle, from the initial idea to project delivery and assessment of benefits. Each process has its own checklist of recommended activities, related responsibilities, and guidance on how to tailor the approach to each unique project environment.

1. **Starting a Project**: Project team is appointed, including project manager, and project brief is produced

2. **Initiating a Project**: Business case is refined and project initiation documentation is assembled

3. **Directing a Project**: How the project board will oversee the project is outlined

4. **Controlling a Stage**: How each stage will be controlled is outlined

5. **Managing Product Delivery**: Link between project manager and team is controlled through formal requirements

6. **Managing Stage Boundaries**: Transitioning from one stage to the next is explained

7. **Closing a Project**: Project is formally decommissioned and evaluated

To some degree, PRINCE2 seems to be running out of steam. Many project management professionals now feel that it's just too hard to implement. PRINCE2 is infamous for being excessively complicated and bureaucratic. And they have recently added *Managing Successful Programmes (MSP)*, which makes it even *more* complicated and even less useful. MSP is more focused on program management—how to run several projects at once, with the resource issues that inevitably come with that. It also covers some of the softer and more strategic parts of project management: benefits management, stakeholder engagement, and transitioning of project outputs into the business. But these areas are complicated enough without adding extra PRINCE2 complexity. Still, many project managers and aspiring project managers consider PRINCE2 the market leader. It remains a popular choice, probably because it's well known and therefore considered a safe option, and it's often mentioned in project management job ads. So, let's take a closer look at the pros and cons of PRINCE2.

Advantages of PRINCE2

» The biggest advantage of PRINCE2 is that major decisions and the project itself are based on a robust business case. The project can't be jump-started based on the off chance of success, or insisted upon by an exuberant executive. It has to stack up commercially with clear return on investment and delivery of benefit that the business needs.

» PRINCE2 is particularly useful for large public-sector projects. Apart from anything else, the public sector, especially in the UK and parts of Europe, is very familiar with it. No one is going to lose their job for using PRINCE2!

» PRINCE2 pushes the project manager, team, and project owner to very high levels of front-end definitions and agreements. Whether this is an advantage or a disadvantage depends on your perspective and your role. Even those who recognize the merit of proper project outline and definition sometimes balk at the levels required for PRINCE2.

» Roles and responsibilities are very well defined in PRINCE2. This makes it easier for people to know their position on the team, what they need to deliver on, by when, and why.

» PRINCE2 delivers high levels of control. Projects can't be started or progressed to the next stage without sign-off.

» It also allows for greater control over which projects can be started and when money can be spent.

» PRINCE2 forces management to engage with the project management process.

» It's great if you are doing one big job (such as building a nuclear power station) because documentation, control, and decision control are excellent. But if project management is just part of your job, it can feel overwhelming.

Disadvantages of PRINCE2

» The biggest drawback of PRINCE2 is that it doesn't actually tell you *how* to do anything, such as how to estimate tasks. It doesn't even tell you how to use Gantt charts, which project managers will almost certainly encounter during their careers. All it does is certify that there is a plan, signed off on by the board. Even with

PRINCE2 you still need PMBOK to explain the *how*. PRINCE2 is a framework, like ISO 9001. You still need this book, or something similar, to execute a PRINCE2 project. To give you a sense of what this means, PRINCE2 goes into a lot of detail about just two tools and techniques, but there are more than one hundred tools and techniques within PMBOK.

» Have a look at the seven stages, and you'll see that there isn't one for planning. How weird is that? In my PMBOK Lite process, steps two through eight—that's seven of the twelve steps—are all about planning, because it's the biggest and most important part of project management.

» PRINCE2 doesn't address or acknowledge the importance of "soft skills" for project management.

» It's overly bureaucratic. As a result, too often those involved in PRINCE2 projects pick and choose parts of it. But which parts? This leads to another questionable acronym: PINO (PRINCE2 In Name Only).

» PRINCE2 is going out of favor because it's so bureaucratic—though it has taken people thirty years to realize that. There is far too much paperwork. Busy PMs don't have the time for all those forms!

» It takes too much time and it's not flexible enough. It's also really dull, especially boring for staff who have other roles and responsibilities to engage in. So in order to avoid all the PRINCE2 forms and controls, people avoid admitting that their project is a project, and the result is that many smaller projects go along under the PRINCE radar and have no controls at all.

» PRINCE2 is expensive to learn and implement. In fact, I've never seen it work successfully in practice. That's because in all the companies I have trained over twenty-five years, I have never seen it being fully used; some give lip service to it, saying they intend to use it or are working toward it, but I've never seen it being used properly, let alone successfully.

> » Project managers don't like it because it controls them too tightly. This is, of course, not all bad, and certainly the project owner often relishes that control, but still, if the key person on a project is unhappy, that's not a good start.

Agile

In many ways, *Agile* is the antithesis of full-on PRINCE2 or PMBOK, which some people consider too complicated and cumbersome. And they may have a point, especially with PRINCE2. But PMBOK gets a bad rap sometimes because people assume they need to know all of it and implement everything, rather than seeing it as a project management toolbox. Just find the tools that work for you in your particular project rather than feeling like you need to do it all.

However, there is little doubt that Agile emerged as simpler and faster. It first appeared in the software development industry. In software development projects, those involved often don't know in detail where they are heading or what is possible, so an iterative and incremental approach makes sense. Agile as we know it today really came into being in 2001 when a group of seventeen software developers got together at a ski resort in Utah to discuss their development methods. The result was the publication of the *Manifesto for Agile Software Development*.

But Agile as a mindset or idea has been around since the 1990s when there emerged a slew of alternatives to the prevailing PMBOK and PRINCE2—which, in certain corners, especially the software industry, were considered excessive, arcane, rigid, and process-obsessed. The new entrants included rapid application development (RAD) in 1991, unified process (UP) and **dynamic systems development method (DSDM)** in 1994, Scrum in 1995, *Crystal Clear* and **Extreme Programming (XP)** in 1996, and feature-driven development in 1997. For software developers, PMBOK and PRINCE2 were not flexible or responsive enough for their projects. Again, in software development this makes some sense. But the differentiator is not whether a project is a software project; the differentiator is whether the project is a structured IT project or an open-ended IT project. PMBOK Lite can work really well for the former, but Agile is better for the latter. However, Agile has since spread beyond the world of software development, and many of the arguments simply don't hold true outside of that industry. Interestingly, despite originating before the **Agile Manifesto**, many of the earlier methodologies are now collectively referred to as Agile.

Today Agile is everywhere. It has become uber-fashionable and is endlessly thrown about in executive meetings. So what is it exactly?

Essentially, Agile involves self-managing teams planning their work in two-week increments (known as *sprints*). *Scrum*, as well as being the name for a short daily meeting in Agile, is also the name of the most common Agile methodology, an iterative and incremental framework for delivering (usually) IT products. Scrum is therefore a subset of Agile. There are many Agile methodologies, and Scrum is one of the main ones. Others include *Kanban*, XP, *feature-driven development (FDD)*, DSDM, Crystal Clear, *Lean*, *Scrumban* and a whole bunch of other buzzwords. In all of these, the team works closely with the customer, adapting the plan and the deliverables as they go along, often with the aim of getting some sort of marketable *minimum viable product (MVP)* as soon as possible. The idea is to deliver the most important deliverables first and the nice-to-haves later, if there is enough time, money, or inclination left. Agile works on the principle that we don't know exactly what will happen in the future and there are too many variables and too many unknowns at the start, so a full plan at the beginning is impossible and therefore a waste of time.

The original Agile Manifesto suggested four overarching values and twelve principles.

Four Agile Values:

»   Individuals and interactions over processes and tools
»   Working software over comprehensive documentation
»   Customer collaboration over contract negotiation
»   Responding to change over following a plan

Of course, these imply that other methodologies value the opposite. For example, we're meant to infer that PMBOK values processes and tools over individuals and interactions, or following a plan over responding to change. This is simply not true, especially with PMBOK Lite. Sure, PMBOK Lite values processes and practical tools, but it also values individuals and interactions. It values enough documentation and a successful outcome, customer collaboration, and responding to change while following an agreed-upon plan.

12 Agile Principles:

1. **Customer Satisfaction:** Agile's highest priority is to keep the customer happy through quick and continuous delivery.

2. **Welcome Changes:** Agile accepts changes, even late changes, and sees change as a way to harness competitive advantage.

3. **Deliver Frequently**: Outcomes need to be delivered quickly, from a couple of weeks to a couple of months, with quicker always being better.

4. **Collaboration Is Key**: Businesspeople, the project owners, and specialists must work together for the duration of the project.

5. **Foster Motivation**: Build projects around motivated individuals. Give them the environment and support they need, and trust them to get the job done.

6. **Face-to-Face Interactions**: The best way to convey information and move the project along is face-to-face conversation.

7. **Minimum Viable Product (MVP)**: A working deliverable, such as working software, is the primary measure of success or progress.

8. **Sustainable Development**: Agile processes promote sustainable development. The sponsors, developers, and users should be able to maintain a constant pace indefinitely.

9. **Constant Improvement**: Continuous attention to technical excellence and good design enhances agility.

10. **Simplicity**: Agile aims for simplicity to maximize the amount of work done and see that it's not done needlessly.

11. **Self-Organizing Teams**: The best outcomes come from self-organizing teams (linking back to point five).

12. **Reflect and Update**: Agile is based on regular reflection to update everyone on the learning. The team fine-tunes and adjusts its collective behavior accordingly, making everyone more effective.

These principles are good, but they are not always relevant to every project. Building a bridge as fast as possible is never ideal, for example, and too much face-to-face interaction, especially with the project owner, can be counterproductive. It is far easier to see the relevance in software development projects. In those types of projects Agile can work well; its success with more traditional projects is open to debate. According to the Project Management Institute, more than 70 percent of organizations have incorporated an Agile approach into their business, and yet the statistics on project failure are still consistently hovering around 70 percent. So is Agile making a difference to success rates? The PMI states that Agile projects are 28 percent more successful than traditional projects, but how can Agile fail when it doesn't even have a starting plan by which to compare the final outcome? Without a finish date, how can an Agile project be delivered late?

My argument against Agile is that it really boils down to "Let's just start and see where we end up before we run out of money and time." Can we really call that project management? Let's take a look at the pros and cons, and I'll let you decide.

Advantages of Agile

» Good for:
  - small projects where overspending doesn't matter
  - software projects where changes can easily be made
  - projects where the objective is unclear at the start

» It's simple and relies on the logic of doing the most important things first in order to deliver the minimum viable product (MVP). Assuming dependencies don't rule that out.

» Agile deliberately stays close to the customer. With PMBOK the customer is closely involved in defining the project, but once it's signed off on, they are not involved that much except to update or negotiate changes. This is deliberate and ensures that everyone is engaged and focused on what the desired outcome and benefits are before starting.

» Some customers like the fact that they don't have to decide up front exactly what they want.

» Motivationally, teams often love working on Agile projects, partly because of the team spirit and partly because there isn't much pressure regarding timelines, deadlines, deliverables, or budget. How nice to be on an Agile team!

» For some things, such as creative processes, you don't know how long it will take, so you can't use PMBOK; you have to use Agile and see how it goes and then work from there.

» Agile has a fun and exciting atmosphere. Where else would you be talking about sprints, scrums, scrum masters, release trains, customer stories, and burndown charts?

Disadvantages of Agile

» Among the key variables of cost, quality, and time, Agile can deliver one or maybe two, but rarely all three. For example, an Agile manager might come back to a customer saying, "We can finish on a particular date, but we can't tell you what we will have done by then." Often, it's quality/scope that suffers as the time and money run out. So the project owner might get a minimum viable product or deliverable, but it rarely includes all the other hoped-for features. To ensure delivery of all three—full brief by a set date within a set budget—PMBOK is probably necessary because right at the start it will tell you either "Yes, we can do it, and here's a plan for delivery" or "No, it's impossible, you'll need more time and money."

» With Agile, there is no overall long-term plan. Yes, that's right, *there really is no overall plan.* Instead, it's week to week, or a two-week sprint and then regroup and decide what to do in the next two-week sprint.

» Unlike software or digital products, physical projects can't be changed partway through. You can't build a house and decide to make it 10 percent larger once the foundation has been laid. This is one of the biggest drawbacks of Agile, especially for projects that rely on the delivery of a physical product or outcome.

» The Agile methodology has sought to expand to cover larger projects, but if you have to commit early on to a design, or if you have to book something like a laboratory or a crane, it'll never be possible, because Agile has no overall plan. Agile users don't look further ahead than two weeks, so they can't really book that crane. Proper project management always has a long-term plan, although sometimes it changes or gets fleshed out in more detail as you go along.

» As part of a larger project, Agile can screw up the overall plan. Imagine a big plan that contains one wobbly component, one "Agile" part that has an unknown duration. Everything else is impacted by that "agility," making success virtually impossible.

» Agile can't measure a success rate relative to an agreed-on plan, because there is no plan to begin with.

» There is always a risk that customers will say at the end, or near the end, "Hang on, I've spent all this time and money and is this all I've got to show for it?" Unless you spell out expectations and deliverables, there will almost always be a gap between what's delivered and what was expected. Agile leaves everyone exposed to too many surprises, and surprises are rarely good. The lack of a target also tends to facilitate a creeping unease or sense of unhappiness with progress.

» Agile can be harder to sell to project owners or customers because they can't be told exactly what they'll get and when, or how much it will cost.

» There might be an idea about a finish date or how much money can be spent, but usually not both at once. Agile cannot promise all three: what will be done, by when, and for what budget.

Figures 7 and 8 will help you compare the three methodologies side by side and break down when they are often used. But don't worry too much about it. PMBOK Lite, which is covered in this book, takes the best of all three and gives you a foolproof way to manage any project without endless meetings or documentation *or* by flying by the seat of your pants.

GRAPHIC

fig. 7

	PMBOK	PRINCE2	AGILE
1. Define the project and agree to start	Yes	Very thorough	Not done
2. List the tasks	Yes	Yes	Yes
3. Estimate the costs and times	Yes	Not covered	A bit
4. Dependencies and critical path	Yes	Not covered	No
5. Speed up the plan	Yes	Not covered	All the time

	PMBOK	PRINCE2	AGILE
6. Gantt Chart	Yes	Not covered	No
7. Plan resources	Yes	Not covered	All the time but only short-term
8. Plan for risks	Yes	Yes	Might do
9. Monitor progress against plan	Yes	Yes	All the time except there isn't a plan
10. Monitor costs and forecast total	Yes	Not covered	Constantly changing
11. Replan when necessary	Yes	Probably	Doing this all the time
12. Review	Yes	Very thorough	Yes

WHEN TO USE PMBOK LITE	WHEN TO USE AGILE
Fairly or very clear spec at the start	Spec is unclear
Spec can be agreed on at the start with only small changes, or definite separate initial scoping phase or definite second "final adjustments" phase	Customer won't know spec till after one or more phases — iterative design process
Times and costs are estimate-able within a range	Task times and costs cannot be listed or estimated
Fixed budget and/or fixed timescale which must be achieved	Budget and timescale are not strongly defined
Most parts of the project depend on others so things have to be done in the right order	Tasks / deliverables are parallel — minimal dependencies
Plan is going to change only by small amounts in a controlled way (signed for)	Plan is going to change a lot

GRAPHIC

fig. 8

WHEN TO USE PMBOK LITE	WHEN TO USE AGILE
PM is taking the risk – price is fixed, or increases will have to be negotiated	Customer accepts the risk and is prepared to pay for it
Large projects where cost forecasting is vital	Cost is low – doubling it won't be significant
Projects which have to be done correctly from the start – later changes are much more expensive, e.g. construction	Software projects where fundamental changes can be made at any time
When you don't want a poor prototype to tarnish your reputation	When you need to get a prototype out quickly
When the whole job needs to be delivered in one successful lump, fully working from day 1	When it's OK to deliver the job in parts, starting with the key parts ASAP

A Quick Word on Software Platforms

Like project management methodologies, there are a lot of software platforms and tools. They include the following, in alphabetical order:

- » Asana
- » Basecamp
- » Celoxis
- » ClickUp
- » GanttPRO
- » Jira
- » LiquidPlanner
- » Microsoft Project
- » Monday.com
- » Smartsheet
- » TeamGantt
- » Teamwork.com
- » Trello
- » Wrike
- » Zoho

It is beyond the scope of this book to review or recommend them individually, but these are the main options at the time of writing. Some are very lightweight (e.g., *Trello* is a list-maker really, though I love it for doing that) and others (e.g., *Wrike*) are very powerful but quite hard to learn. Some (e.g., *Monday* and *Basecamp*) are more communication tools than proper project management software, but they are still useful, since communication is one of the biggest problems when lots of people are doing lots of projects. And, of course, your choice of software will depend on the size of your company, the type of projects you're doing, and how much you like using software. Personally, I like a human element in the process, to keep your feet on the ground. If you automate everything then it's inevitable that you will get a key input wrong and all the plans will be off, and you won't even know! So I like Excel augmented by plenty of meetings. It's simple, everyone already knows how to use it, and it's on most computers. I hope you feel that this is good news: Excel is all you need.

If you want more, you'll need to do your homework, and here is some help with that. My first test for assessing any software platform is this: Does it have Gantt charts? If it doesn't, then it's not real project management software, it's a communication tool—although that might be all you want or need. Related to that, are the Gantt charts based on dependencies between tasks (is there a known critical path?) or are the Gantt charts drawn in by people who are guessing at dates? Proper Gantt charts should always be based on a critical path, as I'll be explaining later in this book.

The next test: How user friendly is the software? How quickly can you get started with a small project? If it's horrible and gives you a headache as soon as you open it, then maybe your IT people will use it, and maybe you will, but nobody else will, and that's no good.

But it's important to note that no software platform is a substitute for steps in the project management process, so in the end it can only be a drawing tool or a communication tool. No software can tell you:

>   … if you have missed a task.
>   … if your time or cost estimates are realistic.
>   … if tasks are dependent on each other.
>   … if your plan looks extremely risky. (And it won't prompt you to add in more contingency if it is risky.)
>   … about resource planning. Software is always weak on resource planning, because it never has all the information needed to make the intuitive judgments required: Dave can do task A but not task B; Louise can do both but is better/faster at task A; Karen would enjoy task A but would learn more from doing task B.

Whatever software you end up using, you'll still have to work all this out yourself. Luckily, I can help you with that.

Chapter Recap

» Despite a baffling array of approaches to project management, there are just three main ones: PMBOK, PRINCE2, and Agile. The other approaches are usually simply tools or subsets of one of these three.

» PMBOK comes from the Project Management Institute (PMI). The PMI is effectively the governing body of project management worldwide. And PMBOK refers to *A Guide to the Project Management Body of Knowledge*, an extensive guidebook of more than one hundred project management tools and techniques. Some of those tools and techniques have been pulled out and given names that imply they're methodologies, but they're really tools within broader methodologies.

» PMBOK is a good idea when the project has clear parameters, when the specifications can be agreed on at the start, and when there is a fixed timeline and budget.

» PRINCE2 is a project management approach that started in information systems projects but has evolved into other industries. It remains most useful for large IT projects and those where documentation, traceability, and control are vital.

» Agile is the antithesis of PMBOK and PRINCE2 and emerged out of the software development industry. In software development, a more agile approach makes sense. But today Agile is everywhere, and its strengths can easily flip into weaknesses in a different industry.

» Agile has four values and twelve principles, but as the name suggests, it is much more fluid and open-ended than PMBOK or PRINCE2. It's basically about starting, making it up as the project moves along, and seeing what happens before running out of time and money.

» There are plenty of software platforms touted as project management software. Some are better than others. Some are too complex for small and medium projects. Stick to Excel; it really is all you'll ever need.

| 3 |
Define the Project – Step 1

Chapter Overview
- » Know your parameters: cost, time and quality
- » The importance of two kick-off meetings
- » The three levels of approval

If you don't know where you are going, how can you expect to get there?
– BASIL S. WALSH

Projects don't just miraculously emerge from thin air. Projects emerge from individuals or teams who are seeking to create something, change something, or make something better. There is always an aspiration that brings the project into being in the first place.

Say your project is building a new house. Perhaps the idea to build a house emerged during a conversation with your partner. Issues with your current house, together with a long-held desire to be a self-builder, nudged you toward the decision to build a new house. But to actually go through with the project, the aspiration "I want to build a house" needs to be broken down and defined, so that everyone involved in the project (both those who own it and those who will actually be doing it) know what success will look like. There is no way you will get the house you and your family want unless you define the project and get really clear on the important parameters. That's what it will take to make a real decision about whether to move forward with the project or not.

Every project starts with a determination to create or deliver something new by a promised date. This would be much easier if projects didn't also come with a required level of quality and scope, and a limit to the money available. That's where the real problems can begin, because it's impossible to deliver an amazing outcome, such as a lovely new house, really quickly with a very limited budget.

The Iron Triangle

> *Project management is like juggling three balls: time, cost, and quality. Program management is like a troupe of circus performers standing in a circle, each juggling three balls and swapping balls from time to time.*
>
> — GEOFF REISS

The *iron triangle* is the combination of cost, quality, and time (figure 9).

THE IRON TRIANGLE

fig. 9

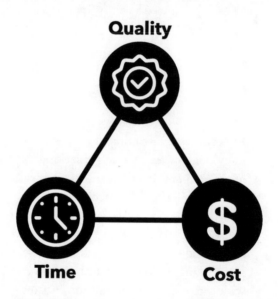

The reason it's called the iron triangle is because, just as iron doesn't give easily, neither does the desire to have it all: low cost, short time, and perfect quality.

Of course, the project owner or customer will always want the highest quality in the fastest time for the least amount of money. This is often what salespeople will promise the customer to secure the project! Often the first task in project management is to explain to the customer that they can't actually have all three. More often, they can have two out of three, because the elements are often related:

» The customer can have top-notch quality, but it will probably cost more or take longer than they want (or both).

» The customer can spend less, but the project will take probably take longer and the quality may be lower.

» Or the project can be completed faster, but it will probably cost more and may also have implications on the quality.

There are always trade-offs to consider (figure 10).

PROJECT TRADE-OFFS

fig. 10

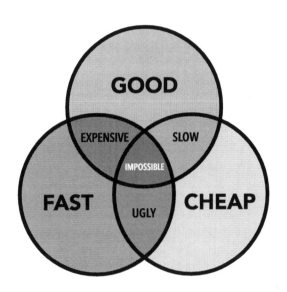

Some authors suggest that scope is a fourth element of every project—distinguishing between how much you get (scope) and how good it is (quality). In truth, it can be very difficult to separate scope and quality, because scope is really a part of quality. For example, the number of people who can log in to a system at any one time sounds like a scope issue—but if that limit means others have to wait to log in (or the system crashes with too many users), isn't that a quality issue too? Similarly, is having the right-sized parking lot or the latest high-speed scanner at a hospital only part of the scope, or does it have implications on quality? In the end it doesn't really matter what you call it. When we talk about quality, we are outlining the answer to the customer's question, "What will I get?" That includes scope.

Once a project has been proposed, as the project manager it's your job to drill down into the customer requirements and figure out if that project can be done. This is achieved through two kick-off meetings. One happens right at the start to work out exactly what the project is, what's needed, to what level of quality, with what specification or scope, and by when. The second kick-off meeting happens once you've taken that information and figured out whether the project can be delivered or not.

First Kick-Off Meeting

> *All things are created twice; first mentally, then physically. The key to creativity is to begin with the end in mind, with a vision and a blueprint of the desired result.*
>
> *– STEPHEN COVEY*

This *first kick-off meeting* involves all the key *stakeholders* in the project. This will include the project owner or the customer, any managers who may be affected by staff pulled in to work on the project, the project manager, and key members of the proposed project team, as well as the person who controls the purse strings.

Watch a short video on the challenges of managing different stakeholders.

To watch the QuickClip, use the camera on your mobile phone to scan the QR code or visit the link below.

or

www.quickclips.io/pm-1

 SCAN ME

 VISIT URL

The aim of this first meeting is for the stakeholders to agree on the objectives. These objectives will almost always vary between different stakeholders. For example, the chief financial officer's primary objective will be to complete the project within a specific budget. The project owner (that is, the person who originally called for the project to be done) may be more focused on what the project will deliver or change, or what benefit they expect. The objective of the team members might be that it is possible to work on the project alongside their existing workload. The level of enthusiasm for the project is also likely to vary depending on ownership. The person who proposed the project is almost always the most vocal and enthusiastic about it.

During this phase, as the project manager, don't try to make any decisions yourself, even if you have strong feelings about what should be delivered or how much should be spent. That's not your job. Your job is to get the stakeholders to make all the decisions and to get agreement from everyone. If *you* choose the specifications, you'll rarely please everyone, and you'll be wide open to criticism later. The stakeholders must agree on what they want and sign up for that, so that when you deliver it they'll have no reason not to be happy.

Behavioral science has demonstrated that we value what we already own far more than what others own, and this extends beyond possessions or skills to ideas. We all harbor a natural bias toward our own ideas and what we think is important. This is known as the ***endowment effect***.

It is naturally given to all men to esteem their own inventions best.
– THOMAS MORE

Not only does everyone in the room want different things from the project, but they are likely to have different feelings about it too. Everyone will have an opinion about what's most important and an explanation for why their priorities are more important than other people's. Their definitions or expectations regarding the three parameters of cost, time, and quality will also be different. Again, your job as project manager is to get all those differences out on the table for discussion so that some decisions can be made concerning the project definition in the first kick-off meeting.

This is often made even harder because these stakeholders are not normally in the same room together, and levels of seniority and authority are likely to vary too. This meeting is about getting the stakeholders to clearly articulate the requirements of the project so you can go away and work out whether it can be done.

To establish that, you will need to leave the first kick-off meeting with the following:

» A top-line understanding of exactly what they want. What does success look like for the project?

» A clear sense of a delivery timeline. When does the project need to be delivered, and is there any wiggle room?

» A clear understanding of the budget and, again, whether there is any wiggle room.

Establish the Key Drivers

Most project owners or customers will know in their heart that it's not possible to have all three elements of the iron triangle exactly as they want them. Given that, during the first kick-off meeting it's extremely important that you establish what the one *key driver* is that will sit at the top of the iron triangle for this project—the one that outweighs or is considered more important than the other two.

Never assume you know what it is. Instead, listen to the stakeholders. Even *they* might not be able to answer the question if you asked them what their key driver was! But the discussion should alert you to any obvious bias toward one of the variables.

For example, ask yourself now: What is likely to be the key driver for the Olympics? What about a nuclear power plant? What about a new school or hospital? And finally, what about your daughter's wedding?

The answers, in case you are stumped: The key driver for the Olympics would be time. The Olympics *must* start on a set day. Athletes and spectators have traveled from all over the world to attend the opening ceremony, and missing the deadline would be catastrophic. For a nuclear power station, the key driver must be quality. The risks of poor quality are so huge they can't even be contemplated. The key driver for a school or hospital is likely to be money, as there is only so much in the public purse, but quality may be a close second. And as for your daughter's wedding, that probably depends on how much you love your daughter, how important you think weddings are, or perhaps who's the boss, you or her! That one is far harder to figure out. As with many projects, it's not obvious.

Asking the customer or project owner outright what is most important to them among time, money, and quality probably won't yield a helpful answer, for a number of reasons. They want all three, or they don't know, or they don't want *you* to know. No one wants to admit that cost is the key driver in their daughter's wedding! Customers can also be reticent to tell you that cost is not an issue, lest you go crazy with the budget.

But you really need to know. Listen to the conversation and pay particular attention to possible clues. Perhaps the owner mentions that a little more money might be available if necessary, or that if delivery slips by a day or two it wouldn't be a disaster. If no one drops any hints, then consider asking these three questions:

» Can you tell me *why* you've set that budget (or time limit or quality level)? The explanation will help you to establish where the emphasis is. If the customer says, "Because that's all there is allocated for the project and we've already been told there will be no more," that's pretty definitive. But if they say, "Because that's how much I think it will cost," then you know that the budget is not really the key driver. Similarly, if you ask about the target finish date and they say, "We thought that sounded like a reasonable date" or "Because that's how long we think it will take," then you know that time is not the key driver.

» Ask "what if" questions involving only small changes to time, money, or scope (bigger changes will always be a problem, so that tells you nothing). What if the project was a week late, or what if the quality was a little lower, or what if we went over budget by 1 percent? The answer—and the passion in the answer—will give you a clue as to the key driver. For example, if the answer to "What happens if we go over the budget?" is "The company goes bust," you can be pretty sure cost is the key driver. What if the Olympics were a couple of days late? "Unthinkable!" What if the wedding dress cost an extra hundred? Much less of a problem.

» Suggest possible trades. You might, for example, suggest increasing the budget to shave a month off the delivery. If they like the idea, then time is clearly more important than money. If they don't like the idea, then money is more important than time. Next, pit time against quality and see which one is more important. The "winner" of these hypothetical face-offs is the key driver. In the case of my website, they told me if I spent a little more money, they could add in some really nice extra features. When I responded, "Like what?" everyone—including me—suddenly knew that money wasn't my key driver.

Knowing the key driver tells you what to focus on if or when things go wrong. You can then use the other two drivers to ensure that the most important one doesn't slip. When you know what the key driver is, you know the project priorities and can better manage the project to the customer's satisfaction. For example, if you know that time is the key driver and the schedule slips, you can get back on track by either reducing the scope a little or spending more money on more people or equipment.

MY TAKE

Whatever you do, don't fail on the key driver, or the customer will see the whole project as a failure. The key driver is their *one thing* that really matters to them, and they will judge the entire project on whether that driver is met.

Don't commit to anything during the first kick-off meeting. You will need to be strong and assertive and resist the temptation to agree to the project without proper assessment and planning. Don't get drawn into any type of commitment, either by being pressured to say yes or by thinking you can deflect the pressure by offering a "maybe." If you say "maybe," the project owners hear "yes." If you agree to something without knowing what you are agreeing to, then it will almost certainly end badly. You may be the hero in the first kick-off meeting, but you'll be the villain when the project starts to go sideways because you agreed to something you didn't understand. Instead, explain that you need some time to look at everything you've been told, consider the requirements, and come back to the stakeholders after you've done some planning to determine whether it's feasible. This is surely a reasonable request. And of course, if the project they are asking for is impossible, you will have the information that proves it.

NOTE

Planning makes you stronger.

Watch me explain key drivers in this short clip.

QUICKCLIP

To watch the QuickClip, use the camera on your mobile phone to scan the QR code or visit the link below.

or

www.quickclips.io/pm-2

📱 SCAN ME

🖥 VISIT URL

Second Kick-Off Meeting

After the first kick-off meeting, you need to go away and analyze whether what the stakeholders want is possible. Can it be done in the time frame, to the specifications, within the budget? Ideally, there needs to be a gap of at least several weeks between the first and second kick-off meetings so you can really drill into the detail and assess what's possible against hopes and expectations. You will be mapping out steps 2 through 4 (list the tasks, set up the running order, estimate the costs and times). You need that detail to be able to make an informed assessment. You could do all of this in a few hours if it didn't involve other people, but inevitably you'll have to get quotes from suppliers and information from internal departments like HR or IT or facilities, and that can require a bit of waiting.

Once you're ready, you set a second kick-off meeting, which is where you tell the stakeholders whether it can be done. There are really only two outcomes. One is a good-news meeting where you get to tell the stakeholders that it can be done. These are rare, unfortunately! The more common option is a bad-news meeting.

Don't ever say yes if you can't do it or if you still don't know if you can do it. You'll end up being the hero at the start but the villain at the end.

A bad-news meeting is when you need to tell the stakeholders that what they want can't be done. It can appear obstructive and negative, which is why planning the project and looking at the requirements are so important. *Planning makes you stronger.* Instead of appearing defeatist and negative, you are able to say, "I'd love to promise you that, but the list of tasks, running order, and time and cost estimates are saying no. But don't worry; I've found a way it can be done. If we can find a way to boost the budget by 5 percent, then we can pull it off, because that will allow us to pay for specialist equipment." Or, "If we can find another four weeks in the timeline, then we can do it." Or, "If we drop the spec in this area and this area, we can do it."

Essentially, you are offering trades between the elements in the iron triangle that you know are not key drivers in the project in order to find a compromise that everyone can get behind. There is no point in offering a trade on the key driver, because meeting that driver—whether it's time, money, or quality—is the one thing that will determine success for the project owner or stakeholders. The key driver must be met, but there is usually wiggle room around the other two.

Be assertive and clear. Lean on your assessment and the planning you've done. I often joke that great project managers are assertive, with a dash of pessimism and a healthy dollop of detail obsession—great people to invite to a party!

» You need the assertiveness so that you don't get pushed around or backed into a corner by a project owner. If the client is more senior than you, which is likely, you may feel a huge amount of pressure to go along with what's been asked for, even if it's highly unlikely to be achieved. Or maybe the client is very assertive and even tries to bully you into agreeing that the project can be done. Don't accept either. Stay strong and use your planning to prove your points.

» You need some pessimism because what can go wrong probably will go wrong. It's always far easier to anticipate those speed bumps, put a bit of a safety margin in, and celebrate if they don't happen, than to cross your fingers and hope they don't show up.

» And the detail obsession is particularly helpful because you need to be thorough; check, double-check, and triple-check for planning every single task that needs to be done.

This is why you need time between the two meetings. You need to get to a position where you are so confident in your planning, even if it's rough planning at this stage, that if you say no, you are doing so not to be difficult but because you know that it simply can't be done within the existing parameters, and you can prove it. But do this in a way that offers solutions, not problems. Again, this is why planning is so crucial between the first and second kick-off meetings: because you will be able to come up with alternative solutions so that the project team can decide on the best outcome and what can be adjusted—price, time, or quality.

 Never hedge your bets and say "maybe" or "I'll do my best." Stakeholders only hear "yes" or "no." Be decisive. Get off the fence by saying either yes or no. Otherwise, you've lost control over what they hear.

It is not your responsibility to decide on changes to the iron triangle. Your job is to present the project owners and decision makers with evidence about whether the project can be done, and if not, to offer various scenarios to make it possible. That is your responsibility. It is the stakeholders' job and responsibility to decide what to do with your information. They must decide which option to go for, or even whether to continue with the project at all. All the stakeholders must agree and commit to what is going to be delivered and agree to be available when needed to deliver on the objective.

So if you're going to say yes, you need to have a good plan so you know you can definitely deliver on that promise. If you're going to say no, you need a good plan so you can prove that more time or money is going to be needed. And if you want to say maybe, then you need a better plan to find out whether it's really a yes or a no. It's all in the planning!

Put All Agreements and Parameters in Writing

Once the kick-off meetings have been concluded and the project has been defined, make sure everything that's agreed on is put in writing.

> *What is not on paper has not been said.*
>
> – ANONYMOUS

Usually, getting things in writing can be as simple as a confirmation email sent after the meeting to outline the outcomes and agreements. You might think it's OK to have it in your head, and in your customer's head, but things always change during the life of any project. Initial agreements and promises get forgotten. There might even be a different customer or set of stakeholders by the end. Having the written documentation at the start acts as a flag in the sand for everyone involved in the project.

It is also useful when things change: you can use those written agreements to alert the project owner to the implication of those changes and negotiate alterations to the iron triangle if necessary. For example, if the quality spec changes during the project, you are able to use the initial agreed-upon spec documented in the confirmation email to show that you need an increase in the budget or the timeline to accommodate that change. Maybe the new spec can be done, or maybe it will require compromise elsewhere (more money or more time), but at least you can have a full and frank discussion about the change to the spec and what that means for project delivery.

In this case, don't worry about being committed to something that you can't deliver. As long as you've done thorough planning and have assessed the project properly, that opening confirmation email will align with what's possible right now and what it will take to deliver the project as originally outlined. It is kind of a constraint, and it can also confirm that you've failed—and even with a great plan you might still fail. But one thing's for sure: if you leave the project open-ended, then you absolutely *will* fail.

Why is that? Because the stakeholders *will* move the goalposts during the project, and they *will* complain afterward that they didn't get what they wanted or expected. Getting it in writing up front helps to prevent both problems. It will alert you to exactly when the stakeholders move the goalposts and will allow you to renegotiate against those altered expectations. The stakeholders probably will get what they want, but they are also forced to acknowledge that they've moved the goalposts and therefore changes to the project parameters are almost inevitable.

Stakeholders aren't always moving goalposts maliciously. Often, people genuinely forget what was agreed to, which means it's only a matter of time before they start to feel like they didn't get what they wanted. Also, the external environment inevitably changes during projects, so requirements will almost certainly change to some degree. Written agreements keep everyone honest and on track. Being able to say, "Look, this is what we agreed on, and we can make changes, but that's going to require some additional resources" makes it easier and less stressful for everyone. And people move in and out of the project team, so having something in writing to bring new people up to speed can be helpful. If you have everything in writing, you have a better chance of success.

> *No major project is ever installed on time, within budget, with the same staff that started it.*
> — EDWARDS, BUTLER, HILL, AND RUSSELL

Three Levels of Approval

This chapter is all about defining the project, which essentially means gaining clarity on what the project is going to be so that decisions can be made regarding whether to continue with it or not. That decision involves getting approval from all the stakeholders. The following three-level approval technique is actually a PRINCE2 technique and it's really useful, especially for larger projects. Overall, I think PRINCE2 is too complex for most people, but this is one of the parts I like. It's an easy addition to your project management repertoire that can save everyone a lot of time. Choose to use it on larger projects.

The idea is that there are three stages of approval, each nesting inside the previous one, like Russian dolls (figure 11).

THREE LEVELS OF APPROVAL

fig. 11

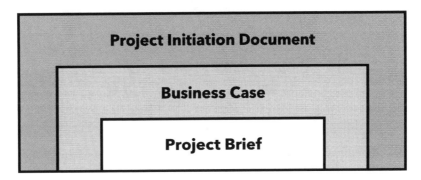

Project Brief

The *project brief* outlines the purpose of the project and communicates that purpose and the agreed-upon approach, so that everyone on the project team is on the same page. It is essentially a "pitch" that explains the project objectives, scope, key deliverables, milestones, and timeline and asks, Is this the kind of thing we want to do?

It is a great first step in the project decision-making process because it is relatively easy to pull together. There is no point in moving to a business case or diving into the detail of a project initiation document (which we'll be discussing shortly) if the project owner looks at the brief and says no.

I have a friend who works in the IT department of a large company. He's been there for years, but his dream is to open up an adventure-vacation business in the Pyrenees. He wants to buy a cottage and a bunch of mountain bikes and run cycling vacations during the summer and skiing vacations in the winter. His dilemma is whether to bite the bullet and do it or stay safe for a few more years in the IT department, saving those activities for retirement—maybe. There is no point in his pricing the mountain bikes, working out how much he can charge for vacations, or checking on the cost of property in his desired location until he's got some sort of approval from the project owner—in this case, his wife. The project would mean a new life in a different country; it's not just *his* decision. So he could write up a project brief, a page or two that outlines his thinking and his plan, and show it to his wife.

If she says, "Oh, that sounds really interesting, what a fun adventure," then he has approval to investigate further. The decision has not been made to move to the Pyrenees, but it's not been knocked on the head. If his wife says, "No way, what about our life here, and our grandkids? I don't want to go." Then (depending on the strength of the marriage!) the project is dead in the water. Either way, the project brief will be enough to either kill the project, saving him a lot of wasted planning time, or warrant further investigation; he has the approval to continue because the idea is appealing, but they still don't know if it can be done with their current resources.

The project brief therefore gives a big-picture overview of what the project is all about, so that everyone can be sure they are talking about the same thing. It creates the groundwork for shared understanding and agreement regarding the nature of the project and whether those involved ultimately approve of the idea. Does it fit with the organization's strategy? Is it a priority?

 A blank, printable template for a project brief is available with your Digital Assets. Use it as a simple guide to completing a project brief without the stress. Access this and more at go.quickstartguides.com/project.

If it's you that's initiating the project idea, then you'll probably prepare it on your own and present it to your boss or the stakeholders. If it's someone else who is asking you to get it approved and do it for them, then you, as the project manager, will prepare the project brief in tandem with the client/your boss and then present it to the other project stakeholders for their approval, before you go ahead with any more planning work.

Despite its name, this first level of approval isn't always especially brief. After all, it's supposed to describe the whole project, even if it's taking a broader view, so it might be anywhere from half a page to several pages long. Regardless of the project's size or shape, a good project brief should always include the following:

» **Title**: What is the project going to be known as?

» **Client**: Who is the client? What is their contact information, type of business, or customer base?

» **Project Definition**: What is the background to the project? What are the required outcomes? What is the scope of the project?

> » **Project Approach:** What processes and procedures are going to be used to achieve the project objective?

> » **Project Objective:** What is the project objective, explained in as much detail as possible? How will success be measured?

> » **Project Details:** Who is the target audience? What are the goals and approximate timelines (estimated, not calculated)? Are there any phases, and if so, how many?

Business Case

Assuming my friend's wife is on board with the idea of setting up an adventure holiday business, it sounds promising—but neither of them has any idea whether it's viable or even what's really involved. And that's where the *business case* comes in.

A blank, printable template for a business case is available with your Digital Assets. Use it as a simple guide to completing a business case without the hassle. Access this and more at go.quickstartguides.com/project.

The business case builds on the project brief, adding more meat to the bones. Specifically, it looks at what is wanted in light of whether or not it makes financial sense to initiate the proposed project. It's interested in cost, return on investment, and other hard financial data. In my friend's case, it will involve things like pricing local real estate and working out how much they might get for their family home and how much it would cost to move. How many skiing packages is he likely to sell and for how much? What about sales and costs of the mountain biking? What's realistic?

At one point in our lives, my wife was really keen to open an internet café and sell coffee and cakes. I wasn't averse to the idea, so it passed the project brief stage. But as soon as we sat down to look at the business case, it fell apart. Considering the costs of rent for premises in our area and how much it would cost to set up the computers with high-speed broadband, compared to the tiny amount that was going to be earned from coffee and cakes, it was unlikely to break even, never mind make money. My wife makes amazing cakes, but there was no way she could sell enough to cover the costs. Unfortunately, it didn't work financially.

The business case sets out to prove to the client, customer, or other stakeholders that the project is a good idea. Can the business afford to start the project? Can the business afford not to? What is the expected return on investment and how long will it take to pay back that investment? Is there an opportunity cost for running this project versus another one?

Compared to a brief, the business case is much more concerned with how the project will benefit the client or business. It weighs the cost, time, and risk of doing the project against the expected benefits. This means that it must be grounded in reality as it examines how the project will impact the business. It looks at the why, what, when, and how of the project. Whereas the brief sets out what is wanted, the business case looks much more closely at the ramifications of the project.

Here is what a robust business case will cover:

» **Reason**: Why is this project being considered? What problem is it seeking to solve?

» **Options**: Are there any other options or ways to solve the problem that would make more financial sense or be faster or more economical?

» **Benefits**: What are the expected benefits of the project? What does the project owner expect to receive or improve as a result of the project?

» **Timescales**: When are these benefits likely to become evident? There are usually two timescales to consider: the length of time to complete the project and the length of time it will take for the return on investment to become evident.

» **Costs**: How much will it cost? No, really, how much will it actually cost? Are there unknowns? How risky are those unknowns, and what is the plan for unexpected costs?

» **Risks**: What could go wrong? It's always best to image the worst-case scenario and have a plan or some type of contingency in place to deal with that risk should it arise.

» **Investment assessment**: Are the investment, disruption, time, and effort really worth it?

The business case is where many projects go to die. They don't pass the test in terms of costs and return on investment—like my wife's lovely café idea. But it's far better to know this up front than to press on regardless and lose a lot of time and money.

People sometimes lie to get their projects approved! Often, it's not even deliberate; it's that their optimism is not grounded in reality, so they overestimate how much can be made or underestimate how much it will cost. Don't be tempted to do it; it almost always ends in disappointment. You'll get approval, but then either the project initiation document (PID) will expose you and your project will get chucked after you've done lots of work or, even worse, you'll push straight into doing a project that will wind up failing.

Project Initiation Document (PID)

The final level of approval is the *project initiation document* (PID). This is a detailed plan of how the project will be executed. It is a continuation and to some extent an amalgamation of the previous two documents, but it goes into much more depth—it's the biggest Russian doll.

A blank, printable template for a PID is available with your Digital Assets. Use it as a simple guide to help you create a more robust PID. Find it at go.quickstartguides.com/project.

In my friend's case, if his wife was on board after the brief and the business case made financial sense, then the investigation would be expanded into a PID, where he would look at everything involved in the project, not just financials. This would include logistics, like assessing how easy it would be to set up a business in the Pyrenees, and whether there are visa requirements or restrictions that might impact the idea. It would analyze how much competition there is, how successful those businesses are. Could he take early retirement to help fund the first few months? Should he rent or buy the mountain bikes and ski gear before he goes, or get them there? The PID digs into these more detailed questions and answers. It is still an essential step, especially for larger projects—but only if the project has passed the previous two approval stages.

The PID also explores the what, why, how, who, when, and how much, and in much greater detail. A project initiation document will cover all this:

» **What**: This defines the project and the scope and will include background on the project to give context and explain what the project is. It will cover the purpose of the project, objectives, scope, deliverables, constraints, exclusions, assumptions, and deal-breakers.

» **Why**: This is where you pull in information from the business case about why the project makes commercial and financial sense. "Why" covers the cost-benefit analysis as well as risk assessment, options, and timing. This is the justification for the project and expected benefits.

» **How and Who**: This defines how the project will be conducted and the roles and responsibilities of the team. It includes organizational charts and structures (specific roles and the relevant reporting lines), who has the ultimate authority, who is project manager, and all the key team members with their roles and job descriptions.

» **When**: This outlines how the project will roll out, by defining timelines, phases, and the resources needed at each phase. It includes assignments (major tasks and milestones), the schedule, human resources needed at each stage, as well as project and quality control—how quality will be measured along the way, etc.

» **How Much**: This delineates the funding for the project and makes it clear what financial resources are needed at each stage.

This looks like a lot of work, but really it's not. You have to plan the project anyway, and steps 2 through 8 will do all this for you, as we'll see.

A thorough PID gives everyone involved in the project the information they need to fully understand the objective and their individual role in delivering that objective. It also gives the project owner enough information to make an informed decision about whether to move forward with the project.

When you move from a project brief to a business case to a PID, it may feel as if you're duplicating work. But this progression makes a lot of sense; there's no point in going straight to a business case or a PID if you don't know whether anyone wants the project. Think of these three similar-yet-distinct documents as incremental steppingstones along the path toward a go/no-go decision. And really, if you did go straight to the PID, you'd still have to outline what the project was and look at the financial case and the costs involved, all as part of the PID. So doing the previous stages actually saves time, either by helping you gather information for your PID or saving you from writing an unnecessary one.

Chapter Recap

> » Every project is constrained (to some extent) by the iron triangle, which consists of three things that are evident in every project and set parameters for the project. They are cost, quality, and time.

> » It's impossible to deliver an amazing outcome really quickly with a very small budget. One of your first jobs as project manager will be to explain to the customer that they can't actually have all three. They can usually have two but not three.

> » Before you can determine whether a project can be done, you need to define the project. This is done in the first kick-off meeting where all the stakeholders come together to decide what they want, so that you can take that information and work out whether it can be done.

> » In order to assess feasibility, you will need to understand what the key driver is for the client or project owner. The key driver is the major variable (time, cost, or quality) that is of greater importance than the other two.

> » Don't ever commit to anything during the first kick-off meeting. You may be the hero in the moment, but you'll be the villain when the project starts to go sideways because you agreed to something you didn't understand.

> » The second kick-off meeting is when you deliver the news of whether the project is possible—and if it's not, what alterations would make it possible. Then the plan gets signed off on.

> » Whatever is agreed on, get it in writing. Projects always change, and having a marker in the sand regarding the opening agreement will allow you to renegotiate, if necessary, should the project scope change.

> » For larger projects, use the sequence of three levels of approval, which can help you filter out projects and save time and stress. The levels are a project brief, a business case, and a project initiation document (PID). Only if the brief is approved do you move to the business case and then the PID.

PART II

MAPPING OUT THE IDEAL PLAN

| 4 |
List the Tasks – Step 2

Chapter Overview
- » The three methods for creating a complete task list
- » Insight into the level of detail required
- » Which approach is right for your project?

The secret of getting ahead is getting started. The secret of getting started is breaking your complex overwhelming tasks into small, manageable tasks, and then starting on the first one.

– MARK TWAIN

Once the stakeholders have defined and agreed to the project, you as project manager need to work out whether it can be accomplished. Step 2 is where that assessment begins in earnest. You have the project objective, you know the time frame and budget available, and you understand the level of quality that's required. Now it's time to list all the tasks that will need to be done to fulfill that objective. These tasks will become the raw material of your planning.

But this is not always easy.

A project always has a finish line, involves something new, and delivers a benefit (but not right away).

Issues at step 2 often arise from the fact that projects involve something new. How can you list all the tasks involved in building a house or opening a new office in Paris if you've never built a house or opened an office in Paris? You can't, really—not one hundred percent perfectly anyway—but there are ways to ensure you create as thorough and complete a list as possible. There will always be some tasks that slip through, but the aim of step 2 is to ensure that those missed tasks are kept to an absolute minimum.

It's very important to try to get all the tasks listed, because missing a task will always impact the project. It will definitely make it more expensive than you expected, it will probably mean the project takes more time than you expected, and you may have to reduce the quality of something else in order to accommodate that missed task. A complete list of tasks will reduce the number of surprises later.

Methods to Ensure a Complete Task List

There are three completely different ways to ensure that your project task list is as complete as possible right from the start. You can use one, two, or all three of them. It's best to think of these methods as steps that will allow you to progressively capture a more complete list of tasks. Aim to do all three steps, in this order, if you have the time.

» Brainstorm
» Use a work breakdown structure (WBS)
» Ask an expert

Brainstorm

A brainstorm is a meeting with your team where you each use the creative right side of your brain to come up with possible tasks for the project.

In his book *The Wisdom of Crowds*, author James Surowiecki demonstrates that if you put together a group of people big enough and diverse enough and ask them to make decisions, the group's decisions over time will be intellectually superior, and their estimates more accurate, than those made by an isolated individual—no matter how smart or well-informed the individual is. In other words, the many are always smarter than the few. This can feel counterintuitive, especially when we've been repeatedly told that experts know best. But we all have something to offer. Brainstorming with your team will always result in more ideas and better ideas because everyone brings their own unique outlook, expertise, life experience, and areas of obsession. Other people will always think of things that you may never have thought of alone. Besides, it would be quite lonely to brainstorm alone!

The key to productive brainstorming is to get as many potential tasks out on the table as possible. This is not a space for assessment, criticism, or judgment. Once the team has run out of ideas, you can collectively look over the list and decide which of the suggested tasks are going to be necessary.

You can try a couple of different methods when brainstorming with a group. One is to brainstorm randomly, with team members encouraged to shout out tasks that they imagine might be needed over the course of the project. Another is to start at the beginning of the project and run a collective thought experiment where you attempt to walk through the project in a logical order.

A thought experiment is really just a logical argument considered in the imagination. If you wanted to build a house, the thought experiment would involve asking yourself, Where do I start? and What comes next? What's needed before any building work can be done? Find a site, get the necessary approvals—both of which can then be broken down into multiple subtasks. You don't really need to know exactly how to build a house to know logically what sort of tasks will be required to pull that off. We all live in a house, so we know about walls and rooms and heating, etc. A thought experiment is simply going through the project in your imagination, each team member doing the same thing so that collectively you can identify as many tasks as possible. Albert Einstein used thought experiments to figure out how things might work. For example, when explaining his theory of special relativity, he would mentally chase beams of light or envision moving trains; for his theory of general relativity, he would picture accelerating elevators, someone falling from a roof, or blind beetles crawling over a curved surface. And honestly, if it was good enough for Einstein, it might be worth a shot.

The other crucial benefit of involving the team up front this way is that you get their buy-in. Pulling off any project successfully requires the concerted effort of the entire project team. Getting their input on what will need to be done not only ensures that more of the tasks are identified, but it connects those tasks to the people in the team, who in turn will be more invested in making sure they are done properly.

Think of the endowment effect, the idea that we instinctively value our own ideas over other people's ideas, and we value what we already own over what others own. Involving the team means that they will be more invested in the project because they had a part in coming up with the list of tasks that they will later be working on.

Work Breakdown Structure (WBS)

The second method for making sure you capture all the tasks is a more structured form of brainstorming. Essentially, you plug the tasks identified in the brainstorm into a more formal structure that will also aid in alerting you to what tasks are still missing. Rather than using the creative right side of the brain to generate ideas, this time the team employs the logical left side of their brains to work through the project process.

One of the best ways to do this is by using a ***work breakdown structure (WBS)***, which is a fancy name for a systematic way to show all the work that will be needed in a project. WBS is in the PMI's PMBOK and is defined as a "deliverable-oriented hierarchical decomposition of the work to be executed by the project team." An easier way to visualize a WBS is as a tree diagram that lists all the tasks and shows the relationship between those tasks. It's like an organizational chart or a family tree; each successive level adds more detail. The last level of the WBS is normally a level that has independent time constraints and responsibilities—in other words, actionable tasks.

There are two types of WBS:
1. Deliverable-based
2. Phase-based

DELIVERABLE-BASED WBS FOR BUILDING A HOUSE

fig. 12

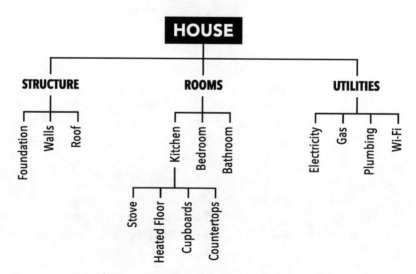

Both can be useful. The main difference is what is identified at the start, or on the first level: is it the jobs to be done (the phases) or what will end up being produced (the deliverables)? Figure 12 is an example of a deliverable-based WBS for building a house. This means that the first level is deliverables: the main structure, the individual rooms, and the utilities or services. Underneath those elements are the subtasks within each one, which may well go down two or three levels. You can see that I've gone into more detail for the kitchen, to show you how it might look.

Often the WBS is produced in an outline format to show the levels. Because of the levels inherent in this approach, it lends itself very well to an Excel spreadsheet (figure 13). It is easy to move things around and add in anything that was initially missed. There are thousands of rows and columns in Excel, so you'll never run out of space, and you can add different worksheets for different projects or different sub-projects within the same project. It's also a program most of us already have on our computers, or can obtain easily, so there is no need for specialist software.

fig. 13

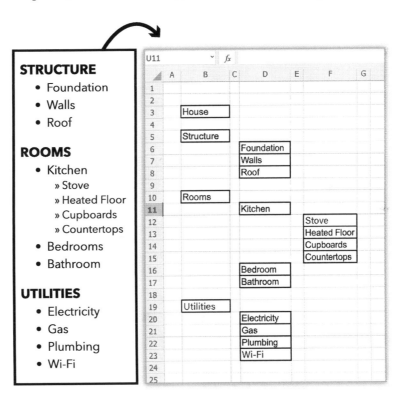

Figure 14 shows a phase-based WBS. As the name would suggest, the first level is focused on the various phases of the house's construction, with more details of these phases underneath. The first example was focused on deliverables, for example, kitchen countertops, but these can also be thought of as jobs to do: install the countertops. This second example, phases, is definitely focusing on jobs to do rather than deliverables, and they are in chronological order.

PHASE-BASED WBS FOR BUILDING A HOUSE

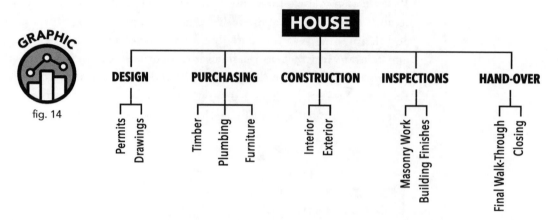

fig. 14

A WBS helps you organize tasks into categories and makes it easier for the team to spot if anything is missing. It can be used in tandem with brainstorming and can alert everyone involved about things that may have been missed when considering either the deliverable or the phase.

Characteristics of a Strong WBS

Personally, I feel that the best work breakdown structures describe the work to be done, rather than the outcomes of that work. The project scope and definition tell you what the project owner wants to achieve; the WBS then outlines everything that needs to happen for that outcome to be delivered.

A robust, useful WBS should exhibit the following characteristics:

» **Well defined:** The tasks should all be described and easily understood by everyone on the project team.

» **Doable:** The tasks should outline a feasible unit of work to be assigned to one individual or one team.

- » **Possible to Estimate:** It should be possible to realistically estimate the amount of time required to complete the task, as well as cost or use of other resources.

- » **Divided into Independent Tasks:** Ideally, each task should stand alone and have minimum dependence on other ongoing elements.

- » **Possible to Measure:** It should be possible to measure the progress of each identified task, and each should have a start and finish date as well as milestones in between.

- » **Adaptable:** Projects are changeable, so a good WBS is flexible so that additions or amendments to the scope can be accommodated.

- » **Clearly Worded:** Always seek to express your milestones as nouns (words used to classify something) and express the tasks as verbs (words that describe an action, or "doing" words). See figure 15 as an example.

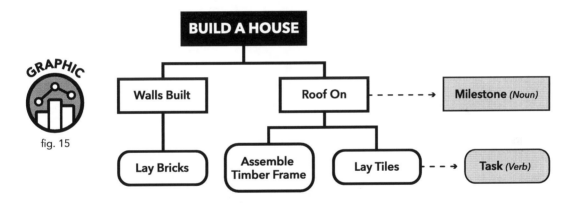

fig. 15

You can put everything into your WBS like this: The top level of the WBS is your project title level. The second level is your list of major deliverables or milestones. The last level should be your list of actual tasks. The main objective is to get *all* the tasks listed, without missing any. The list of tasks needs to be broken down sufficiently so that each one is a separate activity that is the responsibility of one team or one individual.

Ask an Expert

Now we've used our right and left brains for the brainstorm and the WBS. The last way to make sure all the tasks are identified (or as many as possible) is to use *someone else's* brain. This might be an expert in the field or someone who has done a similar project before. That's really all an expert is—someone who has experience in doing what you are attempting to do. They know the potential mistakes because they've probably already made them. Those experiences make experts a valuable resource for understanding all the tasks you'll need to complete. It's always best to ask an expert *after* brainstorming and creating a WBS, because they are especially useful for spotting tasks the other methods have missed. Creating your task list in this order is also more respectful of the expert's time and expertise.

An expert is someone who knows some of the worst mistakes that can be made in their subject, and how to avoid them.

— WERNER HEISENBERG

If you work for a smart organization that insists on project reviews and that documents past projects, then you can also research those past projects. These files on previous projects may be held by the project management office (PMO) if there is one, or they might be held by whichever department has done the projects. If you're lucky, you'll find that a similar project has been documented, which might include objectives, a task list, and learnings you can study. If such documents exist, they can be a rich source of insight into some of the tasks that may not yet be on anyone's radar.

The problem is that most organizations don't have those documents in the first place; maybe there were no written project plans, or the plans weren't kept, or they aren't filed in a way that makes them easily searchable. Or maybe it's all in various people's heads, spread all over the organization. If so, then asking an expert may mean a few conversations with internal people from past projects or external contractors or consultants who can help you to create a thorough and complete task list.

Which Method to Use

Though your project may favor brainstorming, using a WBS, or asking experts, it's not always a question of which single method to use but rather how to use them all together. The three approaches work together in a way similar to the project brief, business case, and PID, where each one leads to the next. Figure 16 illustrates the connection and the optimal order for identifying tasks.

METHODS FOR ENSURING YOUR TASK LIST IS COMPLETE

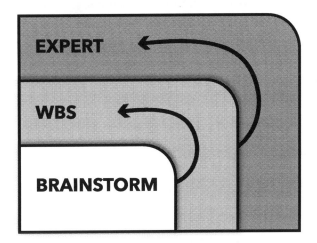

Start off with the brainstorm to activate the right, creative side of your brain and those of your team members. Next use a work breakdown structure to organize the tasks into categories, which will also help to alert you to new tasks or elements that are missing. And finally, give an expert the resulting WBS and ask for their input, or whether you've missed anything. This order is preferable for everyone. The expert isn't wasting their time pointing out the obvious things that you and your team would have identified anyway, and they are also much more likely to see something that you've completely missed. It's always a bit annoying when you realize you've missed something—but it's very useful to the project as a whole!

For large projects, it can also be very beneficial to engage in brainstorms with different groups of people, based on various aspects of the project. And if the project is quite similar to a well-documented previous one, that previous project may be the most sensible starting place. However, for most projects it's best to stick with this order: brainstorm, WBS, expert input. You're always better off using two or three methods to identify all the tasks. Your planning will be more accurate as a result.

Granularity—How Detailed Do You Get?

One of the biggest challenges you are likely to face when listing all the tasks is uncertainty about how detailed you need to get. Fine detail is known as *granularity*. If you get too detailed, you'll waste a load of time, only to end up with a ridiculously complex and unmanageable project plan. But if you don't get detailed enough, then you won't have a good handle on the tasks involved. You won't understand what the high-level tasks actually consist of, which in turn will make your estimates less accurate.

There are no clear, hard rules about this. Deciding on the level of granularity is often a judgment call. For example, if you've installed lots of kitchens before, then you'll know how much they cost and how long they take, so you can probably simply list "kitchen" in your house-building plan. But someone like me who knows nothing about kitchens would have to break the task down to the individual holes to be drilled in order to know how much time and money would be needed. In other words, how detailed your plan needs to be is a personal decision. You are aiming for the Goldilocks zone: not too much detail, but also not too little … just right.

Three Signs That You Need More Detail

It's often hard to know how much detail is just right. This is especially true in projects that involve tasks you've never done before. Here are three signs that should alert you to the fact that you need more detail:

» A Task Too Big to Estimate
» Task Overlaps
» The Forbidden O-Word

The Task Is Too Big to Estimate: If you've identified a task but are finding it impossible to estimate time and cost, then it's almost certainly too big. Going back to the house-building project, you might have identified "install kitchen" as a task. But unless you have experience with this particular task, it's difficult to estimate time or cost because there are too many variables. You need to break it down into increasingly smaller tasks until you reach a "just right" level of detail that allows you to accurately estimate how much that type of kitchen will cost and how long it will take to install.

Tasks Overlap: If you have a task that overlaps with another task, this is usually a sign that you need more granularity. If task A and task B overlap, you need to know exactly when in the process of accomplishing task A that you can start on task B. The best way to handle the overlap is to break the tasks down further.

Suppose, for example, I am going to overlap the painting of the rooms and the fitting of the carpets, in order to get the whole job done quicker.

That's fine, but at which point in the painting can I start on the carpets? One way to think about this is to divide the painting task: as soon as all the rooms that are going to be fitted with carpet have been painted, I can start installing the carpet in those while the painter continues to paint the rooms that will not have carpet. See figure 17 (which we'll be exploring in more detail in the next chapter), which shows how the task of painting has been granulated to increase efficiency.

OPTION 1:
SPLITTING TASKS BY EXTRA GRANULARITY

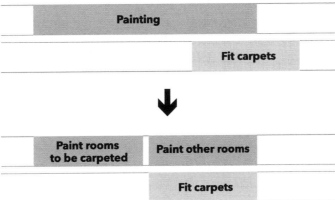

fig. 17

OPTION 2:
SPLITTING TASKS BY EXTRA GRANULARITY

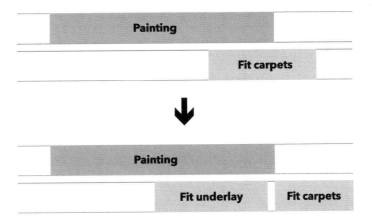

fig. 18

The other way to think about it is to divide the carpeting task into parts that can overlap with painting and parts that can't. Maybe I'll fit the underlay while the painters are working, but I can't fit the finished carpets until the painters have gone. We don't want drips of paint on our carpets! Figure 18 shows the second task (fitting carpets) now granulated into two tasks, fitting carpets and fitting underlay.

The key here is to keep breaking down the task until you hit a point where you can figure out when each task should start.

The O-Word: The forbidden o-word is "ongoing," and it's rumored that it's so bad that whenever anyone utters the o-word in projects, somewhere a kitten dies! At the very least, "ongoing" is a danger signal in project management. In fact, it's the bane of any project manager's life. "Ongoing" really means that there isn't a plan available for the person assigned to that task. Without a firm start or finish date, its execution is lamely labeled "ongoing." Returning to the house-building example, say the electrician tells you that the electrical work is going to be ongoing. In that case, push for clarity. This is a sure sign that there is not enough detail, and no one has enough of a grip on what will actually be done and when.

Of course, it's understandable that some people feel safer with the o-word. If you are asking suppliers or project team members to estimate time and cost, it will take some time, and there may be a reluctance to spend that time if the project has not yet been given the green light. It's your job to remind everyone involved that there is no way the green light will be given on the project without that detail.

Once the project has been given the go-ahead, it's even more important to push back on anyone hoping to get away with using "ongoing" to refer to any ask that's between 10 percent and 90 percent complete. You need to know the exact status or get those involved to admit they don't know the exact status, so they can go and figure it out. You need a weekly plan; otherwise, those tasks will be put off until the last minute and you won't know there is a slip in the timeline until it's too late. Make people commit.

Ideally, you should be aiming for between ten and twenty identified tasks in your main project plan. Depending on the size of the project, that number may go up to thirty—but any more than that and the project will probably start to get too cumbersome.

It's never too late to granulate! If you start to notice an overlap in those ten to twenty tasks, or you can't make the time or cost estimates accurately, then you can always add more granularity and create a more detailed subplan. Or if you need to speed the project up and you decide to do it by overlapping a couple of tasks, you may want to break one of them down to show the overlap more clearly.

If you do find your project nudging past thirty tasks, you might be better off breaking it down into sub-projects to make it more manageable. So, with our house example, rather than our main project plan listing all the tasks associated with building a kitchen, we could list "build kitchen" as a high-level task and create a more detailed subplan, which would list the ten to twenty specific kitchen installation tasks. That way we wouldn't need to be too worried about the kitchen until we were ready to install it, and then, when we needed it, the plan for the installation would be laid out for us, without complicating the main project plan.

Bottom-Up Versus Top-Down Planning

When you are creating the project plan, you will need to decide quite early on whether you are going to create it bottom-up or top-down.

QUICKCLIP

I've made a short video on the difference between bottom-up and top-down planning.

To watch the QuickClip, use the camera on your mobile phone to scan the QR code or visit the link below.

SCAN ME

or

www.quickclips.io/pm-3

VISIT URL

Let me explain …

In a perfect world, you would create your plan using the bottom-up approach to planning. This means working out how long each task or sub-project will take to complete, and how much it will cost, and then feeding that information back into the larger project plan to give you an accurate overview of time and cost.

However, we don't live in a perfect world. Instead, the opposite often happens: top-down planning. In top-down planning, you as the project manager, usually in tandem with the project owner, put your own cost and timeline estimates and constraints into the high-level project plan. Then you tell everyone involved to come back with a plan for how their assigned tasks can be accomplished within the given budget and time frame. The various project team members will then come back with the good news that the tasks are doable or with estimates of how much more time and/or money is actually required. Then you build those changes into the high-level plan and figure out whether that still works for the project owner. The advantages of top-down planning are that it's much quicker and it puts a bit of pressure on each team member, rather than allowing them to take as long as they like. The problem is that you and the project owner may not know enough to be able to estimate every task accurately. Those involved in delivering the project may also spend a lot of unnecessary money keeping to a timescale you estimated, when you could have gotten a more accurate one by asking for more input.

Whatever approach you use, spend some time on step 2. Remember, the tasks are the raw material of your plan; you'll always miss some, but a comprehensive list of tasks up front will massively increase your chance of success and allow you to create the best plan possible.

Remember, once the project goes live, make sure you document any tasks that the client asks for after the project begins and get them to sign for it at the time. This is called scope creep, and although it can seem petty and bureaucratic to push for this sign-off in writing every time, it's important because all the little changes add up. An extra five percent of work could easily halve or even wipe out your profit from the whole project. At the end, when you have spent more than originally agreed, you will be able to point to the folder of these *change request forms* and remind them that there is an additional $100,000 worth of changes that were asked for, agreed on, and acted on.

I've included a change request form template as a Digital Asset. Find it at go.quickstartguides.com/project.

Chapter Recap

» Identifying all the tasks that will need to be done to deliver on a project is not always easy because projects by their nature involve doing something new.

» Missing tasks can negatively impact a project by delaying it, making it more expensive, or requiring a drop in quality. It's always better to spend the time up front to identify as many tasks as possible.

» There are three main ways to accurately identify the tasks of any project: brainstorming, using a work breakdown structure (WBS), and asking experts for their advice.

» Brainstorming uses the creative right side of the brain. Starting from a point without limits means the group usually comes up with more and better task suggestions. Brainstorming also helps the project team buy into the project.

» A work breakdown structure (WBS) activates the logical left side of the brain. It's like an organizational chart, where the tasks identified in the brainstorm are plugged into a more organized and structured plan.

» It can be useful to share your WBS with an expert, someone who has experience doing a similar project. The expert may identify tasks that you and your team would never have identified on your own.

» When listing your tasks, be mindful of granularity, going into enough detail to identify discrete tasks but not so much that the planning becomes overly complicated.

» There are three signs that you need to push for more detail and break the tasks down further: the task is too big to estimate its time or cost; tasks overlap, making it impossible to see clear start and finish dates; and use of the word "ongoing."

» Use more than one method to identify tasks so that you are more likely to capture all of them. Your planning will be better and more accurate as a result.

| 5 |
Set the Running Order – Step 3

Chapter Overview
- » Using Post-its to easily set the running order
- » Critical path method (CPM)
- » Project evaluation and review technique (PERT)

Once you've outlined all the tasks that will need to be done to ensure the project's success, it's time to arrange those tasks into some sort of running order.

Step 3 is really the heart of your project plan. This is where you work out how all the tasks fit together—what has to be done before what—and where you decide how you are actually going to do the project. The project goes from "I have no idea how to do this" to "I have a plan; I know what needs to be done and I know where I'm going to start," which feels much better.

Let's say the project is to set up your own business. You've identified ten to twenty main tasks that need to be done in order to get started. They might include finding premises, getting computers and employees, making a website, and, before all that, getting the funding.

You might be most excited about the first thing you thought of: the state-of-the-art IT that's at the top of *your* task list. But that clearly isn't the starting point for the project, and you need to make sure you don't jump the gun because you're so excited about that one task. Setting the ***running order*** lists all the tasks that need to be done, what needs to happen first and what order the rest of the tasks need to be completed in, so you can determine how long the whole project will take. It is also the first opportunity for you to figure out which tasks are concurrent (those that can be performed at the same time) and which ones are dependent on other tasks being finished first. "What do I need first, the website or the employees? Or can I acquire both at the same time?"

Network Diagrams and the Power of Post-its
A ***network diagram*** is just a posh term for the visual representation of

your project. The approach I'm about to describe for setting the running order and creating that network diagram may seem really low-tech—and it is. But it works wonderfully. Using Post-its means there is no intimidating software, or even a computer, required. No barrier between you and the hands-on planning. And a group of people can all work on it together. Here are the steps to unleash the power of Post-its:

1. Write your identified tasks on Post-it notes. One task per Post-it. Ideally only a few words, and use a thick marker so they are easy to read. Leave space at the bottom of each note to insert the time, which you'll add later. And don't peel your Post-its off the pad upward, because then they won't lie flush on your whiteboard. Use the sideways peeling method.

For a quick tutorial of the sideways peeling method, watch my short video.

To watch the QuickClip, use the camera on your mobile phone to scan the QR code or visit the link below.

www.quickclips.io/pm-4

 SCAN ME   VISIT URL

Each project should have a maximum of thirty tasks, preferably more like ten or fifteen. If your project has more than thirty tasks, you may need to assign some of them to sub-projects. For example, the details of "create website" probably need to be pulled out to form a sub-project called "creation of website." That way, we can have one Post-it for the website on our high-level plan.

2. Transfer the Post-its to a whiteboard or a large sheet of paper.

3. Organize them into a running order.

4. Add arrows between the tasks to connect them. Every Post-it must have at least one arrow pointing in and one pointing out, except, of course, the initial Post-it and the final one, which signify the beginning and the completion point of the project.

Figure 19 is the resulting running order for the project of setting up a new business.

SETTING THE RUNNING ORDER WITH POST-ITS

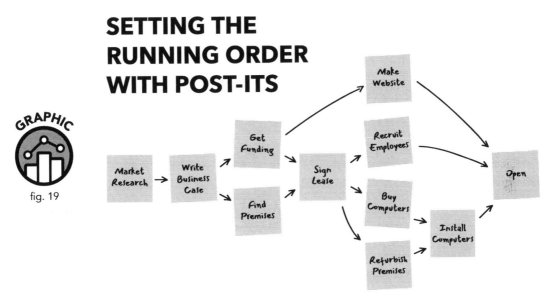

fig. 19

Make sure the outline of your tasks is not too linear and not too parallel. In other words, look out for tasks that roll out one after the other in one long line of Post-its. This is going to result in a poor plan that is too cautious, making the project too slow. Figure 20 shows you what to watch out for.

RUNNING ORDER THAT'S TOO LINEAR

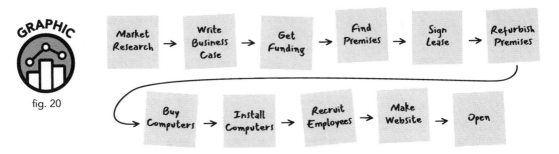

fig. 20

What you are aiming for is efficiency, where you and your team can multitask on various unconnected tasks at the same time. Obviously we can order the computers at the same time as we're refurbishing the premises. The two tasks are not connected or dependent, so we don't have to wait for one to accomplish the other. With very linear-looking projects, for each task ask yourself, "Do we really need to wait until after this task is started or finished to start the next one?" Use the answers to revise the running order of your Post-its.

Alternatively, watch out for a project plan that is too parallel (figure 21), because this can create three problems:

- » **Insufficient resources:** You may not have the resources to do everything in parallel.

- » **Management chaos:** You are more likely to run into management problems trying to keep track of so many tasks all happening at the same time.

- » **Increased risk:** If you have different people working on big key tasks at the same time, there is increased risk that something will happen in the wrong order. For example, you acquire the premises but they are not right for the people, or you don't get the funding but you've already bought the computers and signed the lease.

RUNNING ORDER THAT'S TOO PARALLEL

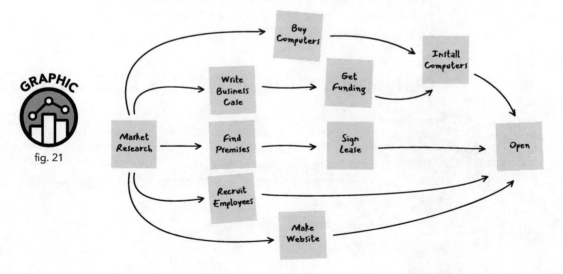

GRAPHIC

fig. 21

The great thing about this Post-it method is that you can immediately see these issues once you put the Post-its on the whiteboard. Of course, some projects are unavoidably linear (for example, bureaucratic projects where they have to get approval at each stage before the next one can go ahead). And some projects are genuinely very parallel, often when time is the key driver and the project has to be rushed through. But the best project plan will be a mix of linear and parallel, as in figure 19.

Nevertheless, even if your project is too linear or too parallel, it's worth drawing out the project plan. It will show your stakeholders why the project is going to take so long or why there is more risk in it than they thought necessary. If you think about it, in a linear project *every* task is a critical one, with the potential to make the project late if it overruns, and the plan will show that. For parallel plans, every task elevates the risk, and at least the project owner can see that and appreciate the ramifications.

The great thing is that the entire process will only take about twenty minutes. You don't need to spend hours putting data into a software program; just stick the tasks on Post-its, put them in a running order, and connect them with arrows. Done!

It can also be fun! You can—and should—involve the project team in producing this Post-it note diagram. Like the brainstorming of step 2, creating the running order together encourages buy-in from the team. Everyone can join in. Perhaps someone will argue that a task needs to be moved; they can come up to the whiteboard and move the Post-it. That gives a very different feeling in the team than if the project manager is hunched over a computer inputting all the changes, with the other team members twiddling their thumbs. It's much more open and organic, and it facilitates more participation from the team members. It's also highly visual, making it much easier for someone in the group to say, "Hang on, that won't work, we need task C done before task B," or "Actually, we could do task B and task C at the same time." If a team member points out a missing task, that task can easily be added to a Post-it and inserted into the running order in the right place. Post-it notes allow us to see the project as an image and move things around until everyone is happy and on board.

There is usually more than one way to successfully complete your project. You might expect project management to be about finding the one right answer, or the *best* answer, but actually it's usually about coming up with a plan that you and your team are happy with, agreeing on that plan with the stakeholders, and sticking to it.

It is possible to use virtual Post-its if you really want to use a computer, or if your team members are working remotely. But the team engagement is always far higher if you can meet in person and play around with little squares of colored paper. Sometimes low-tech really is the best approach.

Advantages of Network Diagrams

As mentioned, once you have created your running order in this way using Post-its, you have effectively created what is known as a network diagram. Shortly we'll explore the different types, *critical path method (CPM)* and *project evaluation and review technique (PERT)*, but right now let's focus on the benefits of creating a network diagram.

» It provides a graphic view of the project, which helps the project team to plan the relationships between the events and activities.

» The running order of the activities allows you to predict the project duration (more on that in step 4).

» The critical path will be easy to identify. This shows the activities (and the events they facilitate) that can't be delayed under any circumstances. In fact, there is no way to find the critical path other than by using a network diagram.

» It allows you to calculate the "float" of each activity. The technical definition of float in a project management context is the difference between when you *could* start something and when you *must* start it, or, on the other end of the project, the difference between when you *could* finish something and when you *must* finish it. It's the wiggle room of each task and tells the project manager how long a particular task can float, or come in a little later, without impacting the project schedule or outcome.

» It increases the visibility of the impact of project changes on the team members and the client or project owner.

» Finally, it helps the project manager to build a strong, cohesive team around the project, as everyone can see what's to be done and how their individual tasks affect other members of the team.

Network Diagrams Versus Flow Diagrams

It's worth noting that network diagrams are not the same as flow diagrams. Flow diagrams can have decisions, branches, if-statements, and loops that go back to a previous point, but network diagrams cannot. If you allow if-statements, you no longer know how long the project will take or what it will cost, because you may or may not have to do extra tasks or even go around a loop and do things more than once. If you are a project manager, this is a pretty major issue.

Say you want to write an article for an industry journal, and you don't know whether you'll need photographs for the article. How long will it take to be published? How much will it cost? You don't know yet, because you don't know about the need for photos.

Figure 22 shows a flow diagram with an if-statement for the article that leads to two possible branches.

BRANCHING FOR A PUBLISHING PROJECT

fig. 22

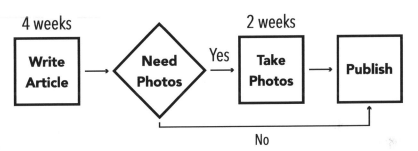

Figure 22 is really two projects displayed on one diagram: one project where the article needs photos and one where it doesn't need photos. Before you can forecast delivery time and budget, you have to know which one you are dealing with. And if you have to quote the time and cost before you know, then you must either base your estimates on the worst-case scenario (photos needed) or you can opt for the most likely case (which might be no photos), with a mention of the possible need for photos in your risk plan. Clearly, not knowing aspects of the project adds risk, which we will discuss further in chapter 10.

So you can't have branches in your project plan: "If it rains … ," "If we don't get planning permission … ," "If the supplier delivers late … ," etc. The project plan has to say what *will* happen, not the various things that *might* happen. This is why network diagrams are stronger.

As well as not being allowed branches, you also can't have loops, where an arrow goes back to an earlier point in your plan. Imagine that in your publishing project you estimate that it will take you four weeks to write the article, with editor approval taking a week. But the editor might ask you to rewrite it. How can you show that in your plan?

If you add this scenario to a flow diagram with an if-statement (see figure 23), how long will it be until the article is published?

FLOW DIAGRAM INFINITE LOOP

fig. 23

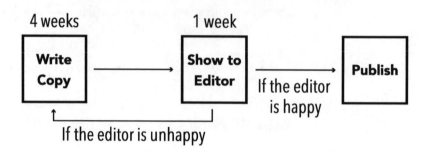

The answer is, we can't possibly tell!

It might take five weeks if we're lucky, but it could easily take ten weeks if one rewrite is needed, or fifteen weeks if there are two rewrites. In theory, it could be infinite. This means that if you attempted to create this flow diagram using computer software, it would tell you that the longest path would be going round and round this loop, which could go on forever. So you can't have loops that circle back to previous points in the flow diagram. Instead, you need to "cut the loop" in your project plan. You have to take one view, such as "I think there will probably be one rewrite" and draw it like that. Figure 24 shows a diagram in which you cut the loop and the whole job takes ten weeks.

CUTTING THE LOOP

fig. 24

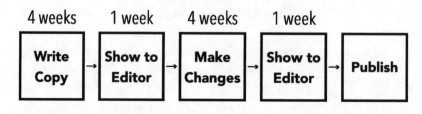

If there is a risk that you'll need more rewrites, you can put that in the original contract and in your risk plan, which we will cover in chapter 10.

In effect, flow diagrams, with their loops and branches, are really lots of projects overlaid on each other. There is one plan where there are no rewrites, another plan where there is one rewrite, another where there are two rewrites, and so on. With a flow diagram, a process can have lots of options, but a project plan shows the one option that we think is most likely to happen.

Two Competing Network Diagram Methodologies
(a Bit Boring but Important!)

This idea of drawing out the flow of your project has many different names: network diagram, Post-it chart, *critical path analysis (CPA)*, flow diagram, PERT, *precedence diagram*, and *dependency chart*, to name the main ones. They're really just names for the same thing. And to keep this book simple and practical, I'd prefer to tell you about the best of these methods and leave it at that.

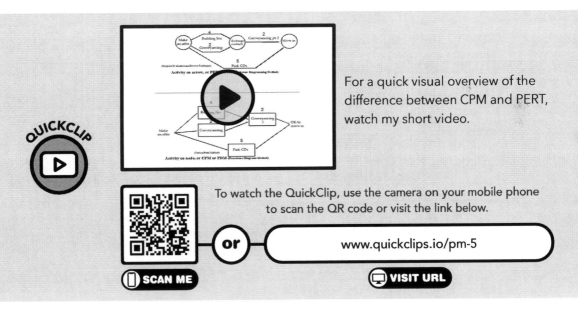

For a quick visual overview of the difference between CPM and PERT, watch my short video.

To watch the QuickClip, use the camera on your mobile phone to scan the QR code or visit the link below.

or www.quickclips.io/pm-5

SCAN ME   VISIT URL

But it will be helpful to appreciate that there are essentially two subtly different ways of creating these running orders. Network diagrams are created with the critical path method (CPM), which focuses on *activities*. Project evaluation and review technique (PERT) is another method that focuses on *events*. These two methodologies are archenemies in the world of project management (figure 25).

GRAPHIC

fig. 25

Every project management book I have ever seen teaches either CPM or PERT, but never both. Of course, there are pros and cons with each method, and it's a good idea to understand what you are gaining and losing when you choose a particular method. Although we have actually already looked at CPM (because the way we did our Post-its diagram uses CPM), it's important to cover PERT as well and explain the pros and cons of both. This will help you understand why I prefer, use, and always recommend CPM.

If you want a simple guide to planning projects and you want to be shown the best way and get on with it, then that's my answer: use CPM. But you might find it interesting and useful to look at both models, especially if you want to really understand project management.

The problem starts because every project is really an alternating sequence of events and activities. For example, a training day might look something like figure 26.

Project managers have realized that, for maximum economy, it's better to pick either the events or the activities for consideration:

Events only (PERT)
9:30 Event – start course
11:00 Event – start coffee break
11:15 Event – end coffee / restart course
1:00 Event – start lunch
1:45 Event – end lunch / restart course
4:00 Event – finish course

or:

Activities only (CPM)
Activity – talk about PRINCE2 and Agile, 1½ hours
Activity – drink coffee and eat cake, 15 minutes
Activity – talk about Post-it notes, 1¼ hours
Activity – eat lunch, 45 minutes
Activity – talk about Gantt charts, 2¾ hours

Which one do you prefer?

EXAMPLE OF TRAINING DAY AS A MIX OF EVENTS AND ACTIVITIES

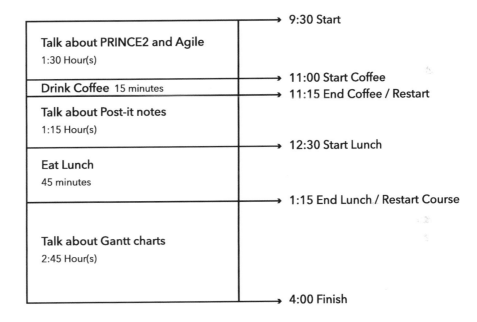

fig. 26

I think you can already see that PERT is better for the customers (When is lunch and when can we go home?) and CPM is better for the trainer (What do I have to do today? Can I fit it all in?). PERT starts with the times and then you fit the work into that, while CPM starts with the work and you see whether you are happy with the times you end up with.

It's worth exploring these two methods in a little more detail. Figure 27 visualizes the different methods side by side. We will unpack both in turn.

CRITICAL PATH METHOD (CPM)
P to U are activities

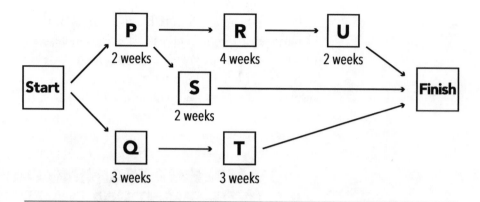

fig. 27

PROJECT EVALUATION AND REVIEW TECHNIQUE (PERT)
1 to 5 are events

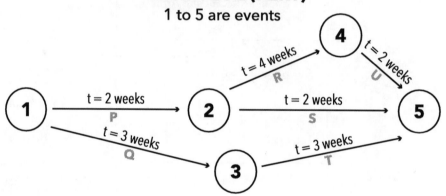

Critical Path Method

You already know a bit about critical path method, because the use of Post-it notes as a visual representation of the running order is essentially CPM. CPM is also known as "activity on node" and occasionally referred to as "precedence diagram method" (PDM). This approach was developed in the late 1950s by Morgan R. Walker of DuPont and James E. Kelley of Remington Rand. Remember, it focuses on activities—the work to be done. It plots the course through the tasks to establish the critical path, or the longest time it will take to complete the project (more on this in chapter 6).

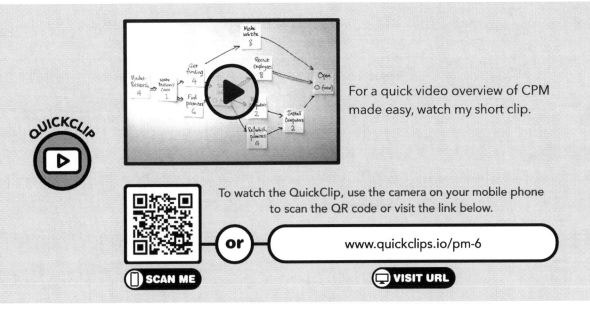

For a quick video overview of CPM made easy, watch my short clip.

To watch the QuickClip, use the camera on your mobile phone to scan the QR code or visit the link below.

or

www.quickclips.io/pm-6

SCAN ME   VISIT URL

Figure 28 shows the CPM diagram for setting up a new business. The tasks (or activities) go in the boxes, along with the durations. The connecting arrows don't represent any span of time; they simply tell you what comes next. Once you've got the durations in the boxes, you can discern the longest path, which is known as the critical path because it dictates how long the project will take. This is usually shown in red or as a double line.

NEW BUSINESS PROJECT USING CPM

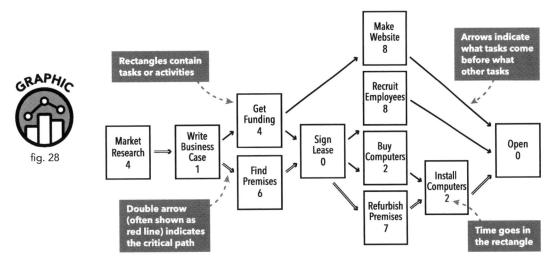

GRAPHIC

fig. 28

This is why step 4 (putting estimates on the tasks) is split from step 3 (setting the running order) in practice. It's very important to get the time estimates as accurate as possible, because they are what will determine the critical path.

You will probably notice that figure 28 is basically the Post-it diagram in figure 19. As a project manager, I personally prefer CPM because it keeps the focus on the work that needs to be done. I find that it's more intuitive, and you can use Post-it notes to do it very effectively. Besides, every project has activities, but not every project has events. More about these advantages later.

Project Evaluation and Review Technique (PERT)

The alternative way to depict your project is by using program evaluation and review technique (PERT), also known as "activity on arrow" and occasionally *arrow diagramming method (ADM)*. PERT focuses on events or deliverables. It was developed by the US Navy Special Projects Office, also in the late 1950s. It was created to simplify the planning and scheduling of large, complex projects like the US Navy's Polaris nuclear submarine project.

Figure 29 shows what our new business project would look like as a PERT diagram.

NEW BUSINESS PROJECT USING PERT

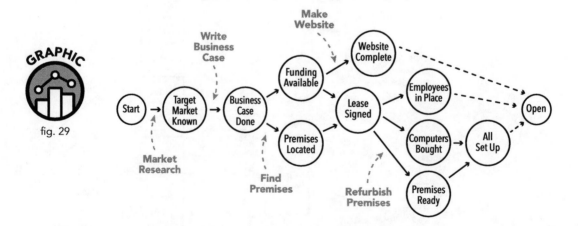

fig. 29

In a PERT diagram, the events are contained in circles. Arrows connect the events and indicate the activities that need to happen and the time it will take to complete those activities. The activity durations go on the arrows rather than within the circles. It's like driving between cities: the time is taken up on the road (the arrows), and the circles indicate where you arrive. On the CPM chart, the arrows take up no time at all; they are instant because they are showing dependencies, but on the PERT chart they incorporate the time spans.

In reality, the decision to use CPM or PERT is often made without the project manager even being aware of it. This happens in step 2, when tasks are listed, because if you list *activities* in a brainstorm or as a work breakdown structure (WBS), then you are going to end up using CPM. But if you list *deliverables* or you have a **product breakdown structure (PBS)**, then your focus is going to be on events and you will probably end up using PERT.

But a big decision has to be made, and it's worth thinking about each method's advantages before you do.

Advantages of CPM

» Every project has activities—jobs to be done—but not every project has events. If you're going to use PERT, you might have to contrive some events so that you have an event in between each activity; the arrows always have to go into a circle.

» To me, it's illogical to have to choose which side of an event the activity goes on. For example, "write business case" is obviously an activity to include in a CPM diagram. But if you're making a PERT diagram and turning that activity into an event, does the circle contain "start writing business case" or "finish writing business case"? If you add "finish business case" to the circle, inevitably you end up with a double event in that circle, because you are writing the business case to help secure funding—another event. Which one do you put in the circle, finish business case or start funding? Do you put both in the circle? You then end up with "finish writing business case and start the funding process" which is pretty clunky (figure 30).

You could create and stick to a convention where you always have events for starting things, or always have events for finishing things (figure 31).

EVENT FOCUS CAN BE ILLOGICAL

fig. 30

PERT USING A START
OR FINISH PROTOCOL

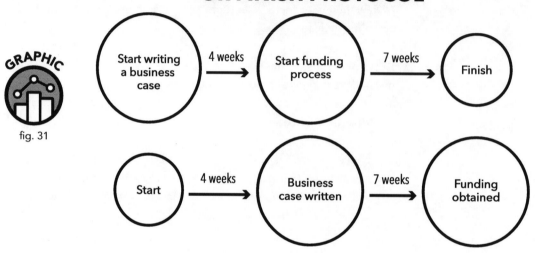

fig. 31

Bearing these wrinkles in mind, it seems much more logical to
have an activity called "write business case" and a second one called
"apply for funding" (figure 32).

ACTIVITY-FOCUSED CPM IS MORE LOGICAL

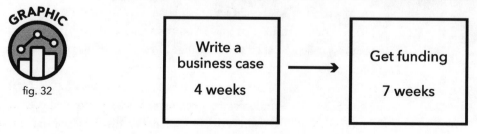

fig. 32

» If you're the project manager, you'll be more interested in the work to be done than in the deliverables, so CPM will feel simpler and more intuitive for you.

» It's easy to move the activities around when they are on Post-its, and the durations (which are also on the Post-its) move around with the activities. Easy! If you try to do this in PERT, you'll have to move the arrows, where the durations live, so the mechanics of actually making the PERT chart are much more difficult. Your options are limited to a very big whiteboard with someone assigned to rubbing out and redrawing duty, or computer software that only one person can use at a time. Neither is as effective as using Post-its for activities.

» Sometimes a particular configuration of tasks can't be drawn on a PERT diagram—but everything can always be drawn on CPM. For instance, going back to our house-building example from chapter 3, if you decide you can't lay the carpet until you've finished painting, which is very sensible, on the CPM diagram you put a dependency from painting to carpet (figure 33).

DEPENDENCIES SHOWN IN CPM

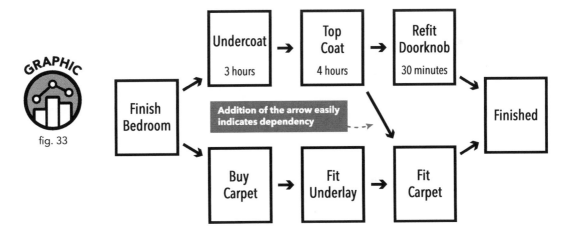

fig. 33

Using PERT, this dependency becomes much more difficult; a line between them would indicate an activity! But there is no activity to be done between the two activities of painting and laying carpet, just a dependency. So PERT people have to resort to a "dummy activity" shown as a dotted line. This is terribly confusing (figure 34).

DEPENDENCIES SHOWN IN PERT

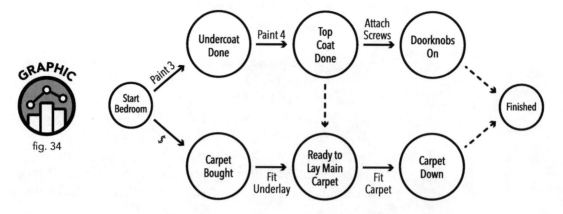

fig. 34

Looking at figures 33 and 34, it's pretty easy to see that CPM is natural and intuitive and PERT isn't, at least when it comes to easy demonstration of dependencies.

Advantages of PERT

» PERT is better at showing events. In fact, pure CPM doesn't have any events at all (though some naughty people like me add the occasional event if we want to). Customers tend to prefer PERT— they can see when they get what.

» Sometimes events are so important (a product launch or agreeing on a contract) that everything feeds into them. In those situations, PERT does have benefits. CPM partisans will argue that you don't need events if they have no duration; all that matters is working out the total time required. But it's not just about time taken but about establishing the running order: what depends on what, so everyone can better understand the project. Therefore, an easy way around this is to use CPM but add the occasional event if there is a key moment or two in the project (figure 35). It is simple to add the event as a circle or a diamond. This example uses a circle.

You can also add an event to a CPM diagram as an activity with a very short duration, say one day or even one minute. Then, if you're using software, the event will be in your plan. A great workaround!

EASY WAY TO ADD AN EVENT TO A CPM DIAGRAM

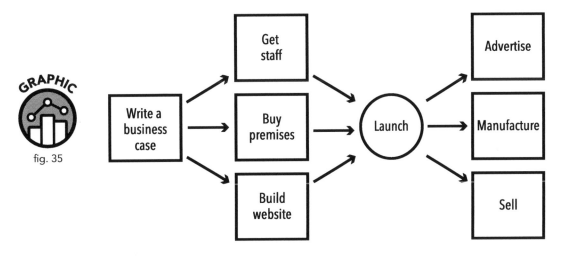

fig. 35

» When PERT is used, events (also known as milestones) will be clearly displayed to everyone, including bosses and customers. This is certainly beneficial, but they will be clearly shown to everyone anyway when they get to the Gantt chart. Whether we use CPM or PERT, we are going to convert the running order into a Gantt chart at some point. We will get our precious milestones whichever method we use.

» PERT might use more comprehensive time estimations. Some proponents claim that PERT is the superior method because it uses three estimates of time (best, average, and worst case). I'll cover estimation in more detail in chapter 6, but my feeling is that this is a potential PERT advantage that can be easily absorbed into CPM; there is nothing stopping a CPM enthusiast from using these estimation techniques.

In case I somehow haven't made it clear by now, I believe CPM is the methodology that wins out in the end.

The key differences between CPM and PERT are outlined in figure 36 as a recap.

fig. 36

PERT	CPM
Circles show events	Rectangles show activities
Activities are on the arrows	Arrows show what comes before what
Time goes on the arrows	Time goes in the boxes

Make a Choice and Stick With It

As far as I'm concerned, for a budding project manager, or a project manager looking for an easier way to do their job, CPM is the superior method.

It works much better for the person doing the actual work, and the events and milestones that the customer or project owner likes can easily be added later in the Gantt chart, so they won't be missing out. Key events can be added to CPM using diamonds or circles. CPM is also better if there are loads of tasks but not many events—which is true of most projects. If you plan to build and launch a new website, there are very few events but plenty of activities that need to happen to make that website a reality.

Whatever approach you decide on, stick with it. And be sure to use the correct shapes so that other project managers know what they're looking at. CPM always uses rectangles for the activities, and PERT always uses circles for the events. Don't mix them! Imagine if you had some of the times on the arrows and some of the times in the boxes—how would you ever find the longest path? How would you avoid double counting? It would be mayhem (figure 37).

ANARCHY OF MIXED METHODOLOGIES

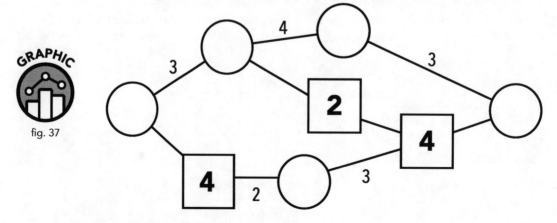

fig. 37

And finally, whatever you do, keep it simple. I have often seen people teaching a really horrible version of CPM where each box is divided up, as in figure 38. Don't do it! It adds an unnecessary level of complexity without a corresponding increase in value.

CPM RECTANGLE ACTIVITY BOXES GONE MAD

fig. 38

Earliest start week	Duration	Earliest finish week
Name of task		
Latest possible start week	Float (earliest minus latest)	Latest possible finish week

We'll cover a little more on this in chapter 6, but the good news is that there is absolutely no need for this level of detail. You just need Post-its with the name and duration of the task, and that's it.

Chapter Recap

» Once you've outlined all the tasks, it's time to get those tasks into some sort of running order. This is the point where you decide how you are actually going to do the project.

» Post-it notes are a low-tech but very effective way to create the running order. Write your identified tasks on Post-its, one task per Post-it. Transfer the Post-its to a whiteboard. Get the Post-its in a running order and connect the tasks by adding arrows. Job done.

» The Post-its essentially create a network diagram, which has multiple benefits.

» Network diagrams are not the same as flowcharts because they don't have decisions, branches, and if-statements that create additional problems like loops. All loops need to be cut before running order can be properly assessed.

» There are two subtly different ways of creating running order and the resulting network diagram: critical path method (CPM), which focuses on activities, and project evaluation and review technique (PERT), which focuses on events or deliverables.

» As a project manager, I much prefer CPM because it keeps the focus on the work that needs to be done. It's much more intuitive, and you can use Post-it notes to do it effectively. Besides, there are always activities to be done in a project but there are not always events.

» Whatever approach you use, make a decision and stick with it.

| 6 |
Put Estimates on the Tasks – Step 4

Chapter Overview
- » The importance of smart estimates
- » The best way to estimate time and money
- » How to easily identify the critical path

If everything seems under control, you're not going fast enough.
— MARIO ANDRETTI

Once you have your Post-its on the whiteboard in what you and the project team believe to be the correct running order, it's time to add time and cost estimates to the tasks. Breaking the project down to the level of tasks that need to be done will help you to get a better sense of the project and what is ahead of you. But until you add the time and cost estimates, you are still flying blind in relation to how long the project will take and how much it will cost. Luckily, the processes for estimating time and money are exactly the same.

Time and cost are two of the three key elements of any project, as outlined in the iron triangle. Step 4 is therefore all about working out whether your project is possible in the allotted time frame for the allotted budget.

Most people, when asked to estimate something, will quote the average. Say I asked you how long it takes for you to get home from work; you might say, "About an hour." But if you input some data from your last fifty journeys into Excel and we looked at the probability distribution of your drive home (this is actually my idea of fun), you would probably get a bell curve (figure 39).

The vast majority of your journeys were around the one-hour mark. But there were some journeys that were a nightmare—traffic was backed way up after a highway accident, or you got a flat tire halfway there. There were also a few (not enough!) where the gods were on your side, every stoplight was green, and traffic was unusually light.

JOURNEY HOME BELL CURVE

fig. 39

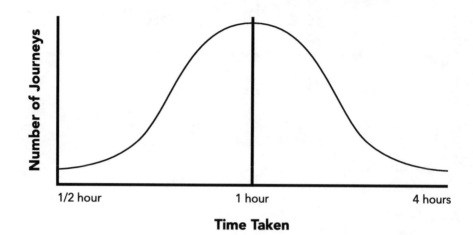

If you look at the numbers on the graph in figure 39 rather than the shape, you'll see that it's actually asymmetrical. And it's deliberately skewed because that's more representative of real life. It's hard to make the journey much faster than the average of one hour because if it was possible, say by taking a shortcut, you would already be driving that better route. But it's easy for the journey to take longer than the average because there are so many variables, such as weather, traffic conditions, and other drivers.

Other drivers never make the journey quicker for you. Neither do road work or detours. Neither does the condition of your car. A flat tire can slow down your journey, but you don't get to your destination quicker because your tires were better than normal!

The same is true for projects. There are so many ways for your project to turn out worse than expected but very few that can make it better. As a project manager you've already worked out the best plan, so if there was a better way to do something you'd already be aware of it and be doing it. But even with a great plan, there are still unknown variables that can cause problems. The range is almost never symmetrical, because that's not how life works.

The question is, what do you tell your family about when you will be home? You need to estimate well, otherwise dinner will be cold and tempers will flare. If you quote the average (and that's what people tend to do), there's a 50 percent chance that you'll be late and irritate your family. You'll have a 50 percent failure rate. It's not going to promote family harmony to remind them that you were early last Tuesday!

On the other hand, promising the average isn't the worst thing to do. The worst thing you can promise your family is the best-case outcome—that you will be home in half an hour. That's a ridiculous promise, with a 99 percent failure rate.

In projects, people make this estimation error all the time. The boss will ask the project manager how long a project will take, and the PM will quote the average. Say in this case it's eight weeks (figure 40).

A WORK EXAMPLE

fig. 40

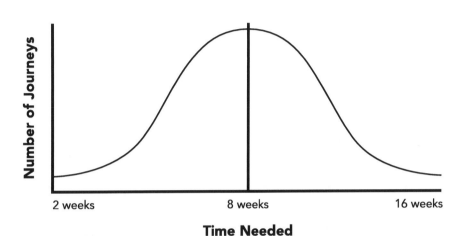

That's already a bad answer. But sometimes the boss puts a bit of pressure on: "We really need this job as soon as possible. If everything goes well, how soon do you think you might be able to get it to me?" And like a fool, the project manager tells them the truth and says that maybe, if everything goes right, with no sickness or supplier problems or IT snags, it can be done in *two* weeks (which is the absolute best-case scenario but a highly unlikely option). It's never going to happen. But all the boss hears is "two weeks," and they will hold that project manager to that commitment. And by the way, if you're a boss, *please don't ask this question!* Asking "what's the best you can do" will only get you a number that is probably unachievable, and you don't want to use that in your planning!

Of course, the project manager can't give a one hundred percent safe estimate and use the worst-case scenario of four months, because they wouldn't get away with that in real life. If you are pitching for a project to be accepted, you're unlikely to get the green light if you estimate with that much safety built in.

Quoting a range doesn't work either; if you tell a customer that a job will take between two and sixteen weeks, they'll think one or more of the following:

a. This person has no idea how long it will take.
b. Two weeks! Great! I'll take it!
c. Sixteen weeks! I can't wait that long; I'll get someone else.

When you think about it, it's pretty unfair that the customer (who may be your boss) is expecting you to provide just one number for how long the project will take (and also one number for the expected cost). This is especially true when it's for a big, complicated project that you've never done before. Even if you have done something similar, even hundreds of times, like driving home from work, you still don't know how long it will take this time. How on earth can you provide a useful, accurate estimate?

In this example, the best estimate to give your boss would be twelve weeks, because it's realistic with a little contingency baked in. The key is to make smart estimates. Smart estimates in this context are realistic, so they have the best possible chance of both acceptance by the project owner and delivery by the project team.

How to Make Smart Estimates

Although this chapter talks about estimates, these time and money estimates can't be produced by pure guesswork. It's too risky.

The best way to arrive at a robust estimate is to work through a process:

1. Use the average with some extra built in. If you get stuck:
2. Break tasks down further. If you are still stuck:
3. Ask someone who has done something similar before.

The first step is to find out the average amount of time and money typically spent on this type of project and use that as a basis. Then include some contingency baked in as a safety margin. *Contingency* is simply the deliberate addition of extra time or money into the plan right at the start. It may not be needed, but it gives you some wiggle room for delivering the outcome. I'll explain how to calculate contingency later in this chapter.

When estimating time, I recommend that you use weeks. Months are too long; things happen more quickly than month to month, at least for many tasks. Days are more accurate, yes, but they are tricky for three reasons:

1. When you add them up, it's too easy to make mistakes. Say you have seven tasks to be done sequentially one after the other:

   » Task 1 = 3 days
   » Task 2 = 2 days
   » Task 3 = 5 days
   » Task 4 = 4 days

   » Task 5 = 1 day
   » Task 6 = 3 days
   » Task 7 = 3 days

   Total = 21 days

   How many weeks is that? Careful … It's not three weeks. Twenty-one days is potentially three weeks, but your team will almost certainly be working five-day weeks, not seven-day weeks, so the answer is more likely to be four weeks and one day. It may be even longer because you can't tell from the list whether certain tasks will be done concurrently or if there are any gaps between tasks.

2. Days are too small of an increment—nothing ever happens that fast. You may be tempted to think you'll be able to do task 1 in a day or task 3 in a day, but projects rarely pan out like that.

3. Using days also encourages confusion of the two types of time. When someone says a task will take two days, do they mean it will take two days of working time (which is cost, really) or do they mean they'll deliver it in two days' time—as in *elapsed* time? Often we assume they are saying the latter when what they are actually saying is that it will take two days of total working hours to do the task, but they haven't told us that it will take a few weeks to get that work slotted in to their schedule. This can lead to delays and disappointments, because we're assuming they will finish the task two days from now, whereas they have scheduled those two days into their work diary for three weeks from now, or gradually over the coming three weeks. It's best to avoid the ambiguity of days by using *hours* for the work involved and *weeks* for the elapsed time.

Time can and will be estimated by different people on different occasions as both hours worked and elapsed time. You absolutely need to know which is which.

There are two types of time: hours worked and elapsed time. For example, an electrician may need to be on-site for three hours to check the connections, but if they can't get to the site for five weeks, then the elapsed time is five weeks. Five weeks is what you need to add as the estimate. The three hours on-site actually represents the cost (figure 41).

TWO TYPES OF TIME

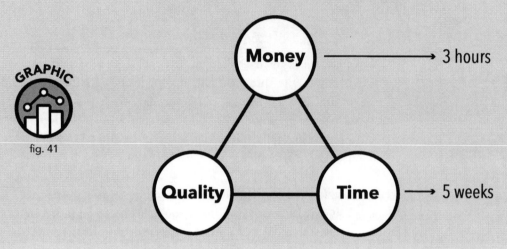

fig. 41

Both cost and duration are useful and important to know; just don't confuse the two. It is always better to estimate hours worked in hours and elapsed time in weeks—no days at all.

If you find that you can't estimate the time or the money, it's a surefire sign that you need to break the tasks down even further until you arrive at a task that you *can* estimate, in terms of both time and money. For example, if you don't know what your kitchen will cost or how long it will take to install, you probably need to break that task down into the component parts. How much for the stove? How long for installing the cabinets? How long and how much to lay the underfloor heating? And so on until you have a complete time and cost estimate for the kitchen.

If you are still unsure, seek out the input of a specialist or someone who has expertise in a similar project. In fact, even if you are pretty sure you're right, show your plan to someone who has done these things many times before, and they'll easily be able to tell you whether your estimates are in the ballpark.

Once you have reliable estimates of *average* times for each task, you can find the critical path. Then—after that—we'll add in some contingency.

Create Your Critical Path

A project without a critical path is like a ship without a rudder.

– D. MEYER

Estimation is vital at this stage because assigning time to our running order will help establish the critical path, which is really only about time. The critical path is simply the longest path through your project. Not the largest number of tasks, but the longest time in total. And the critical tasks are the ones on that path. So "critical" has a very precise meaning in project management. Critical does not mean "mission-critical" tasks or the most expensive or interesting or sexy tasks, or the most difficult or risky ones. Critical is just *slow*. What are the slowest tasks that will define the delivery time of your project?

The critical path is only about time, not cost. Cost estimations are still important, for obvious reasons, but cost estimates don't require any knowledge of the critical path. The total cost of the project is the sum of the costs of *every* task, so that's relatively easy. But the total duration of the project is not the total of the duration of all the tasks, because some tasks will be happening in parallel. (Unfortunately, spending money in parallel doesn't mean we save some of it!) When you're looking at your network diagram with time estimates added, even in its Post-it form, you will see different branches and paths within that diagram, indicating when some tasks are happening in parallel. Some of these paths will be longer than others. The longest route you can take from the beginning of the project to the end is referred to as the *critical path* because it indicates the slowest way through the project.

This, in turn, tells you the minimum amount of time in which you can complete the project. You can't do it any quicker than through the slowest path. If your boss wants you to move to the new premises in four weeks and you figure out that the critical path takes five weeks and three days, then it's not possible to move in four weeks without changes to the budget or the quality. This is essential information for you to have before that second kick-off meeting and before the project is given the go-ahead with your name on it.

The concept of critical path can be confusing to people new to the subject of project management. It was once more commonly referred to as the time-critical path, which made its meaning more obvious, but now it's usually shortened to critical path. The confusion is compounded when the "critical tasks" are discussed. It is vital to understand that the critical tasks may not be the ones you presume them to be; in this case, critical tasks are those that happen to be on the critical path, the slowest path through the project.

Completely trivial, small, easy tasks can also be critical ones, as long as they are on that path. And huge, expensive, difficult, risky, or mission-critical tasks can be noncritical, from a time-based point of view. Don't be tempted to assume you know (or can guess) what's critical. You must create the critical path diagram to find out.

Critical is not mission-critical or the most expensive tasks or the more interesting or sexy tasks or the most difficult or risky tasks. Critical is just slow. What are the slowest tasks that will define the delivery of your project?

Finding the critical path is easy. The problem is that, right now, most people in project management are making the process of working out the critical path far harder and more complicated than it needs to be. If you're struggling to get to sleep some night, do a Google search on critical path analysis or network diagrams, and you'll be out in minutes. It's far more effective than counting sheep. The critical path is usually made insanely complicated. Figures 42, 43, and 44 are some real-life examples that will give you a little flavor of what I mean.

COMPLEX CRITICAL PATH EXAMPLE 1

fig. 42

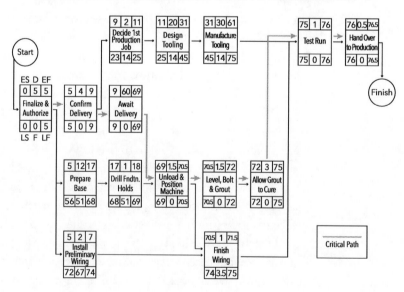

Source: www.bourton.co.uk

COMPLEX CRITICAL PATH EXAMPLE 2

GRAPHIC

fig. 43

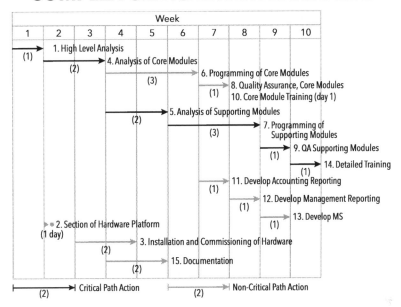

Source: www.brcommunity.com

COMPLEX CRITICAL PATH EXAMPLE 3

GRAPHIC

fig. 44

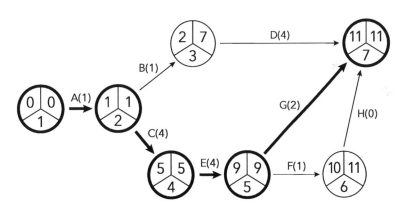

Source: www.designingbuildings.co.uk

Are you asleep yet? All of these, and many more equally riveting examples, are correct and legitimate ways to find that all-important critical path *if you're a computer*, but most people lose the will to live after looking at these for two minutes. No wonder! They are too complicated, never mind incredibly boring and unnecessary!

I've often wondered why critical path has been made so complex. I think it's partially because the intimidating look of these diagrams might make people appear cleverer or more experienced than they really are. But the main reason is probably because *computers* do it this way. All the main project management software employs one of these complex critical path methodologies, so people learn and get used to that particular technique. But the way a computer calculates the critical path is not necessarily the same way a human being would. Humans are actually quite good at seeing patterns and finding answers in them, especially if we can see the information graphically. Maybe there's a better way of determining the critical path that doesn't involve frying our brains. Besides, no one actually has time to do this in real life. Most project managers are running a project as part of their everyday workload. Do they have time to crack that software program, or would they be relieved to find a simpler alternative?

Thankfully, there is a super-simple but highly effective way to discover your critical path—and all you need to do is go back to your Post-its.

Back in step 3 (see chapter 5), you used Post-its to add all the tasks to a whiteboard and connect them with arrows indicating what needs to be done in what order. Now:

» Take the estimates you've established for how long each task will take and write those times on each Post-it. (Use averages for now; we'll add contingency shortly.)

» Find the longest path. What's going to take the longest time? That is the critical path. Can you see what the critical path is in figure 45?

FIND THE CRITICAL PATH

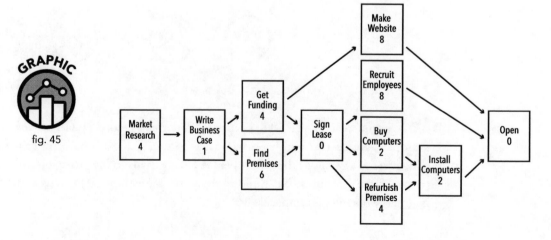

fig. 45

Did you spot it? At each branch you are looking for the route that takes the most time overall. I'm sure you got it right. You can check your answer in figure 46, which shows the correct critical path.

CORRECT CRITICAL PATH

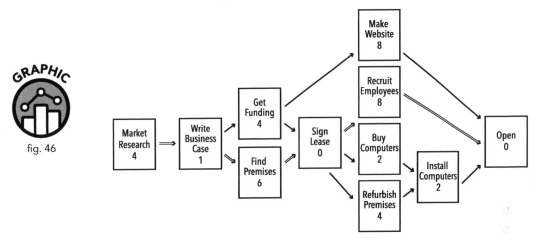

fig. 46

You don't simply take the biggest number at each branch, because a smaller one can lead to a bigger (longer) route later in that branch. For example, if the time to "refurbish premises" had been seven weeks, it would have been on the critical path, even though "recruit employees" is an eight, because the seven is followed by two more weeks to install the computers.

Here are some reasons the critical path gets (and deserves) so much attention:

» It tells you how long the project will take (in this case, nineteen weeks).

» It alerts you to the tasks that have the greatest potential to cause you to err in the promise you make to your boss or customer. Make sure to double-check your time estimates on all the tasks on the critical path.

» It alerts you to the tasks that have the greatest potential to cause problems for delivery. Make sure you use your best people to deliver the tasks on the critical path and that you monitor their progress very carefully.

» It tells you what to shorten if you need to speed up the project (we'll explore that in more depth in chapter 7).

» It saves time. When you add contingency, you only need to add it to the critical path.

» It gives you natural priorities. While your focus will always be on the critical tasks, you can also keep an eye on the tasks that are *nearly critical* as well, since they too can cause problems if they start to go terribly wrong. Tasks that are nowhere near critical are unlikely to be a problem, at least from the time point of view.

Two Critical Paths?

It's very rare, but it's worth briefly explaining what you should do if you find that there are two critical paths.

Occasionally, by pure chance, two paths will have the same length through your project, giving you two critical paths (figure 47). This is not a problem! The methodology still works the same way; you just have more tasks that are critical. On the plus side, it means you are doing the project very fast and efficiently. On the minus side, there are more things that can go wrong and make you deliver late!

TWO CRITICAL PATHS

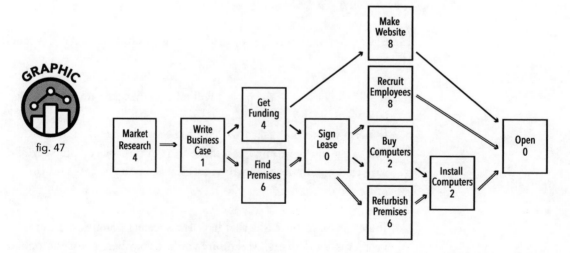

fig. 47

How to Calculate and Add Contingency

You wouldn't dream of telling your family that you'll be home in thirty minutes when the last twenty journeys have been closer to ninety minutes and sometimes longer. And you shouldn't dream of giving the customer or project owner a time or cost estimate that is the absolute, stars-are-aligned, best-case scenario for delivery of a project.

Even the average, which we used to estimate times initially, is going to be 50 percent unreliable (by definition of the word average), and your customer won't thank you for letting them down half the time.

> You need to include contingency for time, money, and sometimes quality/scope. The way it's calculated is always the same.

There are three ways to calculate contingency. I'm duty-bound to tell you about all three, but there is a best way that stands head and shoulders above the other two. Here are the three:

1. Half the difference method (my choice)
2. 10 percent method
3. 1:4:1 method

The Half the Difference Method

This, in my opinion, is the only method you should use to add contingency to your plan. Estimate the average and the worst-case scenario (ideally from previous cases or from an experienced person) and then add half of the difference to the average.

Going back to our driving example: say you're coming home and it usually takes about an hour, but it could be as long as four hours. I recommend that you tell your family you will be home in two and a half hours.

The logic is as follows:
» Worst case = 4 hours
» Average = 1 hour
» Difference = 3 hours
» Half the difference = 1½ hours
» Half the difference added to the average = 2½ hours

Basically, we're going halfway between the average and the worst case. It's quick and easy to work out, and it gives you the number you need (figure 48).

HALF THE DIFFERENCE METHOD
(Ideal Contingency)

GRAPHIC

fig. 48

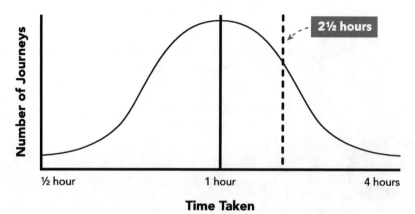

This approach ensures a 90 percent success rate. In other words, if you add half of the difference between your average estimate (time or money) and your worst-case estimate, your project will meet those time or cost parameters 90 percent of the time.

There are some statistics behind this, and I won't bore you with them, but essentially this approach represents one and a half standard deviations from the mean, which is slightly more than 90 percent safe. Only 10 percent of your journeys took more than two and a half hours, so you are 90 percent safe if you tell your family you will be home in two and a half hours.

DETOUR

The *standard deviation* is a statistical term that relates to the amount of variation or dispersion across a data set. A low standard deviation indicates that the values tend to be close to the mean (also called the expected value) of the data set. A high standard deviation indicates that the values are spread out over a wider range.

You're still going to fail 10 percent of the time, on your journey home and on your projects, but you just have to live with that. Most project managers would be delighted with a 90 percent success rate! Obviously, if there is a huge penalty clause based on time, or a really terrible outcome if the project is late, then you would head further toward the worst-case estimate in your planning. If your partner threatened to divorce you the next time you were late, then you would probably quote four hours! But generally, for most situations, 90 percent reliability is an acceptable safety point.

Some project managers are tempted, for strategic reasons, to quote a lower estimate to get the project approved or to win the work. They might quote the average or even the best-case scenario to get the job, assuming that their competitors are all doing the same. But I don't recommend that, because it's far better to build a reputation for reliability and for delivering what you promise time and time again. Start with a robust estimate, and the best way to do that is to quote halfway between the average and the worst.

The 10 Percent Method

As the name suggests, this method dictates that you add 10 percent to the average. In the driving example, that would mean adding 10 percent of one hour, which is an extra six minutes (see figure 49). Logic alone will tell you that's not enough. There are far too many variables in play that could disrupt that journey by far more than six minutes. It's too risky and doesn't give you enough cover. That's the primary flaw of this method—it's almost never enough. This is because it doesn't account for how widely spread the potential distribution is.

10 PERCENT METHOD

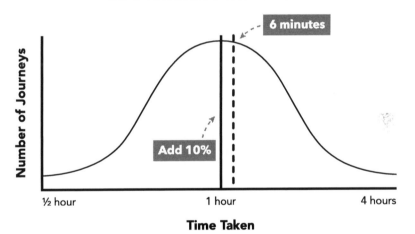

fig. 49

In this driving home example, the spread between the best and the worse is quite wide. If your project is more predictable than a car journey, then it might work out. But projects by their nature are not predictable. That's the problem! The 10 percent method is not consistent enough because sometimes it works and sometimes it doesn't. My recommended method of "half the difference" always works.

The 1:4:1 Method

The final method we'll discuss is known as the 1:4:1 method. Despite being enthusiastically touted in project management textbooks, this is also flawed. Maybe it gets included because it's got a snappy name and looks impressively mathematical.

The idea here is that you add together the best estimate multiplied by one, the average estimate multiplied by four, and the worst estimate multiplied by one. Then divide the total by six. It's basically a weighted average. Figure 50 shows what that would look like for the driving example.

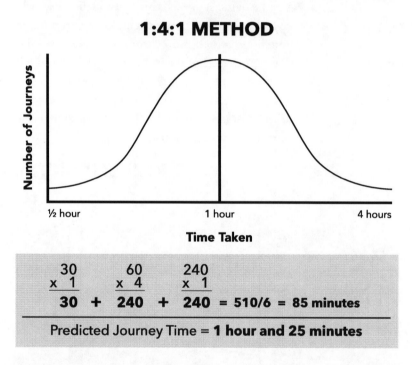

fig. 50

The 1:4:1 method in this example would suggest adding a contingency of twenty-five minutes, which is better than what the 10 percent method recommended. But compared to the half-the-difference method, which adds ninety minutes, the 1:4:1 method still doesn't give you much wiggle room.

The other problem with this approach is that if the best and worst estimates are symmetrically distributed, it comes out at the average! Figure 51 shows what that would look like if the driving example had a symmetrical distribution:

1:4:1 METHOD FOR SYMMETRICAL DISTRIBUTION

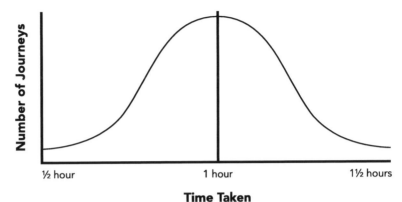

fig. 51

$$\begin{array}{ccc} 30 & 60 & 90 \\ \times\ 1 & \times\ 4 & \times\ 1 \\ \hline 30\ +\ & 240\ +\ & 90\ =\ 360/6\ =\ 60\ \text{minutes} \end{array}$$

Predicted Journey Time = 1 hour
The calculation has added no contingency!

Very rarely in life or project management are the best-case scenario and the worst case equidistant from the mean. It's not the way it works. There are always more ways for something to go wrong than to go right. But you can see that the closer they are together, the less safe the outcome of the 1:4:1 method is going to be. Even if there is lots of uncertainty and the total range is really wide, the 1:4:1 method can often tell you to add almost no safety margin.

Considering that the 10 percent method and the 1:4:1 method don't work all the time, it seems reasonable to stick to the half-the-difference method. It's easier and quicker to figure out, and it works more often. It may not have a sexy name like "1:4:1," but it is rooted in statistics and therefore is 90 percent accurate. Use that method for estimating time and money, and your reputation will soar as you consistently deliver your projects within the time and cost parameters.

Once you have added up your average estimates and discovered your critical path, you need to add the right amount of contingency to the tasks on the critical path. For each of those tasks, ask yourself how long the task *could* take; figure it just like in the car journey scenario, but for every task. Figure 52 shows how we did this for the business project example.

CALCULATING CONTINGENCY			
TASK	CURRENT	WORST CASE	EXTRA ADDED
MARKET RESEARCH	4	4	0
BUSINESS CASE	1	2	1
FIND PREMISES	6	10	4
SIGN LEASE (event)	0	0	0
RECRUIT EMPLOYEES	8	11	3
TOTAL	19	27	8

GRAPHIC

fig. 52

NOTE

You don't have to produce a nice, neat table like this one. In reality, you make a list of all the extra weeks you are adding as you go along the critical path, so you can get a total for the worst possible case.

You might decide you are totally confident that you can do your market research in four weeks. The plan is to spend four weeks doing what you can, and then move on. It won't run over. But writing the business case may take longer than you imagined, perhaps twice as long; so could recruiting staff and finding the premises. When you add up all your estimates, your total worst-case scenario for all the tasks on the critical path, if everything goes totally pear-shaped, is twenty-seven weeks. You have added eight extra weeks.

But you can be 90 percent sure that only *half* the tasks will go fully pear-shaped, or that all the tasks will only go *half* pear-shaped. You'd have to be ridiculously unlucky for nearly all the tasks to go totally pear-shaped, so adding eight weeks is probably a bit excessive.

Imagine you are going to roll some dice five times and you have to promise someone that the total won't go over a certain amount (this is like time or money in a project). What should you promise them? It's very unlikely that you're going to throw five sixes, or even four sixes, or even a mixture of fives and sixes. For the gamblers among you, the average score from one die is (1+2+3+4+5+6)/6 = 3.5, so the average total if you are throwing five dice is 5 x 3.5 = 17.5, and the max is 5 x 6 = 30. Halfway between the average and the max would be 23.75. If you bet (or promised) that the total of five throws would be below 23.75, you'd only go over that estimate 10 percent of the time, and you'd win 90 percent of the time.

So, back to our example where we have added a worst-case maximum of eight weeks to our project. We've already established that adding *half* the difference is the best way to determine contingency, so if you add half of that worst-case extra lateness to the average, that's adding half of eight, which is four, to the average of nineteen, which gives us twenty-three. This is what you should quote to your customer. When they ask how long it will take to set up the business, you can say with absolute (well, 90 percent) confidence that it can be done in twenty-three weeks.

But you still need to spread that time out along the critical path to bake the contingency into the plan. You can't just add it as a lump called "contingency" right before the end. Someone will remove it. Instead, apply it to some of the tasks along the critical path. Ideally, add it to the riskiest tasks where more time is almost certainly going to be needed. Figure 53 shows where that contingency could be added in our "setting up a business" example.

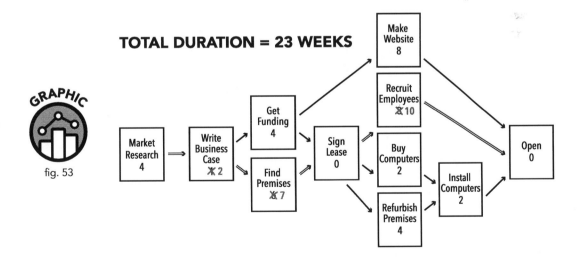

TOTAL DURATION = 23 WEEKS

GRAPHIC

fig. 53

Contingency Is Your Invisible Friend

When I teach about the importance of adding contingency or a safety margin to your estimates, there is always someone in the room who asks whether that is dishonest. Good question, and here is the answer: contingency is not about overinflating the estimate so you can go on holiday and lie in a hammock drinking beer for the last few weeks of the project. I wish! No, it's still a genuine estimate, because we know that something always goes wrong, we just don't know exactly what it's going to be. The margin needs to be added so that we don't let the customer down.

In my experience of project delivery, it's unmanaged expectations that trip us up. We over-promise and under-deliver, and the owner of the project is rightly upset. It is always better to say what you can reliably deliver and then deliver that in the agreed-upon time frame and budget. If your contingency ensures a 90 percent success rate, that means that 90 percent of your projects will be successful by all the usual measures. That, in turn, means happy customers or project owners and a happy boss.

Essentially, you have to account for the multiple ways the project can go sideways that are impossible to plan for. People on the team may leave or get ill, or someone might be pulled from the team to work on another project. Any number of unplanned emergencies may arise. There are always things that are impossible to plan for or predict. The contingency means you are better able to take these things in your stride and still meet the deadlines.

If you promise too much and don't deliver, you fail. If you promise what's doable and you deliver that, you win. If you don't end up using all the contingency and come in before deadline and under budget, you are a legend. It's a no-brainer: add contingency.

But there are a couple of rules.

First, your contingency needs to be hidden. If you make it known to your boss or the customer that there's contingency in there, they will take it out. Even if they don't try to remove it, it will worry them. They may even wrongly assume you don't know what you're doing. This is ironic, considering that the addition of adequate contingency is a sign that you *do* know what you're doing. This is a project; we are surfing the unknown!

In fact, your boss or the project owner doesn't need to know and would probably in some ways rather not know. It's part of your job, so don't worry about keeping secrets. All they really care about is whether you can do the project on time and on budget. Adding adequate contingency massively increases the likelihood of that successful outcome. Besides, once you make your Post-it note network diagram into a Gantt chart in chapter 8, the safety margin is safely hidden in your plan, which is great for everyone.

If they ask you outright about whether your estimate includes contingency, then obviously you shouldn't lie. But instead, say something like, "Yes, I've put in a few days" or "Yes, I've added a few hundred dollars." Besides, if you say no, you look like a bad project manager, since most people in senior roles recognize the need for contingency in project management. But there's no need to get specific about what "a few" actually means.

Repeat after me: "Contingency is my invisible friend."

Chapter Recap

» Once you have your running order and your Post-its on the white-board in what you and the project team believe to be the correct running order, it's time to add time and cost estimates to the tasks.

» Most people, when asked to estimate something, will quote the average. The average is a useful first step but not the end of the story.

» The best way to arrive at a robust estimate is to work through a process: if you get stuck, break tasks down further; if you get stuck doing that, ask an expert.

» Once all the time estimates have been made, they need to be added to the running order so you can establish the critical path. Initially, just add your average estimates to your running order. Then trace the longest path through the project: at each stage, what will take the most time? Connect those tasks. That is your critical path.

» The critical path is the longest path running through the project. Because the project can't be completed without following this path, it tells you the amount of time you need.

» Critical tasks are any tasks that appear on the critical path. This means that completely trivial or simple tasks can be critical ones.

» If there are two critical paths, don't panic. It just means there's more to think about, but they will be managed without issue once everything moves to a Gantt chart (chapter 8).

» Make sure your best people are on the critical tasks. Double-check your time estimates on all the tasks on the critical path, and add contingency.

» There are three ways to calculate the right level of contingency, but the best method is to calculate half the difference between the average and the worst-case scenario and add that amount to the average.

» Contingency is your invisible friend. Don't broadcast your contingency to anyone; keep it close to your chest.

PART III

ADJUSTING THE PLAN FOR REALITY

| 7 |
Crash the Plan – Step 5

Chapter Overview
»   Speed up the plan (or reduce cost)
»   Focus on the critical path tasks
»   Crash the plan using the key drivers

By now, you will have added all the average time estimates to the tasks on your Post-it diagram, identified your critical path, and applied some contingency to that critical path. You have a reliable estimate for the overall duration of your project. You can tell the client or your boss that the new business can be set up in twenty-three weeks (figure 54). This is an accurate picture based on your robust estimating and the addition of smart contingency that you have spread out along the critical path. Your calculations identified the worst case and the average and added half the difference to the plan.

SPREAD CONTINGENCY ALONG THE CRITICAL PATH

TOTAL DURATION = 23 WEEKS

fig. 54

Market Research 4 → Write Business Case 2 → Get Funding 4 / Find Premises 7 → Sign Lease 0 → Make Website 8 / Recruit Employees 10 / Buy Computers 2 / Refurbish Premises 4 → Install Computers 2 → Open 0

In this example, that means adding four weeks to the project, which you have inserted along the critical path by adding one extra week to writing the business case, one extra week to finding the premises, and two extra weeks to recruiting the right staff.

But what happens if, in that first kick-off meeting, your boss or the project owner says that this new business needs to be set up in twenty weeks? Or, after your planning, you've come back to the second kick-off meeting and told everyone that it will need twenty-three weeks, only to be told by the stakeholders that things have changed since you last spoke; the business must be set up in twenty weeks, and you must find a way to do it in that time frame.

You need to consider whether it's possible to *crash the plan*.

"Crashing" in this context means speeding up. Of course, if you speed up the plan, you'll have to pay some sort of price. Let's look at *what* to crash first—which tasks to focus on. And then we'll look at *how* you might crash those tasks.

Don't think about the required delivery date when you start your planning, or it might contaminate your estimating process. For steps 2, 3, and 4, when you are listing all the tasks, establishing a running order, and estimating time and costs, your job is to plan what it will *really* take to deliver that project. Only at step 5 will you then compare what you've discovered against what the project owner wants. At that point, if necessary, you can figure out if it's possible to speed up (or crash) the plan.

Figure 54 shows the high-level plan for setting up the business. Let's use this example to explore some crashing options that may be open to you.

Which Tasks to Crash?

The most important point to remember when looking to crash a plan is that the only tasks that need to be crashed, or sped up—the ones that will ultimately make a difference to delivery times—are those on the critical path. If you look at figure 55, you'll see there is no point in reducing the time it will take to secure funding from four weeks to two weeks because "finding premises" is going to take seven weeks anyway; that's why it's on the critical path. There is no time savings to be gained from speeding up the securing of funding. Similarly, there is no point in reducing the time taken to buy the computers or refurbish the premises, because they are also floating (noncritical) tasks. Recruiting the staff is what's taking the time at this stage; that's why recruiting staff is on the critical path. Crashing floating tasks doesn't save any time.

Only the tasks on the critical path matter when crashing the plan.

That's not to say you can completely ignore the floating tasks. You do still need to keep an eye on them, because if you crash tasks on the critical path, you may inadvertently create a new critical path, especially if there are several paths that are similar in length. In our example, say you crashed "recruit employees" from ten weeks to four weeks (figure 55). You might initially think, "Great! I've crashed the plan by six weeks." But you've not. Can you see why?

DOES CRASHING YOUR PLAN CREATE A NEW CRITICAL PATH?

fig. 55

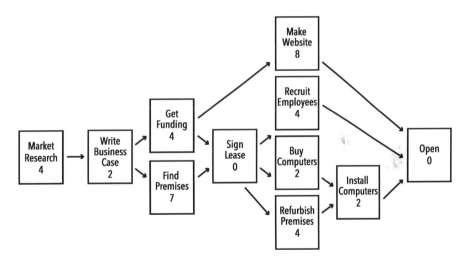

The answer is that refurbishing the premises and installing the computers is still going to take six weeks, so any reduction in recruitment below six weeks isn't going to gain you anything. The path through refurbishing the premises and installing computers has now become the longest route, thus creating a new critical path (figure 56).

This often happens in real life, and without these diagrams, it's easy to become disappointed when you don't get the savings you expected after crashing the plan.

YES, CRASHING THE PLAN CREATES A NEW CRITICAL PATH

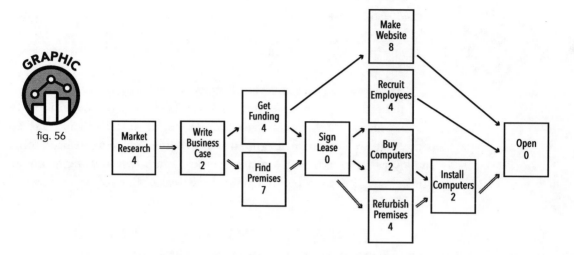

GRAPHIC

fig. 56

It also makes sense to focus on the larger tasks on the critical path. If you are looking to crash the plan for setting up the new business, shortening the writing of the business case isn't going to gain you much time. You've already assigned only two weeks to that task, so the most you could save might be one week. (Then again, in this case we are looking to crash by only three weeks, so it may be worth considering at some point.) Start with tasks on the critical path that are scheduled to take the longest time—they provide the greatest opportunity for crashing. Try to make sure they are not in parallel with other tasks similar in length; otherwise, you will not make the time gains you expect or need.

Crashing the plan is purely about saving time. You might do it by throwing people or money at some of the tasks in the project or by reducing the quality of the project—and this is where the key driver comes back into the picture.

If Time Is the Key Driver

If time is the project's key driver—that is, you've been told that the project *must* be delivered by a certain date or within a certain time frame—then you have to do at least one of the following:

» **Increase the budget:** More money may not be the answer to every problem you face in your project, but most issues can be solved with an increased budget. As long as the money is directed to critical tasks that can genuinely speed up the project, then access to more cash is certainly one solution. In our example, it may be possible to set up the business quicker if you hire outside consultants to do the market research or to recruit staff, but that will probably increase the cost.

» **Reduce the quality**: Reducing quality is rarely a great idea, because quality will be all the project owner cares about once the project is complete. The only way to do this sensibly is if the scope of the project can be reduced slightly without much loss, or if the reduction in quality is focused on tasks where that reduction won't be noticeable once the project is finished. It may be possible to set up the business quicker if you skimp on the market research or write a less thorough business case, for example. Perhaps the results of these tasks won't be visible once the project is complete.

» **Overlap more tasks**: It is possible to speed up the project if you overlap some tasks so that more tasks are happening at once. There is clearly more risk attached to this option, because you need to make sure that the tasks are not dependent on each other, or that part of one task isn't dependent on part of another. In our example, you could increase the overlap between finding the premises and recruiting the staff, but this could mean that you have people showing up for work with no premises available yet! Not ideal. One way to solve this is to break down the overlapping tasks more, so that, for example, you do the interviews (phase one of recruiting staff), but new employees don't actually arrive (phase two) until the premises are available. It does add complexity, but overlapping is often a good option.

If Money Is the Key Driver

If you've been told that the project must be delivered for a set cost and there isn't a cent extra available beyond that amount, and yet you're also under pressure to crash the duration of the project, then you have three similar options:

» **Overlap some tasks**: Apart from the risks and the management hassle of organizing it, overlapping is probably the best way you can save time without spending extra money. Starting to look for premises while you finalize the business case is only risking some real estate agent's time, which might not cost you anything. Of course, if you are doing both tasks yourself then there might be an issue with resources—do you have enough hours in the day to do both?

» **Reduce the quality**: Not all projects are in a position to save money by reducing quality, but in some cases it may be an option. For example, in the hypothetical case we've been examining, it could be possible to save money on the premises if you set up the business at a less prestigious address, and it wouldn't take any longer either. But do you really want to do that? Personally, I always hate reducing the quality of solutions. The quality is remembered long after the cost and the time are forgotten. But in theory, it's an option.

» **Give up on the idea of crashing**: It may turn out that crashing isn't a feasible way to achieve the number one objective of staying within the budget. Adding more time to the whole project may be an unpopular but unavoidable solution. In our example, you may have to deliver the new business three weeks later than hoped for, but within budget. Or if your budget calculations have also come out higher than expected, you might have to do something like reducing the cost of the premises. This may be possible by spending more time searching in a wider area to find somewhere both suitable and inexpensive. It may take longer, but at least you've stayed within the budget.

If Quality Is the Key Driver

If you've been told that the project must be delivered to a specific quality standard, but the project owner wants it done faster, then you have three options:

» **Increase the budget**: With more money you can bring in extra people or other resources to focus on the tasks on the critical path.

» **Overlap some tasks**: Again, you may be able to overlap some tasks to save time, but you need to weigh the risks of any potential impact on quality.

» **Give up on the idea of crashing**: It may be that crashing isn't an option for achieving the number one objective of quality.

Project managers often bring several different crashing options to the second kick-off meeting, and the stakeholders have to choose which is the lesser of the various evils. They can't have everything!

At least now you are 90 percent sure it will take twenty-three weeks, so you can assess the plan using real-world knowledge instead of guesswork or hope. And you won't be as tempted to go along with the project owner's demands or wishes just to avoid conflict. Assertiveness is a key trait of successful project managers. Don't let the stakeholders push you into making a plan that is unlikely to succeed. Everyone will regret it later.

Planning Makes You Stronger.

A good running order and network diagram is a great arguing tool. In the rare situation when you get a boss or a group of stakeholders who say, "I don't care about your plan, find a way to do this thing quicker," then push back against them with something like "I can't see a way to do it. Will you help me look at this plan and see if your greater experience (or higher-level view) can help us find a way to do it?" Try to get them to engage with the plan, because once they look at it, they'll understand the problem.

How to Crash Your Plan Successfully

You can't crash your plan successfully until you know what the plan is in the first place, and that means having completed steps 1 through 4 as fully and thoroughly as possible. The definition of the project is necessary so that you can identify tasks, work out a running order, and apply estimates, but you should not be overly concerned in steps 2 to 4 about what the project owner wants or hopes to achieve in terms or time or cost. Put the required timescale out of your mind until step 5. During steps 2 through 4, your job is to establish what is needed in order to ensure delivery of the project with 90 percent accuracy. Start with what is true.

Don't ever bend your estimates to fit what the project owner wants; all you'll end up with is an inaccurate plan, which will not be executed anyway. There is no benefit to you, or indeed the project owner, if you say, "We'll just have to find the premises in two weeks—it will be fine." Until you know how long it usually takes to find premises and whether you can speed that up, you're guessing or making up numbers. As a result, you are probably creating new, far bigger problems for yourself down the track.

A brilliant project manager manages expectations as well as the project. As long as you are clear about what can and can't be delivered and use your plan to back up your assertions, most clients and project owners would much prefer that you keep your commitments rather than promise the world and fall short. If you promise an unfeasibly fast project delivery, you may be a hero for five minutes, but you will ultimately be the villain, and your reputation as a reliable project manager will suffer.

Expectations are resentments waiting to happen.

— ANNE LAMOTT

Stick to the facts and leave wishful thinking at the door. Estimate what you believe to be accurate and *then* find out whether you have a problem or not. If you do have a problem, crash the plan.

Finally, don't ever try to speed up your plan by removing the contingency. All that does is increase your chance of failure from 10 percent to 50 percent, and the project owner will not thank you for that in the long run. Your crashed plan should still have contingency in it. For example, imagine your plan comes to fifty weeks and you add ten weeks of contingency, taking it to sixty weeks. You then discover, or perhaps you already know, that the customer really needs it in fifty weeks. It might be tempting to take the ten weeks back out again and be done with it, but that leaves you with a higher chance of failure. It's much better to crash the original fifty weeks down to forty and then add back your ten weeks of contingency. Maybe your shorter plan will need less contingency, so you could crash it to forty-two and have eight weeks of contingency. But the key point is that the plan still has contingency, even if it's been shortened. You can crash your plan by adding money or people, reducing quality, or overlapping some tasks, but don't ever take out the contingency.

Chapter Recap

» By now, you will have added all the time estimates to your task list, identified your critical path, and applied some contingency to that critical path. You have a project duration to report to your client or boss, who may require you to consider whether there is a way to crash the plan.

» Crashing the plan means speeding it up by adding additional resources, reducing the quality, or overlapping tasks.

» The first tasks to consider crashing are always those on the critical path.

» Still pay attention to the noncritical or floating tasks, as reduction in time on the critical tasks may inadvertently create a new critical path and thus not save you as much time as you expected.

» When you crash a plan to deliver a project faster, you have three options: increase the budget, reduce the quality, or overlap more tasks.

» Don't ever bend the estimates to fit what the project owner wants; all you'll end up with is an inaccurate plan.

» Don't ever take the contingency out of the plan in order to crash it. All you are doing is increasing your chance of failure. Instead, seek to properly crash the plan by adjusting the iron triangle while maintaining your contingency.

| 8 |

Gantt Charts – Step 6

Chapter Overview
- » The benefits of using Gantt charts
- » Why Excel is the solution
- » How to create a Gantt chart in Excel

The Gantt chart, because of its presentation of facts in their relation to time, is the most notable contribution to the art of management made in this generation.

— **WALLACE CLARK,** *mechanical engineer*

In chapter 5, I explained the importance of network diagrams for helping to establish the running order of your project. The best way to create that diagram is to start with the humble Post-it note. What makes the resulting network diagram so useful is that it provides a visualization of the whole project, and therefore you are unlikely to miss any dependencies.

But by the time we reach step 6 we need a more robust visualization. Network diagrams are all about time, but projects are concerned with more than just time. There are always cost and quality to consider too. Network diagrams assume infinite capacity. In other words, they show the ideal way to execute a project, assuming there are enough resources to do everything in the best order. In reality, some things might be in parallel, happening at the same time, and you might not have enough resources. There is no reference to who is responsible for each task in a network diagram, and they are not good at showing overlaps or the size of tasks. All the tasks, big or small, are represented by equally sized Post-its. And the only way to deal with overlapping tasks is to granulate them down into small parts that *don't* overlap.

If you want to plan your project properly, in a way that shows you have thought of almost everything and you know what needs to be done by whom, when, and at what cost, then you need something more than a network diagram. You need a Gantt chart.

A Gantt chart (figure 57) is a type of horizontal bar chart that illustrates a project schedule. Tasks to be performed are listed on the vertical axis, with time intervals on the horizontal axis. The length of the horizontal bar accompanying each task indicates when that task will be started and its duration. The bars are filled in to indicate which tasks have been done or what proportion of a task has been done.

SIMPLE GANTT CHART

fig. 57

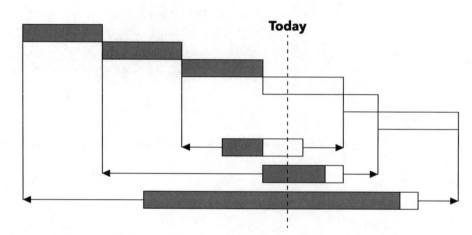

Strictly speaking, Gantt charts should probably be called Adamiecki charts, because Polish engineer Karol Adamiecki was the first person to use this type of tool, in 1896. He even gave it the snappy name "harmonogram," perhaps because it's a picture of working in harmony. But like that of so many brilliant inventors, his work was not widely published or translated—he just used it for his own purposes. Meanwhile, American engineer Henry Gantt designed a similar project visualization tool in 1910, and the name stuck. Gantt charts were used by the United States military during World War I and have been used by every sensible project manager ever since. As well as showing the start, end, and duration of each task, modern Gantt charts can show the dependencies between tasks—that is, when certain tasks can't be started or finished until other, related tasks are completed.

Why Gantt Charts Are Awesome

As you may have figured out by now, I am a huge fan of Gantt charts. Clearly, holding the plan in your head is crazy. It creates needless stress and invites mistakes. Steps 1 to 5, as covered in the last five chapters, ensure that you get the plan out of your head. Step 6 is where you make the plan visible to everyone in the project via the Gantt chart. There are four major benefits of Gantt charts:

- » Improved Communication
- » Better Resource Planning
- » Efficient Progress Monitoring
- » Improved Financial Management

Let's take a look at each of these four benefits in greater detail.

Improved Communication

The Gantt chart allows other people to see the plan, in an instantly intuitive way. This, in turn, improves communication in both directions. First, it allows you to show the plan to your boss or the project owner so they can see that your plan is real, and correct, and usually more complicated than they realized. You can explain it and, if need be, justify it. This can be especially useful in the second kick-off meeting before a project is given the green light (or killed!). If you are unable to give the project owner or your boss the answers they were hoping for, the Gantt chart gives you more power by allowing you to explain why. Those involved can immediately see that you are not being negative, lacking ambition, or being too cautious; evidence that the plan is realistic and sensible should be right in front of them. This makes it easier to demonstrate how complex the plan is, why it's costing so much, or why it's going to take more time than they hoped. It's difficult to argue with a Gantt (figure 58).

The Gantt chart can even be a great sales tool, showing customers why a project needs to take as long as it does or why it's perhaps more expensive than they expected. Even people with no project management training or experience can immediately understand what they are being shown. And if, incredibly, they don't fully understand it, the Gantt chart still assures them that you are organized and that you have an impressive-looking plan that can be trusted. Salespeople often use a simplified or higher-level version of the Gantt chart to walk the customer through the main phases. While these overviews can be useful, I think there's more value in showing the customer how much detail there is in your plan, especially at the sales stage before the contract is signed. Any issues regarding confidentiality can easily be circumvented by using slightly vague descriptions for the tasks, like "design system" or "build assembly," so you're not giving away exactly *how* you will do it.

GANTT CHARTS IMPROVE COMMUNICATION

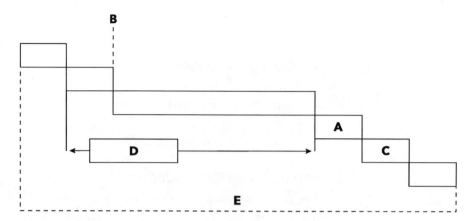

fig. 58

A = Your task

B = Key date when something has been promised, e.g. decision, access, or approval to go ahead

C = "Your task is critical, don't let it run late."

D = "There is some float on your task, so you have some choice about when you do it."

E = "This is why the project takes this long."

The Gantt chart is also useful for communication downward to the team and sideways to other project managers who might need to share resources. For your team, the Gantt chart shows everyone what the plan is and what responsibilities each person has in the delivery of that plan. Each member of the team can also see how their tasks impact other team members and how they are contributing to the overall success of the project, which is great for motivation.

The Gantt chart is a visual reality check for everyone involved in a project, from the project owner to you as the project manager and the project team. Everyone can clearly see their role and how their responsibilities link into other deliverables. Then, if the project is given the go-ahead at the second kick-off meeting, everyone is very clear on what they are committing to right from the start. This also means that later you can hold everyone— including the project owner—accountable for what was agreed to on the Gantt chart. If a customer agrees to make certain resources available to you by certain dates, they too will be held to account if they slip and don't keep their promise. They can also see the effect that any delays will have on the whole project.

Better Resource Planning

Gantt charts are really the only way to properly appreciate and accurately represent resource requirements. They allow you to better manage resources so you can make sure you have enough people for a particularly labor-intensive task or period.

GANTT CHARTS HELP TO BETTER MANAGE RESOURCES

fig. 59

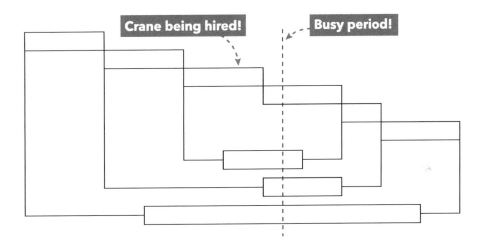

It's very quick and easy to see when your busiest periods are going to be. Also, if you've booked a piece of specialist equipment, such as a crane for a house build (figure 59), you can make sure that you have the required labor available to go with it, so that the expensive equipment doesn't sit idle on the site, costing money every day.

Without the visual information provided by the Gantt, your work becomes akin to driving through fog with no idea of what kinds of problems are going to loom up in front of you. Actually, that's what most companies are doing, and they become proficient at swerving when they suddenly find they have to do several tasks at once. But proceeding that way is expensive and risky. Better to identify potential resource problems early, so you can get them planned well in advance and pull in extra resources when needed, keeping the project on track. Resource clashes, like a crane operator who is needed on two sites at once, can be handled in advance. This can be achieved by moving the start date of one of the jobs or getting more operators in for a short period, both of which will be much easier to arrange with some advance notice.

Gantt charts are also extremely useful when you are resource-planning across several projects, because they allow you to add up the resource profile of each project in order to create a ***Gantt of Gantts*** (more on this later). These master charts help to ensure you have enough people and resources to successfully deliver all the projects on the calendar, or to choose which ones to start now and which ones to leave until later. You can also decide the order in which you will run the projects for maximum efficiency.

Efficient Progress Monitoring

Each task on a Gantt chart starts off as an outlined bar, which indicates that the task is yet to be done. As you start the project and perform the tasks, the bars are colored in to represent how much of each task has been completed (figure 60). You can do this manually, or if you are using software such as ***Microsoft Project*** or ***TeamGantt***, you can indicate the percentage of the task that's finished and the software will automatically color in the bar. As the bars fill in (or don't), you can see if you are falling behind or causing delays elsewhere in the project—say you're holding up task four because you need to finish task three.

GANTT CHARTS HELP TO MONITOR PROGRESS

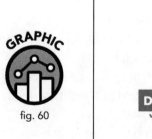

fig. 60

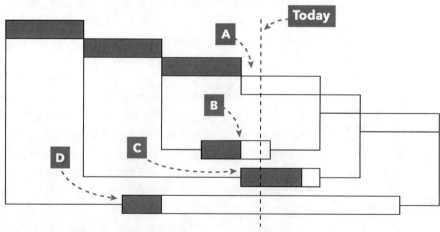

A = This task is not started yet, so we are running late on the critical path.

B = We're running late on a floating task, but there's just enough time to get it done before the deadline.

C = We are ahead on this task.

D = We're badly behind schedule on this floating task. It could cause the whole project to be delivered late.

If you are managing a project or overseeing lots of projects, the number one question you need to ask your team members is, "Can I see your colored-in Gantt chart?" With one sheet (or one screen), you will be able to instantly check on progress. It will alert you to impending issues far faster than a ten-page report or even an executive summary.

It also allows you to work out what to do if someone is behind, and how the team can catch up. Keeping a plan in your head is hard enough, but trying to modify a plan in your head is pretty near impossible, especially if you need to have a conversation with other people about the best way to do it. Looking at the true picture of the project via these colored-in task bars on the Gantt chart allows you to keep a far more accurate grip on the project. And the charts are even more valuable when you have several projects on the go at the same time.

Using a Gantt of Gantts, the CEO or whoever else is responsible for multiple projects can immediately get an overview of all of them. And this will probably take them about one minute a month. Why would any CEO not want that? Have a look at figure 61 and see if you can tell what's going on with projects A, B, C, and D.

GANTT OF GANTTS

fig. 61

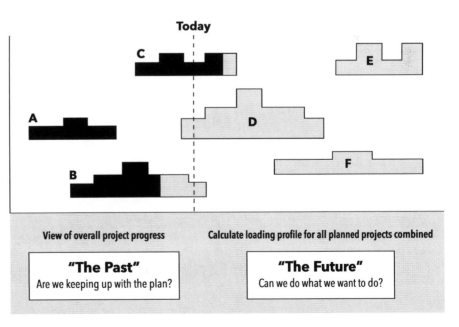

Even if you've just learned about Gantt charts for the first time in this book, you can easily observe in figure 61 that project A is finished, as indeed it should be; project B is behind schedule; project C is ahead of schedule; and project D is already running late because it should have started but it hasn't yet. We can then move straight to asking why it hasn't and, more important, what's going to be done about it. I'm sure you can see how quick and easy it is to gauge progress. No wonder every smart project manager uses Gantt charts! And every smart CEO or business owner asks for them.

Improved Financial Management

We will get into this in much more detail in chapter 12, but for now it's worth knowing that Gantt charts also help you to make sense of financial information and interpret that information accurately.

If you as project manager view only the financial data on a project, you may see that the planned spend and the actual spend are the same, and this could lead you to believe that everything is OK with the project. But you also need to see the progress to determine if that assumption is accurate.

Similarly, you might be pleased to hear that a second project is running under budget. Again, if you don't look at the corresponding Gantt chart to determine progress, you don't really know what's going on. It may be that the project is under budget because it's seriously behind schedule. Without access to the Gantt chart, it's very easy to misinterpret isolated financial data and not realize you have a problem until it's grown much more serious—where you've run out of time or money.

"Underspent" almost always means "late." Late always means you've had problems, which means "overspent" in the long run (especially if you have to spend more to catch up). And, of course, "overspent" always means overspent! Generally, any deviation from the plan means an eventual overspend, because the plan is the best way to execute the project. Anything that is different from what's in the plan is likely to take you longer and cost you more. But rather than guessing, why not check the Gantt?

Gantt charts also allow you to predict your spend profile. You can see what you are going to do when, and therefore where and when you are going to be spending the money in the project. What if you have spent half the money and done half the project, but it was the cheap half and the second half is going to cost much more? This is important to know for forecasting the final cost and making sure that the funds are available when they are needed as the project progresses. It is also even more important if you are managing multiple projects, to help smooth out the cash flow requirement across all the projects. Knowing when large stage payments will need to be made is crucial for managing the project cash flow alongside the other cash requirements of the business.

As you can see, Gantt charts really are a project manager's best friend. And there is no equivalent alternative. Over the last hundred years nobody has come up with anything better! But inexperienced project managers often use a list of tasks instead of a Gantt chart. Sometimes they add start and finish dates for each task on the list, but lists are always a poor substitute. You can't see task overlaps on a list, you can't see dependencies or what tasks might be able to run in tandem. You can't see the effect of lateness on other tasks, or even whether a task is critical or noncritical, and you can't see how much float a task has. Plus, a list is ultimately a guess, and most of the time it's going to be wrong. Without knowing the critical path, you don't know where to focus, and you don't know the effect of one task running late on the rest of the project. So forget lists and use Gantt charts instead.

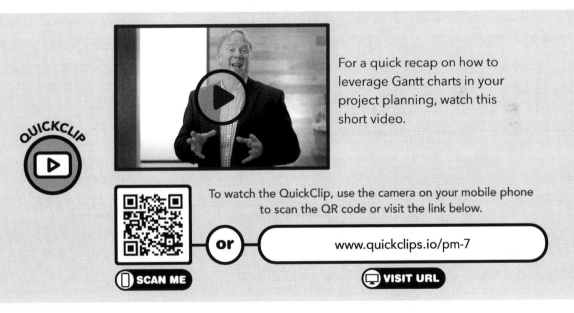

QUICKCLIP

For a quick recap on how to leverage Gantt charts in your project planning, watch this short video.

To watch the QuickClip, use the camera on your mobile phone to scan the QR code or visit the link below.

or

www.quickclips.io/pm-7

SCAN ME   VISIT URL

How to Create a Gantt Chart the Hard Way

Gantts charts are absolutely fabulous for any project, but most people, even those who recognize their value, try to create them *too early* in the planning process and fail. For a Gantt chart to deliver its considerable benefits, you have to create it after step 5, not after step 1. Although it can be tempting to jump to the Gantt chart as soon as the project is defined, this is a mistake. You will run into all sorts of problems and end up wrongly assuming that Gantt charts are very hard to construct, or even that they don't work.

Say you have your project brief and you know what the stakeholders want to achieve. Let's use the "setting up a business" example again. If you jump straight to the Gantt chart, what do you put on the chart? Gantt charts don't help you to identify tasks thoroughly; they certainly don't help in assessing what might be missing. Although they are useful for running order and can illustrate dependencies, you don't yet know what the tasks are, never mind the potential dependencies between those tasks. Also, for Gantt charts to revolutionize your project management capability, they must document the critical path. If you jump straight to creating the Gantt chart, *you don't yet know what the critical path is.*

Unfortunately, inexperienced project managers still try to jump straight to the Gantt chart because they know the Gantt chart is what they want to end up with. They just don't realize that there are some crucial steps in between defining the project and creating the Gantt chart. The chart is a great resource, but it's not a replacement for other forms of preparation, like the Post-it note diagram.

Another suboptimal way to make a Gantt chart is through Microsoft Project or any of the other project management software options. The appeal is obvious because these programs can automatically make a Gantt chart for you. But the program still has to know which tasks depend on which other tasks, and you have to feed it that information. And it's very hard to get all of the dependencies correct if you add them randomly to the Microsoft Project Gantt chart while the computer is creating it. It's much easier and better to think about dependencies by using the Post-it notes—you can look at a nice visual layout and check that you haven't missed anything. In a way, MS Project encourages bad habits like jumping straight to the Gantt chart because it's so temptingly convenient. I've lost count of the number of Gantt charts I've seen that were produced by Microsoft Project that don't even have a critical path on them. They are therefore wrong right from the start. More about this later!

To complicate matters even more, there are countless free or very cheap imitations of Microsoft Project that are even worse than the original licensed software. You end up learning a nonstandard approach that's almost impossible to share because no one else has the same software. But the biggest problem with project management software is that no software will ever be able to accomplish the first five steps we've discussed so far in this book. For example:

» No software will list the tasks for you or flash up a message saying "You've missed a task." If the project is exactly the same as the last one you did, then you can copy the old one, but how often does that ever happen?

» No software can estimate the time or cost required to do a task or question whether your project can really be done in four weeks or for a thousand dollars.

» It cannot possibly alert you to dependencies that you've missed or remind you to do task A before task C.

» Software usually runs on certain assumptions that you may not be aware of and can't see, and these can affect the plan adversely without your knowledge. It is semi-clever, and that's not enough. If you go straight to the Gantt with software, it'll be quick but wrong, and if you try to draw the Gantt chart manually too early, it'll take you hours and will still be wrong.

Always start with the Post-it notes, even if you plan to put that information into Microsoft Project. At least then the dependencies will be correct, so the Gantt chart will be correct.

At their best, even the good software tools are basically drawing tools. You get a nice neat project plan. You can zoom in and out to look at certain parts of your plan in more detail, maybe drop down a level to a subplan. You can also include "what-if experiments" to see the effect of adding tasks or changing durations—for example, if you need to crash the plan or if the customer is asking for a change. Software can therefore be very useful, but it's always best to use it *after* you've manually done the task listing and estimating on Post-its.

The only exception in which you could potentially jump straight to creating a Gantt chart would be if the project was either very linear or very parallel (we talked about those in chapter 5). For example, some public-sector projects can be very linear, where you do a task and then have to get approval before taking the next step, and so on for each task as you work through the project. Nothing, or almost nothing, is done in parallel, since that involves too much risk. It's a simple case of one task following another. You could draw that Gantt chart very easily! Conversely, some commercial projects, particularly where time is the key driver, can be very parallel, with multiple tasks all started at once so everything can be ready as soon as possible. It can be risky, costly, and time-consuming. In the public sector, with public money, it would not be acceptable to take this level of risk, but if commercial success demands a short lead time, then it's the kind of thing a company might need to do, and it could be relatively easy to draw up as a Gantt. But projects like this are very rare in real life, and I would always question a plan that looks mostly linear or mostly parallel. There should always be a mix, where some tasks are being done in tandem to save time—but not too many, to avoid undue risk.

There are a few other typical ways to get Gantt charts wrong or to make their creation tedious and difficult. I'll get back to those at the end of the chapter. But right now, let's attend to the important business of learning the easiest and most efficient way to create great Gantt charts.

How to Create a Gantt Chart the Easy Way: Use Excel

First and foremost, always create the running order with the Post-its from step 3. The human element of seeing the Post-its and manually converting them into the Gantt gives you the ability to get a feel for your project—"Does this plan feel right?" And it gives you two passes at the planning process. Sometimes you notice little errors as you convert the Post-its to the Gantt, because you are seeing it in a different way. You may notice an overlap that isn't possible because you forgot a dependency at the Post-it stage, or you notice that you have forgotten a task, or that one of the estimates doesn't look right when you see the length of the bar on the Gantt chart. If you blindly feed it all into a computer, you'll never know what it's done or what you forgot.

And even with the second look this provides, the whole process can still be super quick! For small projects with less than thirty tasks, it will take about thirty minutes to create the running order with Post-its and then fifteen more minutes to create the Gantt chart. Remember to involve your team if you have one, so you get their buy-in from the start, and you'll get the best possible plan. For larger projects, it might take you an hour to create the running order and maybe thirty minutes for the Gantt chart. Either way, it's always significantly quicker than messing around with project management software. And it's always time well spent!

When your running order is set and it's time to arrange your plan into a Gantt chart, the best and easiest way to do it is with Microsoft Excel. Most people are already familiar with it, and it's very easy to share with all the other stakeholders. It's also part of the Microsoft Office suite of products, so you don't have to pay extra for it. You *would* need to pay extra for Microsoft Project, and sometimes it even tries to argue with you. (For example, MSP will sometimes tell you that you can't move a task because of certain assumptions it has made about your tasks. You won't ever be told what those assumptions are, by the way. If you move the task anyway, MSP will often automatically move other tasks!) Good old Excel doesn't argue; it's stupid and knows nothing. It does what you want it to. Excel is also *better* than Microsoft Project for monitoring costs and for resource planning, since these things are exactly what spreadsheets were made for. In chapter 9 we'll get into more detail on resources for one project and the Gantt of Gantts for resources of multiple projects, and we'll cover costs in chapter 12—all using Excel.

The only major potential drawback to Excel as a project management tool would be if you were a full-time project manager running a number of projects, or one very large one. In that case, you might decide to become proficient in one of the specialist software programs, since you would be using that software every day. But even then, you'd still find it hard to communicate your plan to other mere mortals who don't know the software. If you are a busy professional who wants to get better at project management without the bells and whistles, then Excel is all you need.

Setting Up a Basic Gantt Chart in Excel

The first step is to make sure you can see your Post-it notes running order, aka network diagram (figure 62). If you have created this on a whiteboard, then set up your laptop in front of the whiteboard. Or take a photo of the whiteboard and use that as the start of your Gantt chart. If you're working remotely, you might have used Word or PowerPoint to create the running order via a shared Zoom call, so it's already on your computer. This is really important because these humble Post-its are the heart of your planning.

RUNNING ORDER FOR SETTING UP NEW BUSINESS PROJECT

fig. 62

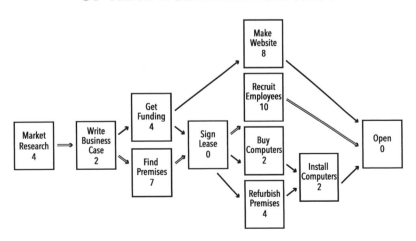

Now you're turning those materials into a Gantt chart. Here's how that process should go:

1. Open a new file in Excel, so you're starting with a blank worksheet. Give your Gantt chart a name and save it. In our example, the project is setting up a new business, so the file may be saved as Gantt Chart for New Business Project.

2. Leaving A1 empty, start listing the tasks from the critical path in column A. Make column A wider to allow the task descriptions to fit in each cell. To do this, hover your mouse over the line between column A and column B until the black cross appears, then left-click and drag the column to the right to make it wider.

3. Next, add all the floating tasks underneath the critical ones (figure 63). They can be in any order, although with experience you'll find that you can put them in an order that will make the Gantt chart as neat as possible—you don't want too many lines crossing over. I'll cover this later, along with other common pitfalls.

LIST ALL THE TASKS

IMAGE

fig. 63

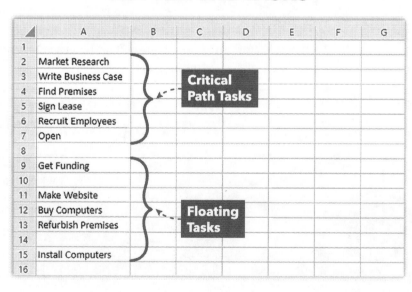

REMEMBER

With Excel you can easily swap tasks up and down as you go along to make your Gantt chart neater.

4. Put the duration of the whole project across the top in row 1. To do this, add up the total duration of the project along the critical path. In our example, the total number of weeks is twenty-three. So we need to insert the numbers 1 to 23, starting with 1 in cell B1, 2 in cell C1, 3 in cell D1, etc., with each column representing one week (figure 64).

ADD THE DURATION OF THE PROJECT ALONG THE TOP

IMAGE

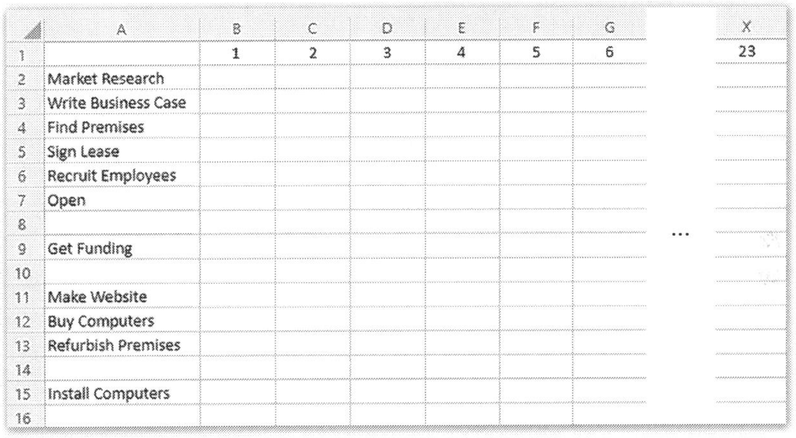

fig. 64

	A	B	C	D	E	F	G		X
1		1	2	3	4	5	6		23
2	Market Research								
3	Write Business Case								
4	Find Premises								
5	Sign Lease								
6	Recruit Employees								
7	Open								
8									
9	Get Funding							...	
10									
11	Make Website								
12	Buy Computers								
13	Refurbish Premises								
14									
15	Install Computers								
16									

Rather than typing in the numbers 1 to 23, you can add 1 in B1 and 2 in C1, then select both cells and you will see a small green square appear in the bottom right-hand corner of C1. Hover your mouse over the square until a black cross appears, then click and drag the cross to the right, and the remaining numbers will be added automatically.

If your project duration goes off the page so you can no longer see the whole project without scrolling to the right, there is an easy fix. Go to the last column, the one indicating the end of the project, and select that column by clicking on the letter in the gray box above the blank spreadsheet. Then, while holding the shift key down, move the cursor to the left and click on the gray box with the letter A above the first column. This will select, or highlight, all the columns. Pull in the first column to narrow it, and Excel will automatically narrow all the other columns by the same amount. While they are highlighted, it's also wise to center the durations as well—it looks much nicer. This is done by clicking the "Center" icon in the "Alignment" section of the ribbon.

Sometimes people ask me to send them a blank Excel template for a Gantt chart, but this isn't possible because you have to put *your* tasks down the side and *your* timescale across the top, including the dates of your project. Besides, once you know how to do it, you'll find it really quick to add the tasks and week numbers. The more complicated you make it, the fewer people will use it. Keep it super simple, as described here. No fancy templates required!

5. Next, you need to add the blocks of time attributed to each task. This is done using "conditional formatting," which sounds scarier than it really is. Select the area covering all the weeks and all the tasks, basically your whole chart apart from the headings and left column, and then under the "Home" tab, click on "Conditional Formatting" and select "Highlight Cells Rules" and then "Greater Than" (figure 65). A new box will pop up: "Format cells that are GREATER THAN." Put zero in the box and click on OK. The worksheet won't look any different, but as soon as you enter anything into those cells, Excel will automatically color it in, which is what you want. This is much quicker than selecting each cell and giving it a color.

CONDITIONAL FORMATTING
TO ADD THE COLOR

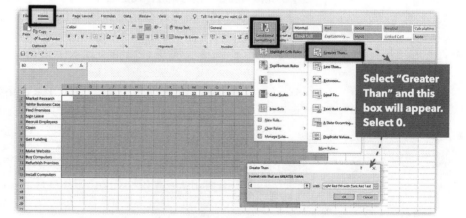

fig. 65

6. Make sure the floating tasks are a different color than the tasks on the critical path. To do this, repeat what you did in step 5, only this time select only the floating tasks—the bottom half of your

Gantt chart. Go to "Conditional Formatting" as before, "Highlight Cells Rules," and "Greater Than." Put zero in the "GREATER THAN" box, and change the color option in the drop-down menu to whatever color you want; I usually use green (figure 66).

CHANGE COLOR FOR FLOATING TASKS

IMAGE

fig. 66

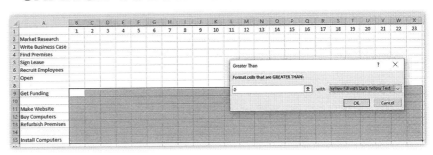

7. Add the durations to each task, starting with the critical path tasks. The easiest way to do this is to put a 1 in each cell that represents duration. In our example, each duration cell represents a week. Adding the 1 tells Excel to color in that cell. I will show you how to make these numbers more useful later in this chapter, but for now, add a 1 for each week that each task takes. For example, "Market Research" takes four weeks, so you would insert a 1 into four cells next to Market Research. "Write Business Plan" takes two weeks, so you would insert a 1 into the two cells corresponding to weeks five and six. See figure 67, which shows all the critical tasks done this way.

CRITICAL PATH TASKS COMPLETE

IMAGE

fig. 67

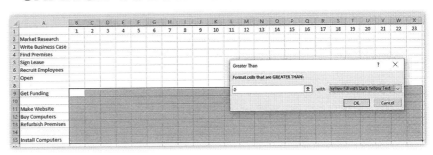

You will notice in our example that there are empty cells next to "Sign Lease" and "Open." That's because these are events, not activities, so they don't take any time and don't get any 1's. But it's useful to record them in the Gantt chart. The way to show events is with a vertical line, made by highlighting the column after the event. In this case, we want column O for "Sign Lease" and column Y for "Open." On the "Home" tab in the "Font" section, click on "Borders" and add

"Left Border." This will add the lines for the events (figure 68). Then, to show which task (event) a line belongs to, you can insert a little diamond on the line. Under the "Insert" tab, in the "Illustrations" section, click on "Shapes." Choose a diamond and move it to where you want it on the chart. In our case, this is on the line next to "Sign Lease" and on the line next to "Open."

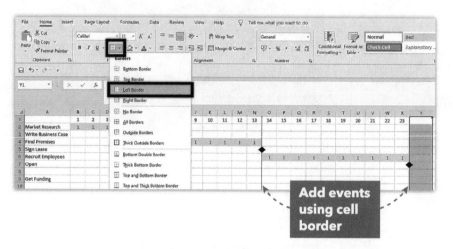

fig. 68

Add events using cell border

8. Next, add the floating tasks. Remember, these are going to show up on your Gantt chart in a different color than the critical tasks. If you look at the Post-it note diagram, you'll see that the first floating task is "Get Funding." The next tasks are "Make Website," "Buy Computers," "Refurbish Premises" and "Install Computers". Taking each in turn, add them to the Gantt chart.

For every floating task, you need to know its constraints, so always ask "What does it come after?" and "What must it come before?"

Think about "Get Funding." This has to happen *after* "Write Business Case" because you will need the business case to secure the funding. Using the Border button that you used to add events, you can add a constraint line after "Write Business Case." The arrow on the Post-it diagram becomes a vertical dependency line on the Gantt chart. Next, ask yourself what getting the funding must be done *before*. The funding has to be secured before you sign the lease, so the other constraint line is where the block starts for "Sign Lease." "Get Funding" will take four weeks, so you'll add a four-week block in between the two constraint lines (figure 69). To show that the task is floating, add an arrow on either side of the task duration.

ADD A FLOATING TASK

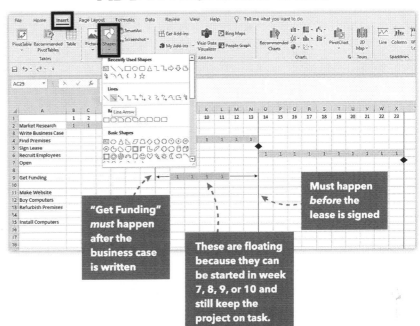

fig. 69

"Get Funding" *must* happen after the business case is written

These are floating because they can be started in week 7, 8, 9, or 10 and still keep the project on task.

Must happen *before* the lease is signed

"Float" means that you have a choice about when to do a task, within time limits. A four-week task floating in a seven-week gap has three weeks of float. Remember, float is the difference between when you *could* start something and when you *must* start it. But actually, the amount of float a task has is just common sense—it's the size of the gaps on either side.

NOTE

To demonstrate that a task is a floating task, add arrows on either side of a task duration. To do this, under the "Insert" tab, click on "Illustrations" and then "Shapes" and select the second line under "Lines." If you right-click on the line you want under "Lines," you will see an option to "Lock Drawing Mode." This will allow you to add all the floating arrows at once instead of having to do them individually.

Figure 70 shows the rest of the floating tasks. Apart from making the website, which can start as soon as we have funding, these must all happen after the lease is signed and before the business opens, but there is latitude about exactly when. You can also use the "insert shape" feature to add a line between tasks to indicate a relationship. For example, you need to buy the computers and refurbish the premises before you can install the computers, so there are lines connecting those on the Gantt chart.

COMPLETE THE FLOATING TASKS

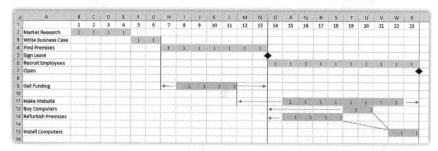

fig. 70

Once you get the hang of it, it really doesn't take long to create a Gantt chart in Excel.

Float Complications

There is some tricky but important information you need to know about floats. Specifically, you must be aware of two "complications" when it comes to putting in the floating tasks. Once you understand those, you'll have everything you need to successfully create Gantt charts in Excel. You can make the biggest Gantt chart in the world for any project of any type, since all project plans are based on these same building blocks.

Complication One: Floaters That Share Float

In our example, "Buy Computers" and "Install Computers" are sharing the gap that comes after we've found the premises and before we open. It's a ten-week gap, because that's how long it takes to recruit the employees on the critical path. Both of these floating tasks are only two weeks in duration; therefore, since ten minus four is six, we have six weeks of float. And that six-week float is shared. If the first task, "Buy Computers," ends up taking an extra five weeks, adding up to seven weeks instead of two, then that's five of the six weeks of float gone. Poor old "Install Computers" has only one week of float. If installation goes over by two weeks, it's going to make the whole project late!

If you have floating tasks sharing float, you need to think about where each goes within the range. If possible, keep some gaps before, between, and after each task, so that you can cope with any changes to the tasks without disturbing anything else. Just add them to your Gantt, with each task on its own line as usual and with a diagonal or stepped line connecting them. The line goes from the end of the first task, across and slightly down, to the beginning of the next task, just to show that they are joined—you can't start the second one till you have finished the first one.

Complication Two: Floaters Hanging Off Floaters
In our example, making the website follows "Get Funding," which is not on the critical path; it's a floating task. So we have a floater, "Make Website," that has a moveable constraint (figure 71).

We still need to ask ourselves the same question: What does it come after? The answer is obviously "Get Funding." Then what must it be done before? It has to be done before the business opens. Don't be fazed by the fact that what it comes after, "Get Funding," is not on the critical path but is a floating task. "Make Website" is just hanging off a floating task rather than a critical one. How much float does the website have? It depends on whether "Get Funding" is floated earlier or later; one of its two constraints is a moveable one, so we don't exactly know. But we can live with that.

FLOATING TASKS HANGING OFF OTHER FLOATING TASKS

fig. 71

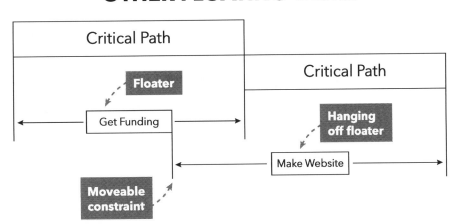

You might wonder what the difference is between these two complications. Why can't "Get Funding" and "Make Website" share float? Why isn't "Buy Computers" a floating task with the floater "Install Computers" hanging off of it? Why does it even matter?

The answer is that in the first example there were no restrictions as to where the two computer-related tasks could be in the floating range. They could both be pulled up to the front or pushed right to the end of the time frame; therefore, you could draw them as a pair of tasks sharing the floating range. But in the second case, there is a restriction on the first floating task. "Get Funding" must be done before week 14 when we are due to start recruiting the employees. So it has an extra constraint; it can't be pushed beyond that point. You draw in "Get Funding" first because you know the starting and ending limits, and then you hang "Make Website" off of it (figure 72).

IT'S THE MIDDLE CONSTRAINT THAT MAKES THE DIFFERENCE

fig. 72

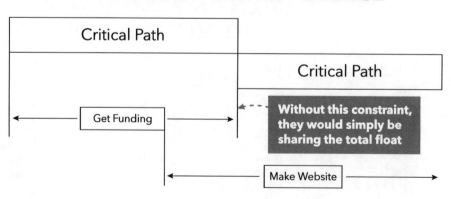

The good news about floating tasks is that if you make a mistake when you're drawing them in, it probably won't matter that much because there's flexibility built in. It's the critical path that must be one hundred percent correct, and, luckily, that's the easy part to create.

Add Dates and Names to the Gantt Chart

Once you've got your basic Gantt chart, it's time to make it look a little nicer and be a bit more useful. In real life, you hardly ever think about a project being at week three or week eight. You are almost always using real dates: "I need to get the funding by July 29th," rather than "I need to get the funding by week five." The next step, therefore, is to add real dates to the chart.

1. To insert the dates, you need to add a new row to your Gantt chart. Click on row 1 to highlight it. On the "Home" tab, click on "Insert," then "Insert Sheet Rows."

   Once you've added the row, enter the start date of your project in the date format of your choice. To see your options, click on the new row to highlight it, then right-click and select "Format Cells." From the drop-down, select "Date," and choose how you would like your dates to be shown. You can also choose your location. For example, in the UK where I live, dates are shown logically as day/month/year. But in the US, dates are usually shown as month/day/year (let's not get into that!). Once you've chosen the date style that suits you, highlight the row again, right-click to select "Format Cells," and click on the "Alignment" tab. The "orientation" will be defaulted to zero. This means the text is shown horizontally. Change that zero to 60 or whatever you prefer, and the text will appear at an angle (figure 73). If you choose 90, the text will display vertically.

DATE FORMAT AND ALIGNMENT

IMAGE

fig. 73

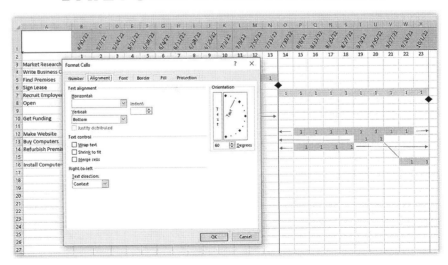

You will need to add the first two dates to the cells so that Excel can figure out the relationship between the dates (whether they're consecutive days, a week apart, a month apart, and so on). Once you've added a date in each of two cells, highlight the two cells and a small green square will appear in the bottom right of the second cell. Click on the square and drag it to the end of your worksheet to display all the dates, based on the relationship between the first two.

NOTE

If your dates appear as a series of hash signs like this, #####, it means that the cell is too narrow to display the date. It should automatically readjust to display properly when you set your alignment. If not, simply expand the column.

When the real dates are in place, it's much easier to get a handle on the whole project. You can see when you need to start certain tasks, which months you're going to be busiest, whether anything serious is going to clash with your vacation or those of any other team members. And you can have a final sanity check concerning which tasks are dependent on other tasks and which tasks are going to take the longest. This is the power of the Gantt: it allows us to see the whole project on one page.

Now it's time to add people to the tasks.

2. The great thing about Excel is that you can add new columns and rows wherever and whenever you need to. To add people to the tasks, highlight column B. On the "Home" tab, select "Insert" and "Insert Sheet Column." A new column will be added before your dates.

Entering who is responsible for the tasks, who will do the actual work, and what department they work in adds another level of detail and usefulness to the Gantt chart (figure 74). Everyone can see their part in the project, commit to delivering their part, and, if necessary, negotiate that delivery in line with other commitments. Either way, dates can be locked into diaries so that everyone is on the same page and knows what they need to deliver.

Using Excel to create your Gantt chart also allows you to calculate when your busy times are and to be aware of when certain people have a lot on their plate. This can help you to better manage those times for the project and the people involved. We can view the expected workload ("load" or "loading") by adding up the hours in each column of the Gantt chart.

ASSIGN TASKS TO PEOPLE/DEPARTMENTS

fig. 74

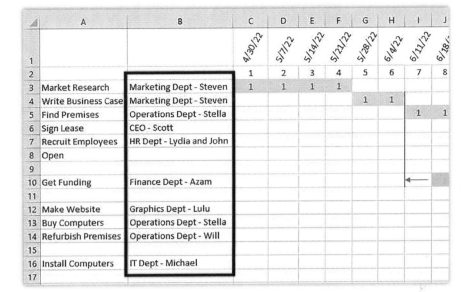

3. To calculate load, highlight the first column, from the first task to below the last floating task. In our Gantt chart, that is C3 to C17. Then in the "Home" tab, under the "Editing" section (top far right of the worksheet), click "AutoSum" (figure 75).

CALCULATE BUSY TIMES

fig. 75

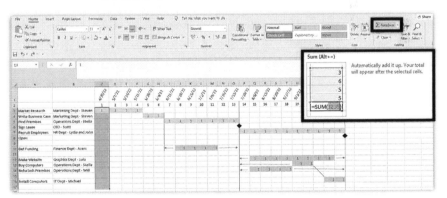

Excel will automatically calculate the total in each column. In the calculation box there will be a small green square on the bottom right of the cell. Simply click on the square and drag to the right to automatically calculate the loading for all the weeks in your project (figure 76).

BUSY TIMES ACROSS THE WHOLE PROJECT

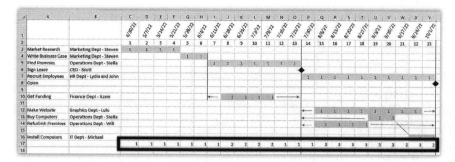

You can immediately see which weeks contain more tasks. This is a simple example, but remember, most projects will have more tasks, sometimes up to thirty, so it can be very useful to identify the busy weeks.

4. If, once you've finished your Gantt chart, you realize that you've not accounted for holidays, such as over the Christmas break when no one is at work, then it's very easy to adjust your Gantt chart. Insert a column at the appropriate place in the timeline and color it yellow or some other distinctive color. Make sure to adjust the dates at the top of your chart to account for that insertion of time off. This will, of course, push the timeline out by however much time you've added.

Add Time and Money to Your Gantt

It's always a good idea to add even more detail to your Gantt chart to allow you to see the load or your "resource profile." The resource profile tells you when and how many resources will be needed to complete a project.

Let's make one sheet for the *hours* we will need to spend each week on our project and a separate sheet for the *money* we will need to spend each week.

1. Adding the hours gives you a much more realistic insight into workload. To achieve this, you need to go through each task and change the 1 in each week to the estimated amount of time that will be needed to work on the task in that week (figure 77). In this example, you can immediately see that weeks 8, 15, and 16 are time-heavy. Moving the floating tasks might be a wise choice to even out the workload.

ADD HOURS TO TASKS

IMAGE

fig. 77

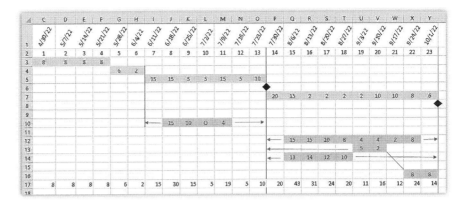

NOTE

Do you notice that the 0 in cell L10 looks funny? In reality, Azam probably isn't going to do anything in week 10, because he will have made the finance submissions in weeks eight and nine. In week 10 he's just waiting for a response. But if you insert a zero, it won't color in the cell. I think it looks better colored in, since that task is still in progress even if nobody is doing any work on it. If you add a letter O, the box will be colored in and will also still calculate properly. Nice!

This gives you an hours or load profile for the project so that you can see how many hours are needed when and by whom. Generally, it should not go above forty hours per person. In fact, ideally it wouldn't go above ten hours, because most people involved in projects are not doing each project full-time and have other responsibilities.

2. It's also possible to make this load profile much more visual with Excel—as a graph. Select the row containing all your totals. In our case, this is C17 to Y17. This tells Excel what data you want to depict in the graph. On the "Insert" tab, in the "Charts" section, click the drop-down arrow next to the bar chart icon and select "2-D Column" or whatever chart type you want (figure 78).

Stretch the graph out to align with the correct weeks, and you can immediately see when the peak loads are and whether you need to do something about them (figure 79).

CREATE A LOAD GRAPH

fig. 78

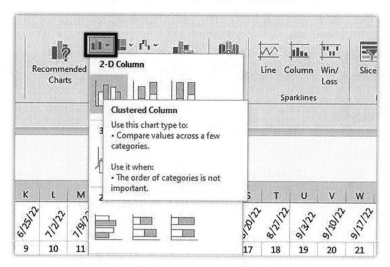

LOAD GRAPH IMMEDIATELY HIGHLIGHTS ISSUES

fig. 79

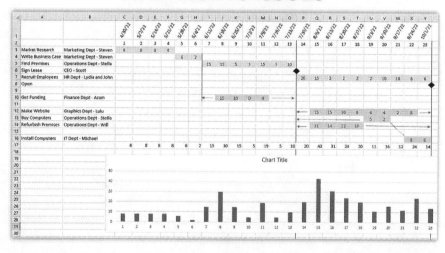

3. We've added vertically to see the total time needed each week, but you can also calculate how much time each *task* requires in total by adding another column at the end, highlighting the task from start to finish, and using the AutoSum feature again to calculate the total time. AutoSum works horizontally as well as vertically. This way you have the hours per *week* as a figure along the bottom and the hours per *task* at the end of each row (figure 80).

IMAGE

fig. 80

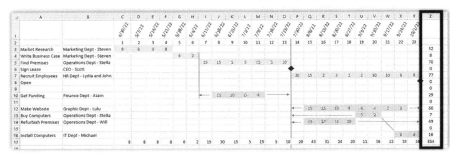

	A	B	1	2	3	4	5	6	7	8	9	10	11	12	13	14	15	16	17	18	19	20	21	22	23	Z
3	Market Research	Marketing Dept - Steven	8																							32
4	Write Business Case	Marketing Dept - Steven	8	8	3	8																				8
5	Find Premises	Operations Dept - Stella					6	2																		70
6	Sign Lease	CEO - Scott						15	15	5	5	15	3	10												0
7	Recruit Employees	HR Dept - Lydia and John													20	15	2	2	1	2	10	10	6			77
8	Open																									0
10	Get Funding	Finance Dept - Azam								15	10	0	4													29
12	Make Website	Graphic Dept - Lulu														15	15	10	8	4	4	2	3			66
13	Buy Computers	Operations Dept - Stella																				5	2			7
14	Refurbish Premises	Operations Dept - Will															13	12	12	10						49
16	Install Computers	IT Dept - Michael																						8	8	16
17			8	8	8	8	6	2	15	30	15	5	19	5	10	20	43	31	24	20	11	16	12	24	14	354

This enables you to sanity-check that the hours on each task look about right. It also lets you reconsider whether the tasks are even worth doing, especially if they are going to take a long time. Maybe there is a better way, maybe they can be subcontracted, maybe they can be omitted from the scope—it's worth considering.

NOTE

Some people get confused by the fact that there are two types of time, elapsed time and hours worked. A task might take six weeks to complete; that's elapsed time, and it is shown by the length of the bar on the Gantt chart. Then there are hours worked (the cost of a task), which are shown by the numbers you put into each week of the bar on the Gantt chart. The two things are not the same. You can have short tasks that are very expensive and long tasks that cost almost nothing, because they require a lot of waiting, or maybe they're cheap, or perhaps they involve work and money spent by someone else. We need insight into both types of time, and both are clearly shown on the Gantt chart: by the length of the bars, and by the numbers (representing either hours or cash) used up each week, written inside the bars.

Finally, it's time to add the *money* to the Gantt chart. To do this, copy the whole worksheet. Go down to the tab in the bottom left corner and right-click on the name of the worksheet you want to copy. (If you've not already given the Gantt chart a name, then do so here in this tab.) To copy, select "Move or Copy," then "(move to end)," then check the "Create a copy" box and click "OK."

4. Rename this worksheet "Money" or "Cost" and then go along each task and replace the hours with costs incurred (figure 81). If something is costing you $1,000 per week, put 1,000 in every box

along the bar that represents that task. And if the spend varies from one week to the next, you can put in the actual numbers; there may be zeros in some weeks, and that's fine. As before, if you put the letter *O* instead of a zero, the bar still colors in, and the calculations are unaffected.

ADD MONEY TO THE GANTT CHART

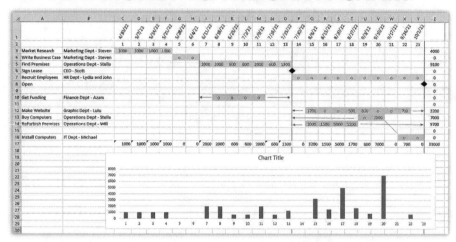

fig. 81

The graph under your Gantt chart is known as your "spend profile," and it can be incredibly useful in managing the monetary side of the project. You can plan for cash flow, you can see how much you are spending in this financial year and the next, and you can check that you have enough cash to do this project. You can also get the spend profile for *all* your projects combined by adding up the spend profiles to create a one-page graph where the horizontal rows represent each project rather than each task. I'll show you how to do that in chapter 9.

Often the cash graph is quite different from the hours graph. It's really useful to be able to see both.

I hope by now you can see how useful a Gantt chart is and how easy it is to create in Excel.

If you are especially visual and would like to see me running through this whole process on video, then check out this clip on making a Gantt chart with Excel.

To watch the QuickClip, use the camera on your mobile phone to scan the QR code or visit the link below.

or www.quickclips.io/pm-8

SCAN ME   VISIT URL

Pitfalls to Avoid When Creating Gantt Charts

Gantt charts are fabulous, but there are a number of mistakes that people commonly make. It's worth going through those so you can avoid them right from the start.

Pitfall 1: No Critical Path

For a Gantt chart to be accurate and useful, it must be built around the critical path. And yet, amazingly, most Gantt charts are made without the critical path.

When the project manager jumps straight to the Gantt chart without creating the running order with Post-its, they are guessing on estimates and dates for each task. It is therefore inevitable that they forget some or most of the dependencies and end up producing a plan that is inaccurate and doesn't contain any information about the amount of float that the noncritical tasks have. Figure 82 shows one of these misguided Gantt charts.

Figure 82 doesn't tell us many of the things we need to know: What depends on what? What happens if a task overruns; does it affect any others? How much can each task run late before it has an effect on the others? *We don't know!*

GANTT CHART WITH NO CRITICAL PATH

GRAPHIC

fig. 82

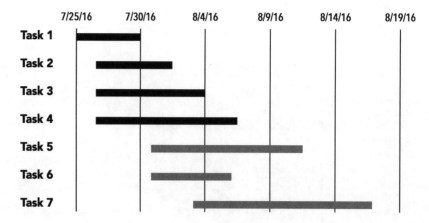

Always start with the critical path that you identified when you created your running order with the Post-its, and this problem will not arise. Remember, the extra time taken to do the Post-its will be worth it when you draw the Gantt chart, making it quick, easy, and correct.

Pitfall 2: No Vertical Lines to Indicate Floating Task Constraints

You'll remember that once you have the critical path created on your Gantt chart, you need to drop vertical lines in the spreadsheet to give boundaries to the floating tasks. For each floating task, you ask, what does it come after, and what must it be done before? This gives you the time frame within which the floating task must be done, and it shows you how much float each task has, or how early and how late you can do the task without impacting delivery.

Even though these vertical lines provide more information and ensure better planning and better outcomes, most PMs don't add them. One reason is maybe because it makes the chart look a bit untidy; sometimes the verticals even have to cut through other tasks on the chart. This is true but not important. The second reason is because they believe that once it's been decided when the task will be done, the options it originally had are no longer relevant. This is not true, and it's a mistake that's important to avoid making. Things will change once the project is underway. The PM will probably end up wanting to move the floating tasks and therefore will need to see those constraints on the chart so they don't get forgotten about later. In fact, they might want to move some of the floating tasks—within their constraints—to level out the resource load before the project even starts.

It's always wise to draw in the vertical lines and leave them in. That way, if you do want to move a floating task later, you will immediately be alerted to the presence of a constraint.

Pitfall 3: Messy Gantt Charts

If the first two pitfalls are crimes against Gantt charts, this one isn't as serious. It's more of a refinement. Optimally, you would plan the order of your floating tasks from the middle toward the outside, so you get a "nesting" effect with a minimal number of lines crossing over. You can see in figure 83 how the top graphic shows the floating tasks nested out from the middle. It is much neater, making the chart easier to understand and follow.

The graphic on the right starts with the floating task that could start soonest, so there is a logic to it, but this means lots of crossing lines and much more potential confusion.

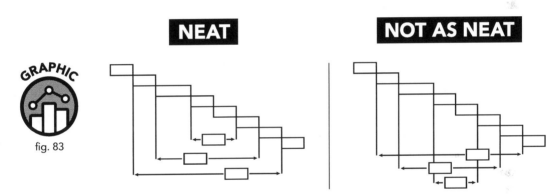

fig. 83

Always aim for neatness because it makes the message clearer and makes mistakes less likely. Of course, one of the great things about Excel is that you can easily drag rows up and down, so if you realize that you should have put one of the floating tasks higher on your Gantt chart, you can easily change it. But with practice you'll immediately see from the Post-its what the best order is for putting the floating tasks into your chart.

Pitfall 4: One Big Task

This is an easy one to avoid once you've seen it on your Gantt chart (figure 84).

The problem with this plan is that once you start task 3, the largest task by many weeks, you don't know where you are any more. Is it half finished?

Almost finished? You can color in roughly half of it if you think you've done half, but without more detail on what the task actually entails, you don't really know. For example, say someone less experienced was asked to create a plan for setting up a new business, and they lumped all the marketing activities together in task 3. Perhaps that included market research, creating the logo and marketing collaterals, and building the website. Once that "Marketing" task was started, you wouldn't have a clue about what was actually happening.

ONE BIG TASK

fig. 84

If one task is significantly bigger than the others, you need to break it down into smaller subtasks or chunks. Remember, we talked about this in chapter 4. You need to granulate the big task or break it down further so you can get better control over what is actually happening in your project. If you find yourself looking at a large task and not really being able to estimate how long it will take (or have any real sense of how well it's going) then chances are you need to break it down.

Pay attention to this problem in any plan, especially one that someone else has made for you.

Pitfall 5: Unspecified Overlap

If your Gantt has unspecified overlaps, then it's going to be hard to know if the plan is on track or not. Take a look at the section of a Gantt chart in figure 85.

You'll immediately notice that the critical path has two tasks, task 3 and task 4, overlapping. Now we already know that *floating* tasks can be overlapping, but overlapping tasks on the critical path can cause problems, because it's not clear exactly when the second task can start.

From figure 85, it looks as if we can start task 4 once we are two weeks into task 3, but if task 3 is slightly behind, can we still start task 4? What exactly needs to be done in task 3 before we can start task 4? And does all of task 3 need to be done before we can do the second half of task 4? It's impossible to tell.

UNSPECIFIED OVERLAP

fig. 85

▲	A	B	C	D	E	F	G	H	I	J	K	L	M	N	O	P	Q	R	S	T	U
1		4/30/22	5/7/22	5/14/22	5/21/22	5/28/22	6/4/22	6/11/22	6/18/22	6/25/22	7/2/22	7/9/22	7/16/22	7/23/22	7/30/22	8/6/22	8/13/22	8/20/22	8/27/22	9/3/22	9/10/22
2		1	2	3	4	5	6	7	8	9	10	11	12	13	14	15	16	17	18	19	20
3	Task 1	1	1																		
4	Task 2			1																	
5	Task 3				1	1	1	1													
6	Task 4						1	1	1	1	1	1									
7	Task 5												1	1							
8	Task 6															1	1	1			
9	Task 7																		1			
10	Task 8																			1	1	
11																					

It's much better to granulate tasks 3 and 4 down to more manageable and distinct chunks. You may even find that one of those subtasks becomes a floating task. Whatever the outcome, more granularity will give you much more control. Overlaps are always messy and should be avoided if possible.

Pitfall 6: Too Linear

This pitfall is also pretty easy to spot. Is your Gantt chart too linear? Could you in fact do the project more quickly? Are you playing it too safe? Figure 84 demonstrated a Gantt chart that was too linear.

It's definitely worth asking yourself a few questions to establish whether more tasks can be done in parallel. We talked about projects that are too linear in chapter 5. They are rare, but occasionally they do happen, so it's worth double-checking.

It's also worth noting that in a linear project pretty much every task is critical, so although it looks quite leisurely from the resource point of view, there is actually a lot of risk. *Any* task running late will make the whole project late unless you can throw more resources at it or reduce the quality, neither of which is ideal.

Pitfall 7: Too Parallel

This is the reverse of pitfall 6; this time all your tasks are bunched on top of each other (figure 86).

TOO PARALLEL

fig. 86

	A	B	C	D	E	F	G	H	I
		4/30/22	5/7/22	5/14/22	5/21/22	5/28/22	6/4/22	6/11/22	6/...
1									
2		1	2	3	4	5	6	7	8
3	Task 1	1	1	1	1				
4	Task 2					1	1	1	
5	Task 3	←	1	1	→				
6	Task 4	←	1	1	1			→	
7	Task 5	←		1	1	1		→	
8	Task 6	←		1	1			→	
9	Task 7	←		1	1			→	
10	Task 8	←		1	1	1	1	1	
11	Task 9	←		1	1	1	1	→	
12									

You need to ask yourself:

» Do I have enough resources? Am I able to get more so I can cope with all the work that needs to be done at the same time?
» Am I *sure* that nothing depends on anything else?
» If there's a problem with one of the tasks, am I sure I'm OK with the fact that all the others probably will have started?

Ideally, your project should be a nice mixture of parallel and linear.

Chapter Recap

» A Gantt chart is a type of horizontal bar chart that illustrates a project schedule. Tasks are listed down the vertical axis, with time intervals on the horizontal axis. The horizontal bar for each task indicates when the task will be started and its duration.

» There are four major benefits of Gantt charts: improved communication, better resource planning, efficient progress monitoring, and improved financial management.

» Gantts charts are immensely suitable for any project, but you have to create them at the right point in the project planning process. The hard way is to jump straight to the Gantt chart once you've defined the project. You also need to know the critical path before you begin.

» The easy way to create a Gantt chart is to determine the running order with Post-its first. Then convert those Post-its to a Gantt chart using Excel.

» Put in the critical path first and then hang all the floating tasks off of that.

» Look out for common pitfalls: no critical path; no vertical lines to illustrate constraints on the floating tasks; one task much bigger than the others, making it impossible to monitor accurately; overlap instead of tasks being broken down further; a plan that's too linear (one task after another), which makes it too slow; or a plan that's too parallel (many tasks at the same time), which increases risk.

| 9 |
Resource Planning – Step 7

A friend of mine is the IT director of a large company. He has a team of about fifty people, with about thirty projects moving at any one time. Every month, he goes to the monthly management meeting with all the other directors, and every time they ask him how certain projects are going. They'll say something like, "How's the bar-code-reading project getting on?" And he'll say, "Oh, it's going really well, it'll be ready by the seventeenth of July." He pulls a date out of thin air. It's a complete guess! When I discovered this, I was scandalized. I couldn't believe he was making stuff up about progress and delivery dates. I was sure he was going to get caught, and I told him so. He didn't agree. "No, no, it'll be all right," he assured me, adding this explanation: "What I do after each meeting is I go back to my team and assign a bunch of people to the bar-code-reading project and we get it done by the seventeenth as promised."

When I asked him what happens to the other projects, he did admit that there is often a negative effect on *their* delivery. "And what happens if you don't deliver by the seventeenth?" I asked. He told me that occasionally this happens, but more often they don't even notice, because by that point they've moved on to the next flavor of the month and don't check up on whether the last one made its deadline. On the rare occasions when they do check, he baffles them with science: "Oh yes, we had terrible problems reconfiguring the server protocol stack architecture, but I've got my best team on it, and it'll be ready by the eleventh of August." And that's that; no one gets in trouble.

Of course, this is madness, because he's promising everything to the other directors and failing quite often. Presumably these projects are needed for important purposes, and if they are not implemented, it could adversely affect the company's bottom line. Plus, he's taking all the strain on himself, hoping he doesn't get found out, which must be stressful. But the biggest problem is that, as a group of senior business leaders, they're not able to make proper decisions. Ideally, my friend would be able to say to his fellow directors, "I can't do all the projects; I can only do five out of the eight you want. Which one do you want first?" This could lead to a prioritization discussion about which projects they really want acted on and why. They might decide to give him more resources so he can do more projects (he is currently covering up his lack of resources). Or they could push some of the projects out into next year. Instead, they ask for everything, he promises everything, and then he doesn't deliver. This is why project prioritization is one of the most important roles of that top team. It's a key part of planning and achieving the business's strategic objectives for the coming years. As my friend's experience illustrates, sometimes it's a discussion that will not be had unless you insist on it.

You're probably reading this and smiling because you recognize the situation. Perhaps you and your company are going through the same sort of thing. In my experience working with companies all over the world, most organizations don't have enough plans, and they certainly don't have one big master plan. In their absence, however, the business loses time and money while putting additional and unnecessary stress on everyone involved in projects. What's needed instead is proper resource planning and some honest conversations.

As I mentioned in chapter 8, one of the reasons Gantt charts are so useful is that they allow for better resource planning. Resources in this context might mean money—being able to see when the big expenditures are due in the project so you can manage cash flow accordingly. Specialist equipment may also be considered resources; it's important to be able to know ahead of time when cranes or laboratories will be needed for a project so they can be booked in advance. But the main resource is *people*. In most organizations, it's the availability of people that limits the number of projects you can do. Making sure you have the right number of people available to get all the tasks done by the project delivery deadline is a top priority. Of course, this will always change when people are sick, on vacation, or if they leave the company, but making sure that all the people you need are available when you need them is a crucial part of project planning and keeping a project on track.

Levels of Resource Planning

There are, in effect, three levels of resource planning:

> » Level 1: Back at step 3, when planning the project with Post-it notes, we initially assumed infinite capacity. In other words, the

Post-its showed the optimal running order of the tasks, and they assumed that as soon as we completed one task, we could move straight to the next. Various tasks might be planned to happen in parallel, without taking into consideration how many people would be needed. Basically, we ignore the issue of resourcing when we're doing the Post-its. We do this deliberately because it's hard enough to think about which tasks need to come before and after which other tasks without clouding the issue still further with resources.

Of course, in real life we are always limited by resources, especially the number of people we can have working on a project at any one time, so we need to go beyond the Post-its ideal view of the world with infinite capacity.

» **Level 2**: People tend to be the key resource because they are usually our biggest cost. We leave them to the second (and third) level of resource planning. At level 2, we need to plan resources for each individual project. Have we got enough people to get this project done? Looking at the overlap of tasks, are there any points where we won't have enough people to get our plan to happen?

» **Level 3**: Once we have all the individual projects planned and resources allocated, we need to look at all the projects together to see if we can do them with the resources we have. If not, we need to work out which ones take priority and which ones will have to be acted on at a later date.

So, in step 6, the drawing of the Gantt chart, we find out what resources are actually needed to deliver the project, and then in step 7, resource planning, we visualize this extra constraint in detail. In step 6 we put in the people that we would like to have, and in step 7, when we add it all up, we discover whether we really can have as many people as we want (and the actual individuals we want). And sometimes we have to make compromises. We find out what resources are available compared to what's needed—first for one project, and then for all the projects we're managing (or that the business is implementing). This process helps to identify any shortfalls in any resources so we can take action ahead of time to get more people or to amend the plan.

Options to Manage Resource Shortfall in One Project

You've completed your Gantt charts for your single project, and you've created your resource profile by calculating when the busy times are, or when the most expensive tasks of the project kick in. Now you will be able to work out what to do about any issues you identified.

For an overview of your options when you don't have enough resources, check out this video.

To watch the QuickClip, use the camera on your mobile phone to scan the QR code or visit the link below.

or

www.quickclips.io/pm-9

SCAN ME   **VISIT URL**

Essentially, you have seven options for managing any identified shortfall:

1. Move the floating tasks
2. Get more resources
3. Extend the project duration
4. Split the tasks
5. Overlap the tasks
6. Reduce quality (last resort!)
7. Move other projects

Move the Floating Tasks

The first and simplest option is to move the floating tasks, evening out your demand on resources.

The floating tasks in any project are all those that are not on the critical path. This does not mean they're not important; it means that other tasks take longer, which gives the floating tasks flexibility about when they get done.

Figure 87 shows the resource profile for our project of setting up a new business. You can see that in week 8 there is a requirement of thirty hours, and in week 15 a requirement of forty-three hours.

IDENTIFY PEAK TIMES

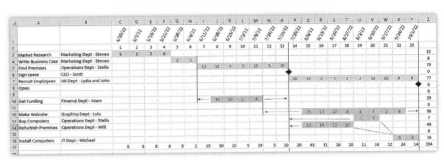

fig. 87

Even though these tasks are being done by different people, it's always best not to use too many resources at once on your project, especially if those resources, such as people, are being borrowed or drafted in from other parts of the business. Being mindful of everyone's other commitments is always going to keep you in their good graces. In our Gantt chart, "Get Funding" starts in week 8, but it doesn't *need* to start that week, so by moving that floating task one week to start in week 9 instead, the total hours being taken up by our project are smoothed out. Similarly, figure 87 shows that "Refurbish Premises" starts in week 15. But as long as it is finished by week 23, it could easily start a little later without impacting project delivery. After moving that floating task to week 17, the week with forty-three hours now shows a much more manageable thirty hours (figure 88).

MOVE FLOATING TASKS

fig. 88

If you do need to resolve a clash of resources, whether you move the floating tasks forward or back within their possible range will depend on a number of factors.

Reason to move a floating task to start earlier:

» **Safety.** If the task may take longer than estimated, it is always safer to pull it forward. That way, if it does take longer it won't end up affecting anything that comes after it.

Reasons to move a floating task to start later:

» **Money.** The sooner you start a task, the sooner you have to pay for it, which brings up cash flow considerations. Is it possible to delay the kick-in of those costs without impacting the delivery of the project? If so, then delaying a floating task may smooth out cash flow requirements.

» **Information is coming in.** If your boss or customer is likely to change anything, or if the external environment is volatile, it's best to delay the tasks that might change until everything has been finalized or there is less volatility. If you know a key decision or event is due at the end of June, try to delay your floating tasks until July, if that's still within their floating range.

MY TAKE

There's nothing worse than doing a task nice and early and then having something change. I remember in college doing a writing assignment way ahead of the due date, and then the tutor changed the question!

» **Storage.** If the floating task involves buying equipment such as computers, furniture, or machinery, you'll have to store those items somewhere where they will not get damaged. Moving the task until later can cut down on storage time, which in some cases can save on resources like space or money.

» **Gaps.** If there is a large gap after a floating task, you might want to delay the task. For example, if you choose a supplier a long time before you place your order, there is a risk that they might go out of business, or a better supplier might come along during the wait. Better to close the gap between the first task and the second and push that first one (choose supplier) further along its float range.

Reasons to move a floating task either way:

» **Inconvenience for the people assigned to tasks.** If you or the people assigned to a floating task are particularly busy during a certain time (or away on vacation), then the task can be moved to an earlier or later time to better accommodate you as the project manager or the other person. There is no point in making life harder for anyone if it can be easily avoided by moving the floating task.

In our example, there was no point in moving "Refurbish Premises" forward a week to start in week 14, because it would have made the forty-three hours worse, at forty-four hours. And it was too risky to move that task much later than week 17, because there would be less room to manage any challenges that refurbishing might present. What happens if a contractor accidentally punches through a water pipe? You've cut it too close to get any issues sorted out in time. In situations like these you can use common sense to work out whether to move floating tasks forward or backward.

Sometimes the order of certain tasks is not absolutely essential but is vastly preferable. In our example, the installation of the computers should occur after the refurbishing has been finished or, at the very least, after the big jobs like installing drywall, painting, and laying carpets have been done. You don't want someone spilling paint on a brand-new computer! We would float the tasks so that the refurbishing is completely done before we install the computers.

This process of moving floating tasks is especially important if the tasks in any one week are going to be done by the same person. In most cases, the project they are working on will be part of their normal work week, so they won't have unlimited time available for your project. If you figure out that Lulu from the graphic design department is due to spend thirty-five hours on your project in one week, then clearly that is a problem, because how is Lulu expected to get the rest of her work done? As the project manager, you need to stay mindful of everyone's other commitments so that their efforts on your project don't make their lives impossible elsewhere.

Get More Resources

The next option for making up a shortfall between the resources you need and the resources you have is to get more! Let's continue with the earlier example, where you figure out that Lulu from graphic design is due to spend thirty-five hours on the project in a single week. Maybe the problem was created when another task was added to the Gantt chart requiring Lulu to create all the marketing collaterals for the new business, including brochures, company logo, stationery, and business cards (figure 89).

LOOK FOR BOTTLENECKS

fig. 89

#	Task	Resource	1	2	3	4	5	6	7	8	9	10	11	12	13	14	15	16	17	18	19	20	21	22	23	Total
3	Market Research	Marketing Dept - Steven	8	8	8	8																				32
4	Write Business Case	Marketing Dept - Steven					6	2																		8
5	Find Premises	Operations Dept - Stella							15	15	5	5	15	5	10											70
6	Sign Lease	CEO - Scott																								0
7	Recruit Employees	HR Dept - Lydia and John														20	15	2	2	2	2	10	10	8	6	77
8	Open																									0
9																										0
10	Get Funding	Finance Dept - Azam									15	10	0	4												29
11																										0
12	Make Website	Graphic Dept - Lulu														20	20	20								60
13	Marketing Collaterals	Graphic Dept - Lulu															15	16	15	10	4	5	8			66
14	Buy Computers	Operations Dept - Stella																				5	2			7
15	Refurbish Premises	Operations Dept - Will																13	14	12	10					49
16																										0
17	Install Computers	IT Dept - Michael																						8	8	16
18			8	8	8	8	6	2	15	15	20	15	15	9	10	40	50	37	25	24	23	26	12	24	14	414

You can see that in week 15, Lulu is expected to work on the project for thirty-five hours, but with her other projects and her everyday work, this is too much. One option might be to move the floating tasks so her involvement is spread out within that floating range, but you could also decide to outsource the marketing collaterals to a design agency that you use from time to time.

This is only an option if time is the key driver and the project owner is willing to add more money to the budget to buy those missing resources. But of course, Lulu represents a cost too. Internal resources are often regarded as free, because we've already paid for them, and it can be really hard to get external resources signed off on. This isn't entirely logical. To take it to an extreme, imagine if you could recruit a graphic designer for one hundred dollars, which would free up six months of Lulu's time. Would you do it? I think you should!

Extend the Duration of the Project
If budget is the key driver and it's not possible to move the floating tasks, then the only option is to take longer to complete the project. Instead of hiring an outside design agency, which would increase the budget, Lulu would simply be given more time to get all the tasks done (figure 90).

EXTEND THE DURATION OF THE PROJECT

fig. 90

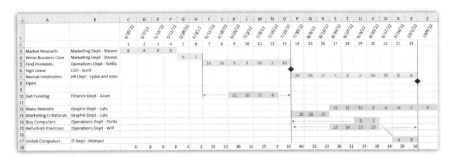

Can you see what this does to the plan?

That's right! We've created a new critical path! The new longest path has been created by a shortage of resources, something we would never have thought about at the Post-it note stage. Therefore, figure 91 now shows both of Lulu's tasks ("Make Website" and "Marketing Collaterals") as part of the critical path, with "Recruit Employees" now showing as a floating task with one week of float.

LOOK OUT FOR NEW CRITICAL PATH

fig. 91

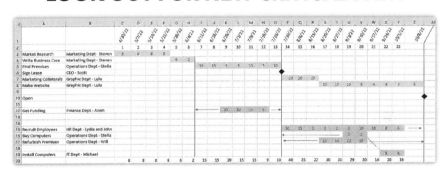

Split the Tasks

Another option for addressing a shortfall in resources is to split the tasks. If there's a peak of demand and not enough time to get all the tasks done, you may be able to split a task and do some before the peak and some after it. Going back to Lulu again, the most important task regarding the marketing collaterals is the branding and logo, because they will be featured on the website, so she could do those parts of the task before the website was created. The stationery and marketing brochures could be done later, closer to opening, although you would still need to allow for printing time.

SPLIT THE TASKS

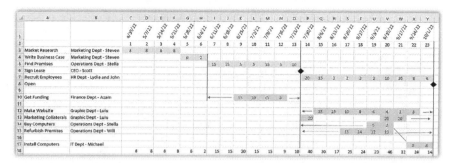

fig. 92

You can see in figure 92 that Lulu would start on the branding work in week 14, then move to the website build. When that got less intense in weeks 20 and 21, she would revert back to the stationery and marketing collaterals.

Like moving the floating tasks, splitting tasks is all about common sense. How can the task be divided to make its execution more manageable, to manage resources, and to keep the project on track? Some tasks can be split easily because they break down into distinct chunks, such as logo and brochures. If they don't break down neatly, then it's probably not a good idea to split them, because you won't know where you are in the task.

Overlap the Tasks

Sometimes it's also possible to manage resources by overlapping the tasks. In our case, we could overlap the tasks of marketing collateral and finding our premises (figure 93).

OVERLAP TASKS

fig. 93

Normally, we wouldn't start any designing until we had premises, but Lulu could start thinking about marketing a bit early. Just one week of overlap would mean that she could finish the design before the website went live, so she would no longer have the resource overlap problem.

Reduce Quality

The option of last resort is to reduce the quality of the output of the task. Personally, I don't ever like this option, because regardless of the key driver for the duration of the project, as soon as the project is over the only thing that will matter or be talked about is the quality. Even if you meet the time and money criteria, reducing the quality to manage resources may come back to bite you. Remember that you can reduce scope rather than quality—give them fewer features or a smaller outcome but still high quality, like a hospital with fewer beds that still has great doctors. But even this will be remembered as a problem long after the price and time are forgotten.

Nevertheless, it can sometimes be your only way out of resourcing challenges. If the client agrees to it, then it's OK. In our example, say it was decided that Lulu would spend only twenty hours on the marketing collaterals instead of sixty (figure 94). This might solve the resourcing issue, but the quality of the output will be lower than it would have been if she'd had more time. This is clearly an option if time or money is an issue, but it's rarely a great idea.

REDUCE QUALITY

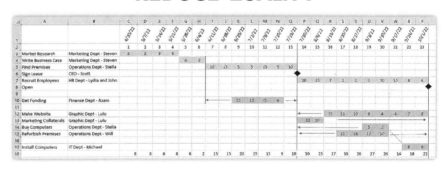

fig. 94

Move Other Projects

This solution is slightly different than the others because it's a resource solution for someone managing multiple projects rather than resource planning for one individual project. Still, it's still worth having up your sleeve as a project manager.

If you discover that you don't have the resources you need to complete your project, there might be a parallel project that can be moved. Or perhaps there are floating tasks within that other project that can be moved, without any problem, in order to free up some resources for you.

If they can delay something from February until March, you can have that resource for February in *your* project.

If you have too many projects and not enough resources, and you're trying to work out how to fit them all in, then a good way to simplify the problem is to start by distinguishing between the projects that are time-limited and those that are resource-limited. You can plan the time-limited ones first, since they can't be moved. That will tell you how many of the various resources you have left for the moveable projects. You can then figure out how many of those projects you can fit in using the remaining resources. It may be that it's just not possible to do all the projects, in which case you call a meeting with all the various stakeholders and discuss priorities: "I can only do three of the eight that you want. Which three should I prioritize?"

Splitting the projects in this way is often far easier to negotiate, because the project owners are better able to see the differences and appreciate that their project may have to wait. For example, say one of the aforementioned projects is to upgrade the IT infrastructure. The company has been experiencing far too many problems with the old system, and it's impacting customers and their experience of the business. This is having an effect on repeat business and must be fixed by a known date. As passionate as the project owner may be about more exciting projects on the list, it is immediately obvious that the IT infrastructure project must take priority, because it can affect so many other facets of the overall business.

How to Manage Resources on Multiple Projects

I've always found it amazing how few companies have genuine project management proficiency. Without that built-in capability, businesses will waste money and time, and their growth will be inhibited. It's inevitable. Even those that do show project management capability often stop at single projects. In other words, there are lots of people running reasonably successful projects, but there is no all-seeing eye or all-knowing brain managing how those projects fit together. Instead, there are lots of project owners almost competing with each other to get their stuff done. In many ways, this type of project management further separates the silos that emerge in business, with each department behaving almost like a separate company or a different team. Clearly, this is not conducive to good, profitable business.

It's vitally important for the prosperity of the company to have people who are aware of all the projects and can make conscious, considered choices about resource management, rather than letting project selection come down to random chance or whoever makes the most noise.

I'll tell you a little story to illustrate the challenges that emerge if you don't manage multiple projects properly. A large local company I spoke with had a clear business plan. To achieve everything outlined in the business plan, the company needed to complete a whole lot of projects, which they listed in a book. In many ways, this book gave them a false sense of control over the projects.

Looking through the book, I counted up how many projects were included. There were 305! Many of them were small, but still, this was going to add up to a lot of people and money. I asked the program manager, "Can you do all 305 of these projects?" He immediately confirmed my suspicions by saying, "Oh no, I don't think so." I asked him how many he thought they could do, and he said he thought maybe they could pull off fifty.

I asked him if he'd told his boss that 255 projects were not going to get done. Of course, he said no; he "didn't want to cause a fuss." I asked what would happen at the end of the year when his boss found out. He shrugged and said, "Oh, I guess I'll be in trouble again, as usual. But what can you do? They've never fired me up to now. I think they know it's impossible to do all 305 anyway!" Presumably he'd only been able to deliver around fifty projects in previous years as well.

There was a pattern, and it wasn't all his fault; both the manager and his boss were to blame for this situation. They hadn't made a plan, and they didn't know what resources would be needed to deliver on those 305 projects. As a result, they weren't able to decide what was impossible and didn't have the additional information they needed to prioritize the projects. Unsurprisingly, promises were not being kept because the initial demands were unrealistic.

Then I had one more thought. I asked him *which* fifty projects would get done. He answered: "Oh, that's easy! I do the ones I want to do."

Clearly, this is not ideal. Rather than relying on a sense of his organization's priorities or an overall strategy, he was implementing projects based on personal preference. Whether he was choosing them based on ease of execution or his areas of interest, these decisions were not made from a strategic perspective or a collective resource management perspective.

His boss could have immediately uncovered all this by asking a simple question: "Can I see your plan?"

The Cube

The reason people don't do these big-picture plans is because it's a little bit difficult. And the reason it's tricky is because the information forms sort of a "cube," so it can't be represented on one spreadsheet (figure 95).

THE RESOURCES CUBE

fig. 95

One axis is a list of all the projects. Another axis is all the resources available to do those projects. And then you've got time on the third axis. You are trying to work out whether each person is available for a specific project on a certain date. And sorting out that cube is very difficult. You have to decide which slice of the cube you want to look at.

If you think about it, a Gantt chart is one aspect, or slice, of the cube: it shows the resources and time for *one project*. It's looking at all the tasks and people on a project over time, but it doesn't show all the other tasks on the other projects or any overlaps that may exist. Your Gantt chart assumes infinite capacity, and certainly it ignores all the other Gantts for all the other projects.

A personal calendar, which is essentially one person's individual log of what they're doing and how much time it takes, is another slice of the cube: it shows projects and time for *one resource*. It looks at one person's view of all the tasks from all the projects, but it doesn't take into account anyone else's diary.

The third slice—resources and projects for *one interval of time*—is what could be called a short-term team planning board. It asks and answers "Who is doing what this week?" It's great for working out how we'll split the work between us, but its weakness is that it's only for this week.

To sum it up, the three aspects, or slices, of the cube are as follows:

» A Gantt chart: one *project*, showing people and time
» A personal calendar: one *person*, showing projects and time
» A weekly planning board: one *time*, showing people and projects but only for one period (e.g., a week)

Each one is flawed because each one is missing an aspect or dimension. We need something better. We need a Gantt of Gantts, because it shows projects, resources, and time in one diagram. And they can even be color-coded to indicate different skill groups.

Don't panic, because they are very easy to create.

A Gantt of Gantts

Before we dive in and learn how to easily create a Gantt of Gantts in Excel, let's take a moment to recap why it's so important to think about all your projects, and to have a resource plan that covers them all.

1. You don't want to promise things that you can't deliver. It will impact your professional reputation as a PM and, perhaps more important, it will send your stress levels through the roof. It's very dangerous to say yes to a project when you don't actually know whether you can do it.

2. The Gantt of Gantts will allow you to spot bottlenecks well in advance, so you can maneuver projects around without having to throw more time or money at them. Perhaps you'll start one of the projects earlier so that it's finished before the bottleneck, thus preventing it. Clearly, the sooner you know there's a bottleneck looming, the sooner you can navigate past it without emergency (and often costly) measures.

3. It will allow you and the project owners to properly prioritize the projects rather than using personal preference or potluck. One of the key duties of the top people in any business is to prioritize which projects get done; they need enough information to recognize that they can only do five projects out of the proposed thirty, and they rarely have this. If they had a Gantt of Gantts then they would be able to have a sensible and informed discussion about the merits of each of the projects so they could decide which five to choose. That way, the right projects would be acted on in line with the strategy.

To get an indication of how useful a Gantt of Gantts is, have a look at figure 96.

GANTT OF GANTTS

fig. 96

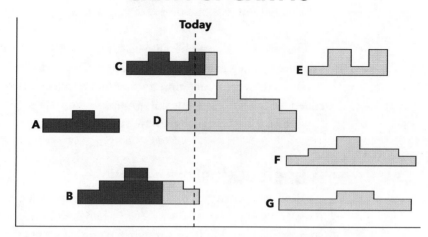

» **What can you tell me about project A?**
- If you thought it was finished, you're right.

» **What about project B?**
- Looking at project B in relation to the "today" line, it's obvious that project B is running a bit late. It should be about 90 percent finished by now, but it's closer to 70 percent.

» **What about project C?**
- You may not know why, but project C is further along than it should have been at this stage, so it's ahead of schedule. Although it's potentially a positive thing, you still need to investigate why this is ahead of schedule.

» **What about project D?**
- It hasn't been started, and it should have been, so it's already behind schedule. This would raise a flag for investigation.

» **Finally, why do you think projects E, F, and G are on the Gantt of Gantts?**
- Because it allows you to look at all the upcoming projects. You can see that they are due to be running at about the same time—peaking together, in fact. Will it be possible to deliver?

If not, you need to have a conversation with the projects' owners or your boss and ask them which one you should do first and which one is going to be pushed back until later. It's not up to you to decide. You will do whatever they want, but *they* need to decide on their priorities.

The Gantt of Gantts shows you the past and the future. The past: have you done what you should have done? And the future: can you do what you need to do? The answers to these questions inform your present.

If I were a CEO, I would want a Gantt of Gantts so I could monitor the overall progress of all the business's projects quickly and easily. It would also enable me to consider what's coming up and choose the most important projects to prioritize, if it turned out that not all of them were possible with the current resources.

If I were the head of any department, I would want a Gantt of Gantts because I could immediately see the pressures placed on my own people as a result of additional projects, and I could decide how best to manage those commitments and get the day-to-day work done.

And finally, if I were part of a senior-level team, I would want a Gantt of Gantts because I could use it to keep track of everything I'm managing. It could also function as an arguing tool if I needed to say to the CEO, "I can't do all the projects you want from me, and here's the proof. Would you like to give me some more resources, and if not, then which of the projects would you like to leave until next year?" Imagine having proof that you needed more people—that would be great!

QUICK CLIP

Check out my short video on the Gantt of Gantts.

To watch the QuickClip, use the camera on your mobile phone to scan the QR code or visit the link below.

or   www.quickclips.io/pm-10

SCAN ME   VISIT URL

How to Create a Gantt of Gantts

Where do the Gantt of Gantts shapes like those in figure 96 come from?

When it comes to creating a Gantt of Gantts, there is the ideal way and there is the realistic way. Let me explain.

The ideal way is to create a Gantt chart for every project. You should have this anyway (for all sorts of other good reasons, such as progress monitoring), and then it's super easy to copy the total time resources from the bottom of each project and paste them all onto your Gantt of Gantts summary.

To illustrate this, let's go back to our "setting up a new business" project example. Once you've done your Gantt chart, you have a tally of the time resources at the bottom of your worksheet. Highlight the row of total resources, and select "Copy" from the "Clipboard" section. Open a new worksheet by clicking on the "+" at the bottom left of the worksheet. Choose a cell, right-click to bring up "Paste Options," and select "Values (V)" (figure 97). This will copy only the numbers and not the formula, which you don't need.

CREATING A GANTT OF GANTTS USING REAL FIGURES

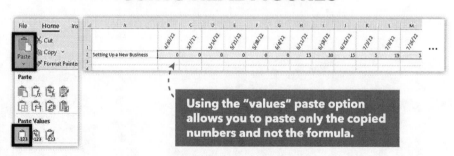

fig. 97

Using the "values" paste option allows you to paste only the copied numbers and not the formula.

Repeat this process for all your projects, adding the numbers into the new Gantt of Gantts from your other projects (figure 98). And you can see the shape of those resources' requirements by adding a 2D bar chart and stretching it out to fit the timeline like you did with your single-project Gantt chart.

GANTT OF GANTTS EXAMPLE

IMAGE

fig. 98

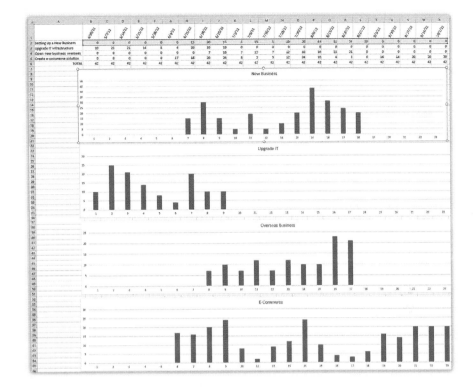

In this case, three other projects are going on during the same time frame: an IT upgrade, a new overseas arm of the business, and an e-commerce platform. By pulling all the resource information from each one, you can get a total resource profile (using the "AutoSum" feature). Be sure to change "Chart Title" to the name of your project so you can see which bar chart relates to which project. Just double-click on "Chart Title" and change the name.

Many people only copy the numbers and don't bother with the graphs. I like the graphs, but I certainly agree that they take time to set up, and they take up a lot of space on the page. If you are going to add up more than about five projects, then the graphs will probably have to go.

This is the precise and correct way to make your Gantt of Gantts.

By now you may have recognized the possible flaw in this method. Even though it's the standard, you may not have completed detailed Gantt charts for all the projects. For example, maybe the e-commerce platform is only in the discussion stage, so you didn't bother with a chart. But you still need to know whether those discussions should be nipped in the bud because there is already too much going on. Or at least you want to be able to give the project owner a heads-up on when it could be done.

Which brings us to the more realistic way to create a Gantt of Gantts chart: by guessing!

This method is not as random as it sounds. Wherever you have real figures from the Gantt chart, you use them. But wherever those figures are missing, you talk to the project owner and make an educated guess. For example, you would ask the IT manager how long they thought the e-commerce platform would take. They might say that it would take three people six weeks to complete. If only one person is available from IT because everyone else is working on the IT upgrade, then it may take one person three months to complete. The Gantt of Gantts is going to be fairly rough, but still significantly better than having nothing at all. And the guess may not be too far off, especially if the person you ask is experienced with similar projects.

If you also calculate one or two projects properly using a Gantt chart and add up the resources for those, then you are "calibrated," having built up some valuable knowledge in how projects work and how long they take, which will help with future estimating. In time, you will be able to say, "This one is about half the size of that one" and be pretty accurate.

Honestly, so few people use a Gantt of Gantts at all that even a rough one will put you ahead of the game. Don't try to get too clever. Don't try to automate it, for example; there are too many variables. Use the figures you do have to make an educated guess for the rest. Manual and rough is best.

Planning for Bottlenecks

One more thought about your Gantt of Gantts: it can be especially helpful in figuring out solutions to bottlenecks. For example, what if some of your projects require surveyors, and surveyors are in short supply in your organization? They are your potential bottleneck, so it makes sense to plan around them. Projects that don't need surveyors can be done any time, while projects that require a lot of surveyor time need to be considered very carefully.

If you know what your bottleneck is, then it's really easy to do a Gantt of

Gantts for just that resource. Figure 99 is a Gantt of Gantts for the surveying department, not the whole company. Put the surveyor parts of each project on the Gantt of Gantts. Maybe project A is huge, but the surveyors only have a small part to play, as shown by the small shape in A in Figure 99. Meanwhile, maybe project B is really small but is almost all surveying work, so it looks quite large on the Surveyor Gantt of Gantts.

GANTT OF GANTTS FOR SURVEYORS

fig. 99

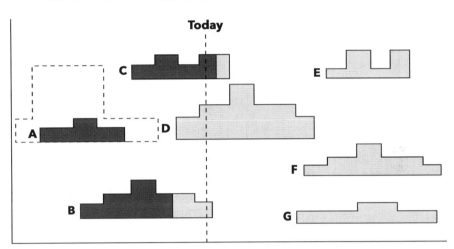

This allows us to look at how much surveying time is needed and when, so we can move on to figuring out whether it can be done. If the surveyors can do their parts of the project, then the rest of the company should be able to do theirs too.

And if you're not sure which department is the bottleneck, then make a Gantt of Gantts for each department, keeping it up to date as each new project comes in. You might also keep a Gantt of Gantts for yourself, or for your team's total workload.

Imagine that a new project comes along and, by looking at the Gantt chart or estimating from experience, you know you'll need to do twenty hours a week for all of March and April (or you'll need to allocate two of your team for that time period). You can add that into your Gantt of Gantts. It's like a graph of your personal calendar, really. And if you are already busy in April, you can alert your team and say, "I can't do it—can anyone else cover this new project, or my existing work?" Or you can have a discussion with the senior team/stakeholders to work out whether the project can be started earlier or later. "Or can my part of the project be started earlier or later, if it's a floating task? Or, failing all of those, can I have more resources on my team?"

With an up-to-date Gantt of Gantts for the bottleneck resource, you are less likely to be surprised by issues with resources, which is a great situation to be in.

Chapter Recap

» Too often, resource planning is contained within individual projects without consideration of all the projects as a whole. This is a recipe for disaster.

» "Resources" can mean money or specialist equipment, but the main resource is usually people. You need the right number of people available to complete all tasks and meet your deadlines.

» During step 3, we assume infinite capacity and ignore the issue of resourcing. But in real life, we're always limited by resources. In step 6, we find out what resources are needed, and in step 7 we find out what resources are actually available—first for one project, then for all the projects we're managing. This helps us to identify potential shortfalls ahead of time.

» There are seven ways to maneuver around resourcing issues. You can move floating tasks to a less busy time, get more resources, extend the project duration, split the tasks, overlap the tasks, reduce the quality (last resort), or establish which projects are time-limited and which are resource-limited and prioritize the time-limited one.

» Managing multiple projects is very challenging because of the "cube." You are trying to figure out whether each person is available for a certain project on a certain date. You have to decide which aspect or slice of the cube you want to look at.

» A Gantt of Gantts offers an overview of all projects for optimal resource planning.

» There are two ways to create a Gantt of Gantts. One is to create Gantt charts for each of the projects and transfer the total resource figures into a new worksheet. The second way is to make an educated guess. Sometimes you might use a combination of both.

» You might want to make a Gantt of Gantts especially for your bottleneck resources, such as departments that are under pressure or have critical skills that are utilized across multiple projects.

| 10 |
Risk Planning – Step 8

Chapter Overview
» Identifying the risks in your project
» Assigning likelihood and seriousness scores
» How to mitigate as much risk as possible

Why do so many professionals say they are project managing, when what they are actually doing is fire-fighting?

– COLIN BENTLEY

I mentioned earlier that all projects are risky because, by their very nature, they involve doing things that we haven't done before. Step 8, which is the final step of the planning part of your project, is to think more specifically about what those risks might be.

Some people don't want to think about risk, as though forethought is inviting exposure or tempting fate in some way. But this is nonsense. Clearly, as the project manager, you want to make sure that you have thought of all the risks that could impact your project and taken steps to prevent as many of them as you can. You'll also need to have a plan ready to deal with the remaining risks, should they crop up.

This is not just good business and common sense; robust risk planning, like all planning, also strengthens your relationship with your customers and colleagues. Your boss, the project owner, and any number of other stakeholders need to know the risks inherent in the project, preferably before they give it the go-ahead. They may not *want* to know about the risks, and they may wave them away, but you still need to inform them. That way, they can't ever come back to you and complain that they weren't informed.

Besides, despite their possible reluctance to engage with the risks, once they understand your risk plan they are likely to feel even more confident in your project management skills. They will be relieved that you know the risks and have taken steps to mitigate as many as possible up front, rather than merely hoping they don't materialize. All project owners want their PMs to have a handle on the project, and that includes risk planning.

The objective of step 8 is to identify the possible risks and make them less of a problem where possible. The risks that are left after mitigation are then reported to your boss, customer, and/or stakeholders so they can decide whether to proceed or not. To use the posh project management term for this, step 8 is about figuring out the *risk exposure* after you've identified your risks and taken all of your mitigating actions.

Identify the Risks

The first thing to do is to create a list of all the possible risks to your project. Essentially you need to have a think about all the things that could go wrong.

Anything that can go wrong will go wrong.

– MURPHY'S LAW

Start by focusing on the tasks on the critical path and think about what could go wrong with those, because they're going to be the main risks. Certainly, they'll be the ones that affect the time the project takes. But, of course, the floating tasks can still negatively affect the cost of the project, and also the time required for the project if they go *very* wrong, so you'll need to consider those too. Here are a couple ideas for flagging risks:

» **Brainstorm with the Team:** Honestly, this can be fun! Get everyone together. Start with the critical tasks and ask, "What could go wrong?" for each task and then "What else could go wrong?" Keep asking until you get an exhaustive list for each task.

» **Look at Past Projects:** What does history tell you about similar projects? Do you have a depressing list of every problem that's ever occurred on any project? If not, start one now. It will be an invaluable resource and will cut the time taken for risk planning in half! If there is limited documentation, consider seeking out people who were involved in similar projects and pick their brains about problems they encountered, or even things they wish they'd thought about up front last time.

Once you have the list of potential risks, transfer them to a risk assessment chart (figure 100).

A blank, fillable template for risk assessment is available with your Digital Assets at go.quickstartguides.com/project. Use this as a simple guide to assessing the risks on any project so you know what you can do to mitigate those risks and what risks, if any, remain.

RISK ASSESSMENT CHART

fig. 100

Description of project:						
Description of possible problem	Risk factor (how likely) 1–5	Impact factor (how serious) 1–5	Weighted factor (risk x impact) 1–25	If weighted factor > 5		
				Preventative action plan (reduce likelihood)	Protective action plan (reduce impact)	Risk x impact = weighted factor after mitigation

All your risks should be listed in the "description of possible problem" column. You can have as many risks as you like—start a second page if you need to. Then assign each possible problem a risk factor that indicates how likely it is to occur (1 = highly unlikely, 5 = virtually certain to happen) and an impact factor for how serious it would be if it happened (1 = you'll hardly notice, 5 = catastrophic) (figure 101).

RISK PLANNING FOR NEW BUSINESS

fig. 101

Description of project: New Business Project						
Description of possible problem	Risk factor (how likely) 1–5	Impact factor (how serious) 1–5	Weighted factor (risk x impact) 1–25	If weighted factor > 5		
				Preventative action plan (reduce likelihood)	Protective action plan (reduce impact)	Risk x impact = weighted factor after mitigation
MR throws up false insight.	2	2	4			
Can't find suitable premises.	4	5	20			
Can't find suitable staff.	3	5	15			

Looking through this example, let's imagine that Steven, who is conducting the market research, has a huge amount of experience in this area, so the chances of his getting it wrong are low, maybe 2. It's also not that serious because even if he is wrong, it will come out in the business case, so it's certainly not a disaster. As the total weighed factor is 4 (2 x 2), we can immediately discount that risk. The accepted wisdom in project management is that only risks that score over 5 need to be mitigated. We have to draw a line somewhere!

Elsewhere in this example, the risk when it comes to both the premises and the staff is that you won't find what you're looking for. Let's say the likelihood of not finding the right premises is high because commercial real estate is scarce in your area, so the score for likelihood is 4. Obviously, it's serious if the premises can't be found, so that scores a maximum of 5 for seriousness, with a resulting risk weighting of 20. Not finding the right staff is less likely but just as serious, resulting in a weighted score of 15. Therefore, both warrant attention.

How scientific is this? Well, some would say "not very." The score for likelihood is a guess, often based on a very small sample of previous occurrences, and the seriousness is often an opinion. This worries some people, but it shouldn't. It's certainly a good starting point for discussion. Your boss or customer might feel that one of your identified risks is more likely than you say, or less serious than you're assuming. Or they might ask you to justify your score. All discussion makes the risk plan better. Besides, whether you enter a 3 or a 4 probably won't affect the result; if the total comes to more than 5, you should work on mitigating it. The difference between a 12 and a 16 doesn't matter much once you realize it's reasonably high. It's not a perfect method, but it's good enough and much better than doing nothing.

Mitigate the Risks

Risk assessment is not just about alerting everyone on the team and the project owners to potential risks. It's also about mitigating as much risk as possible, to reduce the chance of any nasty surprises during the project. You're aiming to reduce the likelihood and potential seriousness of every risk with a total score above 5. You can nearly always do one or the other, sometimes both.

Prevention is always better than cure. It is always better, less costly, and less stressful for everyone involved to seek to reduce the chance of issues arising than to wait until they happen and tackle them then.

Going back to our example: what could you do to reduce those risks?

There is nothing much you can do to reduce the likelihood of not finding suitable premises, except maybe getting a local real estate agent on the case. But you could reduce the seriousness of the risk by ensuring that home-working capability is fast-tracked. This could reduce the score to 4 x 1 = 4.

As for the employee risk, you could reduce the likelihood of not finding the right people by hiring recruitment consultants to locate and weed out the people who are unsuitable. This would come with additional cost, but you could flag that with the project owner for them to decide. If they like the idea, then the risk factor drops to 1 x 5 = 5 (figure 102).

RISK PLANNING FOR NEW BUSINESS

Description of project: New Business Project						
Description of possible problem	Risk factor (how likely) 1-5	Impact factor (how serious) 1-5	Weighted factor (risk x impact) 1-25	If weighted factor > 5		
				Preventative action plan (reduce likelihood)	Protective action plan (reduce impact)	Risk x impact = weighted factor after mitigation
MR throws up false insight.	2	2	4			N/A
Can't find suitable premises.	4	5	20		Ensure home working capability.	4 x 1 = 4
Can't find suitable staff.	3	5	15	Engage recruitment consultant to pre-select.		1 x 5 = 5

GRAPHIC

fig. 102

NOTE

From this example you will probably notice that risk assessment involves a lot of judgment and opinion. That's OK. As I've said, an educated guess is always better than nothing.

Identify and Communicate Remaining Risk Exposure

Once you have run through the risk assessment process and mitigated as many of the potential risks as possible, there may still be risks that have a score higher than 5. It is essential that you report the risks you can't eliminate to your customer, boss, or other stakeholders.

It is also essential that you explain the impact of mitigation. Mitigating actions may need to be fed back into the plan as new tasks. If so, there is almost always going to be some time or cost involved. The stakeholders need to be made aware of this and agree to it.

The risk assessment simply tells you where to focus. It becomes the basis for discussion and points to obvious mitigating actions. Stakeholders may disagree, which is fine. But at least you and the stakeholders know this up front and can make choices based on that information. They can't say they were never told about the risks. Forewarned is forearmed.

Understanding Loops

As I said at the start of this chapter, risk planning is the final step in the planning stage. So, now we've finished our planning—or have we?

Before we can press the Go button and start implementing the project, we may need to take at least one loop back. Figure 103 demonstrates where the loops are that feed back into earlier parts of the planning process.

LOOPS IN THE PLANNING STAGE

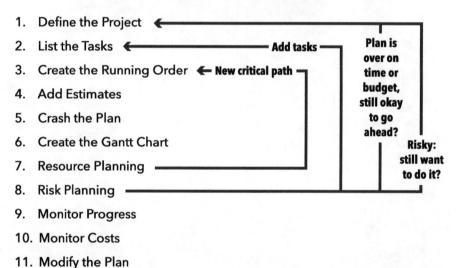

1. Define the Project
2. List the Tasks ← — Add tasks
3. Create the Running Order ← New critical path
4. Add Estimates
5. Crash the Plan
6. Create the Gantt Chart
7. Resource Planning
8. Risk Planning
9. Monitor Progress
10. Monitor Costs
11. Modify the Plan
12. Review

Plan is over on time or budget, still okay to go ahead?

Risky: still want to do it?

GRAPHIC

fig. 103

If you're working on a very simple project, you might talk to the customer at step 1 and find out what they want, say "yes, I can do that," and then go off to plan it and do it. But most projects aren't like that. Most projects are much more complicated, so once you've found out what the customer or project owner wants, you need to do the planning to check whether it's feasible. Can you really deliver the quality they are looking for within the budget and time frame they want? To decide accurately, you need to complete steps 2 through 7. List the tasks, create the running order with the Post-its, add the estimates, crash the plan if necessary, make it into a Gantt chart, determine the resources you will need to successfully deliver the project, and analyze the risks involved.

Once you've done all that, you can go back to the customer, at the second kick-off meeting, and either tell them you can deliver what they want or report that you can't do it in the timescale they're hoping for. And you can use your Gantt chart as an arguing tool, so the customer knows that your response is based on fact, rather than opinion.

Remember, planning makes you stronger.

You might also go back to the customer and tell them that, although you can't do it in the timescale they want, you could do it with more time. If time is their key driver, they may say there isn't any more time, but there is more money to speed up the project. This may be your first loop, because you will then need to rework the plan to see how much time can be saved with the additional budget. In this case, you would loop back to step 5, crash the plan. If their key driver is money, then they may opt to give you more time. And again, you would need to loop back to the plan to confirm that the additional time given was enough.

That's all to say that you might go around this loop more than once. But don't worry about that, because having done the work once, it doesn't take much time to go back through your plan and tweak it for new circumstances.

The biggest loop is that after all eight steps of the planning stage, you go back to the stakeholders and get the final plan approved (or not!). Are they happy with the cost and time, and are they happy with the risks? That's where step 8 can feed back to step 2. When you do the risk planning, sometimes you identify extra tasks that need to be done to mitigate those risks, which then need to be added into the project plan. This should be done before going back to the customers with the whole finished plan. But you'll also remember from the last chapter that there can be a loop from step 7, resource planning, that goes back and affects the critical path. If you have a resource that is in high demand, it can become the critical path, so step 7 can feed back into step 3.

Finally, new loops are likely to be introduced once the project begins (figure 104). Perhaps halfway through the project, as it has changed or evolved, we might need to loop back and add new tasks or change the time and cost estimates or crash the current plan, which in turn changes the Gantt chart and might also affect the risks.

LOOPS IN THE IMPLEMENTATION STAGE

fig. 104

1. Define the Project
2. List the Tasks
3. Create the Running Order
4. Add Estimates
5. Crash the Plan ←
6. Create the Gantt Chart ←
7. Resource Planning
8. Risk Planning   **Running late or over budget = replan**
9. Monitor Progress
10. Monitor Costs
11. Modify the Plan ————
12. Review

A lot of people think of project planning as linear, but really, it's not. We know things will change, and sometimes we have to go back and change parts of the plan. That's OK. That's just real life. At any point in time, we have the best plan we can have, based on the information we have at that moment, and we can adjust the plan as needed. Plus, we know the effects of making those changes. We have a baseline plan for comparison. Good planning makes additional planning easier.

Chapter Recap

» As the project manager, you want to make sure that you think of all the risks that could impact your project and take steps to prevent as many of them as you can. You'll also need to have a plan ready to deal with the remaining risks that might crop up.

» Your boss, the project owner, and any number of other stakeholders need to know the risks inherent in the project, preferably before they give the project the go-ahead. Identify as many risks as possible, focusing initially on the critical path tasks. Ideas for flagging risks include brainstorming with the team and looking at past projects.

» Transfer all the risks to an assessment chart, where you'll use your knowledge, opinion, and common sense to assign each risk a likelihood score and a seriousness score, multiplied together for a weighted risk factor.

» Any risks with a weighted risk factor score of 5 or higher need to be mitigated, either by interventions to reduce likelihood or actions to reduce seriousness—preferably both, especially if they can be instigated without additional time or cost.

» There may still be risks that you can't eliminate that have a score higher than 5. It is essential that you report these risks to your customer, boss, or other stakeholders.

» It is crucial that you explain the impact of mitigation. Mitigating actions may need to be fed back into the plan as new tasks. If so, there will almost always be some extra time or cost involved.

» There are distinct "loops" in the planning stage from listing the tasks (step 2) to resource planning (step 7). Assessing risks, for example, may require you to loop back to the stakeholders to flag any remaining risks. There is also another smaller loop back to listing tasks (step 2) because the act of mitigating your risk may add additional tasks to your plan.

PART IV

MANAGING THE IMPLEMENTATION OF YOUR PROJECT

| 11 |

Monitor Progress – Step 9

Chapter Overview
» The necessity of using the plan during implementation
» Comparing what was supposed to happen to what did happen
» How to color in the Gantt chart to visualize progress

Now that the planning is finished and you've got the green light for your project, it's time to implement it and monitor its progress.

There are those who believe that planning is just about getting the project over the starting line so that the team can begin, and after that's done, the project manager's main responsibility is the plan, not the subsequent work. But that's crazy. Sure, the planning allows you to fully appreciate what's involved and whether what the stakeholder wants can be done on time and within budget, but all that wonderful planning will go to waste if the plan is shoved in a drawer as soon as the stakeholder agrees to the project. Besides, monitoring progress on your Gantt chart is so quick and easy, you'd be mad not to do it.

Your plan, especially the resulting Gantt chart, is a living document that should guide you and the project team throughout the project. Used properly and kept up to date with what's actually been done, the Gantt chart will make the project visible to you. You will be able to tell, within seconds of looking at it, exactly where the project is against the plan and expectations. This gives you a huge amount of power, because it alerts you to tasks that are not on schedule, and it does so quickly enough that you can do something about those issues before the project gets too far off track. All your hard work and planning goes to waste if you don't keep looking at your plan as you move through the tasks.

The colored-in Gantt chart will be the primary document during the project and should be brought to every project meeting. The regularity of those meetings will depend on the length of the project. They could be daily but are more likely to be weekly or even monthly.

Back to the Gantt Chart

Once you have your project Gantt chart and the project is in progress, you need to keep it up to date. The chart should be showing which tasks have been done, which tasks are in progress, and which tasks are still left to do. This progress is noted by coloring in the Gantt chart.

> *Being a Project Manager is like being an artist: you have the different colored process streams combining into a work of art.*
>
> – GREG CIMMARRUSTI

There are two ways to color in your Gantt chart. You can either use "proportional coloring" or "color-when-complete." Proportional coloring is where you color in part of the bar if you have done part of the task. It provides more detail, but it's not always easy to estimate how complete a task is. For example, how can we tell how complete "Get Funding" is? Azam may fill out all the applications and submit them to the relevant bodies, but does that mean it's 90 percent complete because he's done all he can, or does that mean it's only 20 percent complete because his part of the task is actually quite small? There is always an element of opinion or judgment involved in proportional coloring. As a result, project managers, especially those who are under pressure, can be tempted to be overly optimistic with their marker pen: "Oh yes, that task is definitely nearly finished, the remaining part is going to be easy; let's call it 90 percent."

There are those who claim that only "color-when-complete" is 100 percent accurate—a task isn't done until it's done, because full completion is the only certainty. And though I agree with that sentiment, for a project manager it's far more important to get a handle on what's happening and whether something looks like it might be heading off track, than to be certain something is finished. If you use color-when-complete, you will have no idea how much progress has been made, only that it's not done. In our example, this could mean that Azam hasn't even started looking for funding, or that he's mostly done and is waiting for final confirmations.

Always use proportional coloring in your Gantt charts. It may be an estimate, but at least you will be able to see that tasks have been started, and you will have a much better handle on what might be slipping.

This doesn't mean that proportional coloring is perfect as it is. To make this technique even more effective and insightful, I always recommend that you use sub-Gantt charts for a more accurate view. That way you get more granularity on exactly what tasks need to be done to complete the main task, and whether they have been started, finished, or are only partially done.

For example, you might work with Lulu to make a sub-Gantt for "Make Website" so that it is easier to gauge exactly how that task is progressing. Instead of asking Lulu to estimate how much of "Make Website" she's done, you can both look at the sub-Gantt and see that "Domain Registration," "Logo and Branding," "Site Plan/Architecture," and "Copy for all Webpages" have been completed. "Create Pages" is only 50 percent complete, as there are still four more pages to add, and "SEO" has not been started. This level of detail gives you and Lulu a much better handle on exactly what is happening regarding the task "Make Website."

And the great thing is that you don't need to worry about the detail until you get there. Of course, the high-level Gantt chart may have been used to help estimate the time and cost originally, but after that you can use it—with a maximum of thirty tasks on it—to easily see what's going on with the whole project. Then, when you reach a larger or riskier task, perhaps with a less experienced person doing it, you can drill down to the sub-Gantt and micromanage or micro-monitor that particular task. But each time you feel the urge to drill down deeper, ask yourself whether you really need to. If Lulu is an experienced designer who has built countless websites, then you probably don't need the sub-Gantt. But if this is her first one, then the sub-Gantt is helpful for everyone. It's all about trust and who is going to be responsible for delivering that particular task. As a project manager, it may be appropriate for you to give that person a chance to prove themselves and develop.

Never mix proportional coloring and color-when-complete, because you won't know which tasks are which. That task that hasn't been colored in at all—has it not been started (proportional coloring), or might it be 90 percent complete (color-when-complete)? Stick with one method, ideally proportional coloring with sub-Gantts for additional detail and granularity around the tasks. This combination will let you know how the project is actually progressing.

When you update your Gantt chart, save it as a new file with that day's date at the end. It can be fascinating to look back and see the progression of the project and also how accurate your estimates were. This will help you to hone your project management skills for the next project.

The colored-in Gantt chart provides a really helpful snapshot of what's happening for everyone involved, but especially for you if you are the project manager or if you are managing the project manager.

How to Insert Color in Your Gantt Chart

1. First you need to introduce a "Now" or "Today" line into the Gantt chart. On the "Home" tab of your chart, select the column that shows today or the week you are currently in. In the "Font" section, click on "Fill Color." This is the little icon that looks like a tilted bucket of paint. Choose the color you want to use to represent "The present time." In our example, imagine that it's the week of 06/11/22; that becomes the "Now" marker (figure 105).

ADD "NOW" OR "TODAY" COLUMN

fig. 105

2. To color in the tasks that you have done, add a different color to them. However, you will not be able to change the color without a little Excel wizardry, because those tasks are color-formatted to denote whether they're critical tasks or floating tasks. To get around that, add the "task completed" color to another cell somewhere else in the spreadsheet. While the cursor is in the cell with the new color, click on "Format Painter" in the "Clipboard" section of the "Home" tab and then click on all the sections you want to color in (figure 106).

What can you tell about the new business project from the colored-in Gantt chart in figure 106?

That's right: we are behind schedule. How can you tell? Because the coloring is not keeping up with the "Now" line. The project is only a week behind at the moment, but Steven needs to get that business case finished, pronto. And we should probably tell Stella that she can't start yet, and maybe talk with her about how she might be able to do her seven-week task in six weeks, so we can get back on schedule.

COLOR IN GANTT CHART TO INDICATE PROGRESS

IMAGE

fig. 106

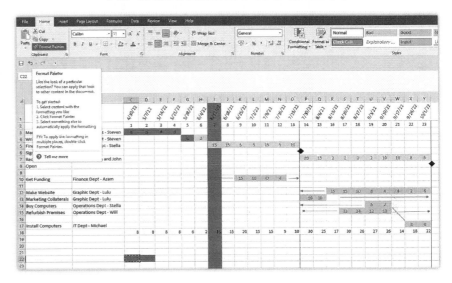

NOTE

You can't partially color in a cell in Excel, but you can color in the task that relates to that week. For example, "Write Business Plan" will take two weeks. I can see from figure 106 that one week has been colored in and one week hasn't, so that task is 50 percent done.

Communicating to Stakeholders

Another key part of monitoring progress is communicating with stakeholders and keeping them up to date with how the project is going.

How this communication should occur may have been decided and agreed on in step 1, via a *communications plan*. That's how it should work in theory, anyway—but it rarely does. If the project has not been given the go-ahead at step 1, deciding how everyone will be kept in the loop is usually considered premature. Instead, the communications plan usually comes into play in step 9 when the project is live and you need to make sure that, as well as monitoring progress, you keep the relevant stakeholders informed of that progress in a way they find acceptable. It is very easy to get into hot water as a project manager because of poor communication. And keeping key stakeholders in the dark, whether deliberately or not, is never wise.

Consult with the stakeholders to be sure you are communicating with them in a way that is appreciated. It may be that you only need to update people once a month via email. Maybe they want a daily phone call, or a written report every week. The type and frequency of the communication will depend on the stakeholder, the size of the project, and your experience as a project manager.

There is room for negotiation here. If the communication they want is verging on micro-management, then you may have to push back and tell them that it will take too much of your time and will therefore damage the project.

One final aspect of communication with stakeholders: are you going to *inform* them after you have made decisions, or are you going to *consult* them before you make decisions? It might be clear that small stuff like delaying a floating task would be in the "inform after" category, and big things like employing an extra team member would fall under "consult before," but what about asking the client for some extra funding? Do you consult your boss beforehand or inform them afterward? And for the client, if you are going to use a slightly different color of paint, do you need to consult them beforehand or can you inform them afterward? In the case of large, well-documented projects there should be a discussion, at either step 1 or step 9, where borderline cases are listed as one or the other.

Make sure you keep the right people informed of progress in the right way for them, for you, and for the project. So many of the problems that arise in projects are not even project-related; they are results of poor communication and unmet expectations. So make sure that everyone knows what to expect, how they will be kept in the loop, and how often they can expect updates on progress.

Chapter Recap

» Now that the planning is finished and you've got the green light for your project, it's time to implement the plan and monitor progress.

» Once you have your Gantt chart and the project is in progress, you need to keep it up to date so the chart shows what tasks have been done, what tasks are in progress, and what tasks are still left to do. This is done by coloring in the Gantt chart.

» There are two ways to color in your Gantt chart. You can use either proportional coloring or color-when-complete. Proportional coloring gives more detail on the Gantt chart because it allows you to see how much of a task has been done, but it relies on estimation and judgment. Color-when-complete is 100 percent accurate and gives the project manager more certainty, but it doesn't tell you whether an incomplete task has been started.

» It's always best to use proportional coloring in your Gantt charts. It may be an estimate, but at least you will be able to see that tasks have been started and will have a much better handle on what might be slipping.

» To make the proportional coloring even more effective and insightful, use it in conjunction with sub-Gantt charts for a more accurate view. You get more granularity on exactly what tasks need to be done to complete the main task and whether they have been started, finished, or are only partially done.

» To color in your Gantt charts, add a "Today" or "Now" line in the column that relates to "the present time," and then add a different color to the tasks that have been completed or partially completed.

» Always make sure that key stakeholders are kept informed about progress.

| 12 |

Monitor Costs – Step 10

Chapter Overview

- » Getting the right data is crucial
- » Overspending and underspending
- » How to institute monthly monitoring

The most likely cause of disastrous financial surprises in any business is *projects*. They can be really dangerous if you don't monitor them correctly. So in this chapter you will learn how to avoid financial surprises, in a quick and easy way. A business will rarely overspend or get a nasty surprise because they have more people in the marketing department than expected, or they bought more steel than usual. Accountants are very good at controlling the costs of each department every month because they know what the regular wage or supplier bill is and have usually been informed of any extra spending. These continuous/process numbers are easy to measure and don't fluctuate much. And if they do, we already know it because we have consciously changed them—you can't buy more steel or recruit more people without making an effort. And they are compartmentalized, so they're easy to measure.

Projects are very different. Projects often spread across a number of departments, with hugely varying spends each month, and actual progress can be hard to see or measure.

What often happens with projects is that a project budget is agreed on for, say, $10 million over two years. At the end of the two-year period, the $10 million is spent and the accountants are happy. They believe the project has ended, and finished on budget. Only the project manager is thinking, "Oh no, I still need another million to finish it." The project is $1 million in the red and the accountants don't even know about it yet. This is very common. When companies overspend, it's almost always on projects.

Projects are rarely finished *quicker* than planned or end up costing less than expected. They almost always run late and the budget is always overspent. This is practically inevitable, even with exceptional planning. Things are very rarely cheaper than you expected, and there are always extra tasks that were missed, and thus any deviation from the plan will incur additional time and cost. It's critical, therefore, that you monitor costs every month.

Get the Data

In order to monitor the costs, you need to get the numbers from the accounting department every week or every month. And if those numbers aren't sent to you, ask for them, because you've got to keep an eye on the money. Never ignore or skim through those figures.

You also need to know what system your accounting department uses. They will use one of two methods: *cash accounting* or *accrual accounting*. In other words, they will either record only what has actually been spent and received (cash accounting) or they will also include what is due to be spent or due to be received (accrual accounting).

Both have merit. Cash accounting is more definitive and definite, but it doesn't forecast. For example, the figures from the accounting department might tell you that you have spent $100,000. If your budget is $250,000, that might mean that you have $150,000 left to spend on the project. But if you know that another $100,000 is already scheduled to be spent in four weeks' time (you have placed the order but not paid yet) then you really have only $50,000 left to spend. If you don't know this, you could easily spend money that you don't actually have, and that could blow the budget.

Accrual accounting is therefore more accurate, because it accounts for all the commitments that are coming up. On the other hand, things can and do change, so it may end up giving an inaccurate financial picture, particularly for incoming money. Imagine you are due a stage payment of $300,000 next month; you could, theoretically, start spending that money now. Accrual accounting would say that you can afford it, while cash accounting would say it's not yours until it's in the bank. The caution of cash accounting could turn into an advantage if there's a problem with that $300,000 payment.

Whatever system your accounting department uses, it's always smart to supplement it with your own spreadsheet so that you can anticipate upcoming costs and adjust actual costs against expected costs in real time. In fact, the safest way to work would be to supplement the accounts information using accrual accounting for spending (as soon as you place the order the money's gone) and cash accounting for income (it's not yours until it's in the bank). This can get a little confusing and also give an unduly negative picture, but you reduce the risk of being caught out financially.

One other thing to look out for: the numbers you get from the accounting department will always contain a lag time, sometimes a month or more. By the time they've waited till end of the month, gathered together all the figures on spend, corrected the errors, and sent those summarized costs to you, the figures will be out of date. That's why project managers should always keep their own spreadsheets of what they've spent and then look at both accounting's costs and their own tally of costs (and payments) to ensure a more accurate real-time picture of the financial side of the project.

You also need to pay close attention to the accountants' figures to make sure that costs have been allocated to your project correctly. It's often quite hard for accountants to know what's been spent on what. Departmental spending is easy for them to figure out, but often projects cut across departments and, in the confusion, costs may be allocated to your project that belong in a different project or department.

By drawing on the accounting data and your own up-to-date spreadsheet on project costs, you can make sure the numbers agree. If there is a discrepancy, look for costs that have been wrongly attributed to your project. Remember, there is always a lag time between accounting's figures and live figures, so your anticipated costs may also help to explain any discrepancy. Doing all this will give you a firm grip on the money side of a project, and you will know exactly how much you have available at any one time.

What's Happening Now?

Clearly, the cost-related progress of a project is connected to the time-related progress of the project. Still, it's very easy to forget this or be confused by the data that you gather regarding both time and cost.

I am constantly reminded of this when I meet with clients. For example, I was meeting with the project manager of a large public project to build a road. It was a $40 million project, and it was expected to take five years to complete. In our meeting, one year into the project, the project manager told me everything was going well. They had spent $8 million, which he thought meant everything was fine. Assuming that $40 million over five years means an allocation of $8 million a year is a logical conclusion—at least in theory. Was he right to be feeling optimistic about the project?

I'm sure you've already realized that it's impossible to say. Even if the spend really is due to be the same in each year (year 1 was supposed to cost $8 million), we still don't know what they have done with that $8 million. What if they have actually finished only 10 percent of the work but it has cost $8 million? That would mean the whole project is going to end up costing $80 million. How will the project owners feel when they discover that their road didn't cost $40 million as promised, but rather $80 million? And when will they discover this? Maybe when the spend reaches $40 million at the end of year five and they find that the road is only half finished! Clearly, they need to monitor progress.

There are only two ways to know what's actually been done. First, you could drive out to the road and see what's been done. But if you are not a road-building expert, that probably won't tell you very much. You might see lots of trucks driving around and people digging holes, but is that what's supposed to be happening at this point? You just wouldn't know.

The quicker, easier, and much more accurate way to assess the progress is to revisit the Gantt chart. Your colored-in Gantt chart will tell you if you are on track timewise, and your spend profile Gantt chart will tell you if you are on track cost-wise.

NOTE Accountants often assume a linear spend profile over time. In other words, they assume a project will spend the same amount each month—but this almost never happens in project management. They always spend different amounts at different times in the project.

The key when monitoring your cost is to compare costs to progress. If you're underspent, it quite often means you haven't done the work. And actually, if you're underspent and you haven't done the work, that means you haven't done the work for a reason. There's been some sort of a problem—maybe you forgot a task, or something had to be done twice. In the end, you'll probably end up being overspent.

So "underspent halfway through" usually means overspent at the end. And of course, *overspent* halfway through usually means very overspent by the end. This is not that surprising. If you divert from the plan, then your project will suffer, because the plan, by definition, is the best way to do the job.

The Six Combinations of Cost Performance

The good news is that there are only ever six possible combinations of lateness and cost that flag *how much* your project is behind or ahead of schedule and *how much* the project is over or under budget. Once you understand these, you understand project finance. Let's run through them briefly so you know what to look out for. For each one, have a look at the Gantt chart first to see if you can figure out what it's telling you, and then read on to find out if you were right.

1. Accountant = "Disaster," Real Situation = ?

If you showed figure 107 to your accounting department, chances are they would not be happy. In fact, these six scenarios are in order of increasing accountant happiness, meaning number one represents maximum accountant *un*happiness.

fig. 107

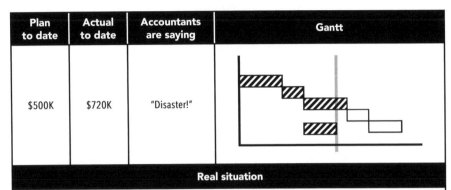

Plan to date	Actual to date	Accountants are saying	Gantt
$500K	$720K	"Disaster!"	
Real situation			
Slightly ahead but very overspent. Looks bad, but may not be quite as bad as it looks if the overspend is due to being ahead of schedule. May be OK if time is the key driver.			

In this project you're meant to have spent $500,000 so far, but you've actually spent $720,000. The accountant thinks the project is a disaster. But you remain calm and look at the Gantt chart. Is this really a disaster?

It's not, is it? Certainly it's not as bad as it looks from the numbers alone. The Gantt chart shows that the project is slightly ahead of schedule. Remember the idea of linear spend, each task costing roughly the same. If this is the case, then we are not ahead enough to explain the $220,000 overspend, but at least some of it is due to our being ahead. It's not as bad as the accountant thinks.

And if the spend is nonlinear, where some tasks cost more than others, it may be that the extra work does indeed account for that $220,000. Perhaps a large, expensive purchase was made a little earlier than planned because the exchange rate was favorable. Or the supplier offered a discount if the purchase was made earlier. It would be very easy to check on that and calm the accountant down.

All we have to do is look at what the task is on the Gantt chart and see if it helps to explain the $220,000. Also look at the colored-in tasks on the Gantt chart—are they enough to explain the overspend, or at least some of it?

Using the traffic light system, you might allocate this project an amber status. In this context it's amber and not red because you can still get back on budget. Red means that you are not going to be able to get back on budget.

How happy would you be if this was your project? My guess is you'd be reasonably happy. Again, your assessment would come back to the key drivers for the project. If time was the key driver, then the project owner would probably be quite happy with this project. If cost was the key driver, they would probably share the accountant's concern, and you would need to take some action to get the project back on budget (or at least not let the overspend get any worse!).

2. Accountant = "Over Budget," Real Situation = ?

If you showed figure 108 to your accounting department, they would be unhappy—although not as unhappy as with the first scenario.

GRAPHIC

fig. 108

Plan to date	Actual to date	Accountants are saying	Gantt
$500K	$650K	"Over budget!"	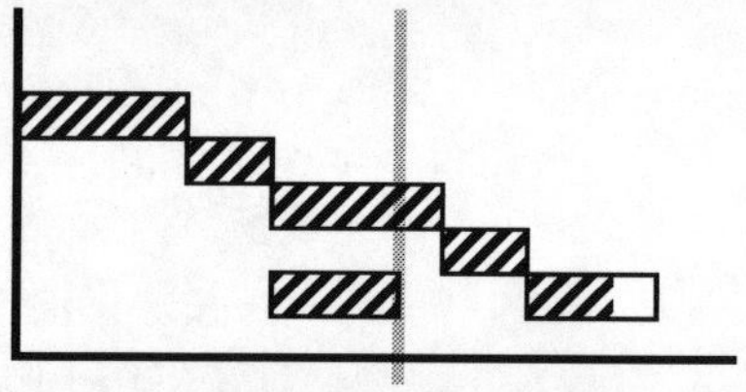
Real situation			
The overspend may be because the project is nearly finished. May come in ahead of time and under budget, although this is very rare. This scenario should make you wonder if the quality is OK and if your estimates were correct.			

Again, you would make the accountant a nice cup of tea and remain calm. This scenario looks similar to the first scenario in that there is an overspend. But you are a smart project manager, so you look at the Gantt chart to get a more accurate view of the project.

It's immediately clear that this scenario is very different. First, the degree of overspend is significantly smaller. You've only spent $650,000 instead of $720,000. But more important, the project is ahead of schedule by quite a margin. You can see that you are "very ahead" and "only a little bit overspent." You've done maybe $900,000 worth of work for only

$650,000. Unlike the first example, it looks as if you're going to be coming in *under* budget.

The first question that springs to mind is, "Is the quality OK? Have we missed anything on the scope?" This project does look suspiciously good!

But assuming that the quality is fine, the real situation is probably double green: green on time and green on budget, not the red "over budget" that the accountants see. It's not the accountants' fault that they've misjudged the project; all they're doing is adding up the money, which is fine. Someone needs to do that, and it's often not easy to do. But the money is only half the story. The Gantt chart provides the full story because you can see what the money has achieved.

One detail you will need to check for on the Gantt is *nonlinear spend*. What if the last bit of work still to be done is going to be expensive? Then you're not really under budget at all. It's easy to quickly check for this; just have a look at your Gantt chart and see what the remaining tasks are. Are they expensive? Look along the bar to see the actual expected cost of the remaining work to make sure there will be no nasty surprises later on.

It's worth noting that this second scenario rarely happens! It's only here for theoretical completeness and as an example of something we can all aspire to.

3. **Accountant = "Slightly Over Budget," Real Situation = ?**
If you showed figure 109 to your accounting department, they would still be a bit unhappy because it still shows a project that is over budget, albeit slightly.

But what is the Gantt chart of figure 109 telling you? It tells you that you are behind *and* overspent—never a great combination. This is more of a problem than it first appears. You've spent $550,000 instead of $500,000, but you've only done $450,000 worth of the work. The situation is considerably worse than the accountants believe it is, because the overspend is not $50,000. It's $100,000. By the time you've done the work you should have done, you'll be over by that amount. The overspend and the delay multiply to make the financial reality worse than the numbers would indicate, because the other $50,000 is hidden by the fact that you haven't done all the work yet.

GRAPHIC

fig. 109

Plan to date	Actual to date	Accountants are saying	Gantt
$500K	$550K	"Slightly over budget"	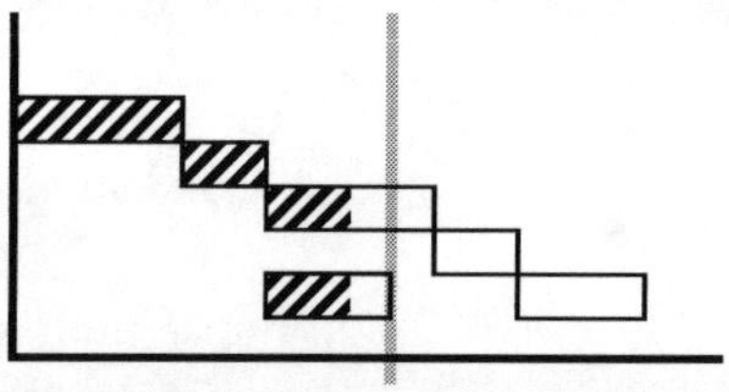

Real situation

Indicates "project creep," which is common. Worse than it looks because the overspend is partly hidden by lateness. The project is only a little bit late, and only a little bit overspent, but these combine and multiply!

This is called project creep. Many projects drift or creep slowly, getting a little bit later and a little bit more overspent. If you saw this scenario, you would know that you had to get a grip on this project before it crept any further out. If you've overspent by $100,000 now, but it looks like only $50,000, the project could easily overspend by $200,000 by the time it's done, and no one would be expecting it until it became visible near the end!

Both time and money are amber on this project, because there is still enough scope to catch up. In real life, however, it is very hard to catch up on both time and money, so this should be classified as a red project: "Can't be fixed."

This scenario is the most common of the six. It's very easy to get a little bit behind and a little bit overspent. All you need to do is forget one task or have one problem. Maybe you need to repeat one task, or one supplier lets you down. Then this outcome is almost inevitable. It's also very dangerous because it doesn't look as bad as it is. So: common, worse than it looks, and can't be fixed.

4. Accountant = "Spot On," Real Situation = ?

If you showed figure 110 to your accounting department, they would be delighted. They might even make *you* a nice cup of tea. Your project is exactly as it should be. Or is it?

fig. 110

Plan to date	Actual to date	Accountants are saying	Gantt
$500K	$500K	"Spot on"	

Real situation

Spent to plan but done less than planned, so the project is both late and over budget. This looks better than it really is and is hard to spot. Nobody will know there's a problem until the end.

Looking at the corresponding Gantt chart, we can immediately see that the picture is not quite as rosy as the accountants think it is. Sure, you have spent the expected amount of money on the project, but you haven't done all the work you should have done by now. Not only that, but the task that is behind is a critical task, even though the floating task has been done. (From the perspective of finishing the project on time, it would have been better to have focused on the critical task.)

The bottom line is that you've spent the money but you haven't done all the work for that budget. You're therefore overspent so far, and this almost certainly means an overspend by the time the project has ended. If this was your project, you would know that you were overspent and late! While the accountant is giving it the green and patting you on the back, you know that the project is actually "double amber." Again, there is very little chance of making up both time and money—which makes this a red project overall.

You may think this scenario isn't very likely to happen in real life, because surely the spend is never spot-on like this, but it could be if your project is "people only." If you've got a team of people working on something, say software programmers, they will cost exactly what you expect every week or every month. They are booked into your project at a certain repeatable cost. They just haven't done as much work as we all hoped. The spend can easily be spot-on and then it doesn't take much—a missed task, some bad estimating, or someone off work—to fall behind. This scenario is really quite common.

5. Accountant = "Good," Real Situation = ?

If you showed figure 111 to your accounting department, they would be making you cups of tea and bringing out the cake.

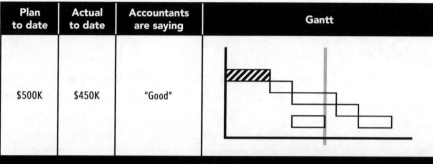

Plan to date	Actual to date	Accountants are saying	Gantt
$500K	$450K	"Good"	
Real situation			

Time to dust off your CV! Although you've underspent, the project is significantly behind schedule, which means that it will be significantly overspent by the end. This is a total disaster although it's invisible to the accountants.

As a savvy project manager, you eat your cake and enjoy the praise and then go have a look at the Gantt chart. You have been around the block enough times to know that under budget halfway through usually means over budget by the end. And, sure enough, you look at figure 111 and it's obvious that the project is running late. In fact, you're *really* late; only one task has been done so far! Check the Gantt chart to find out how much that first task should have cost. It's possible that that one task was exceptionally expensive and all the other tasks will only take $50,000 to complete, but it's unlikely.

What's more likely is that you have a major problem. This situation is probably a total disaster; it's very late and it's very overspent. I sometimes jokingly call this a "time to leave the company" situation—you'll still get a glowing reference because the project looks great at the moment! Or you could have a very frank and open discussion with the accountants about expectations and whether the project should be continued. It might not be your fault. It could have been caused by all sorts of issues. But everybody needs to know about it and talk about it very soon, and it is your fault if you don't tell them. This is the best example of why you should *always* check the Gantt chart when you get cost information on your project. The cost information is only half the story.

6. Accountant = "Very Good," Real Situation = ?

If you showed figure 112 to your accounting department, they would be pulling out the chocolate cake to go with that nice cup of tea. But is it really as peachy as it looks?

GRAPHIC

fig. 112

Plan to date	Actual to date	Accountants are saying	Gantt
$500K	$410K	"Very good!"	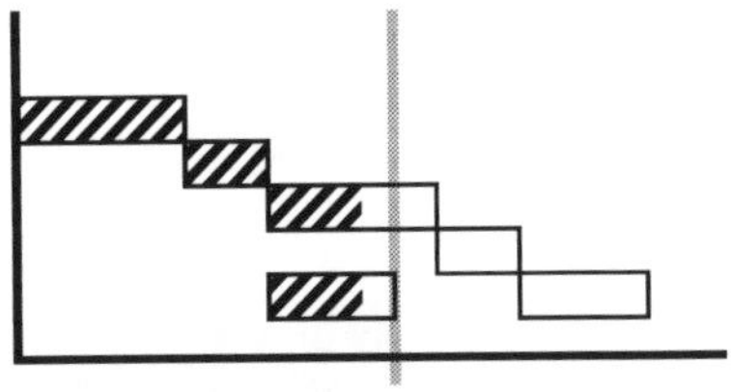

Real situation
You've spent less but also done less than planned. Check that the work you haven't done is not something expensive. And you probably have the option to use some of the spare money to crash some tasks and make up some of the time, if you want.

This last scenario is the best one from the accountants' point of view: you've only spent $410,000 instead of $500,000. They are thrilled and are already wondering where to spend that saved $90,000. You scarf down your chocolate cake and disappear back to your office to have a look at the Gantt chart.

As you suspected, it's not as great as they imagine. Sure, you'd give it a green for the cost, but it's at best an amber for the progress. You've done maybe $480,000 of the work instead of $500,000, and you only spent $410,000. You are under budget but not by as much as the accountants think, so they can't be reallocating all of that $90,000 yet.

You have a couple of options. You can use the smaller underspend you do have to catch up. But again, it will depend on what your key driver is. If it's money, then you might want to hang on to that underspend. If the key driver is time, then you might use some of that money to catch up.

This examination is called *earned value analysis* (EVA). Unfortunately, the way it's normally taught in project management is really torturous, with lots of equations involving things like "budgeted cost of work performed divided by actual cost of work forecast." There's loads of math and it's really confusing. The great thing about these six combinations is that you don't need any of the math. You don't even have to memorize the six. All you have to do is apply some common sense. Have a look at the Gantt chart and see how much you've done, always keeping nonlinear spend in mind as a possibility. Look at how much you've spent and then see which of my six pictures it looks most like. These six pictures are unique to this book, but they're analogous to most real-life situations and make monitoring where you really are in a project so much easier.

You can't monitor progress or cost effectively without a Gantt chart. You can't be a successful project manager without a Gantt chart.

A printable list of all six scenarios with a recap of the answer for each one is available with your Digital Assets at go.quickstartguides.com/project. Once you get used to recognizing them in your Gantt charts, you'll see that you only need common sense. Look at the progress on the Gantt chart and then interpret what the spend means. Keep the list handy.

It is possible that your accounting department will send you the numbers in graph form. Usually, graphs are much easier to interpret than the numbers alone, but in this case they tend to be more confusing. Make sure to ask for the figures instead of a graph, and then use your own spreadsheet to get a clearer picture of what's actually going on, comparing it with the Gantt chart at all times.

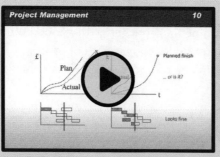

Watch a short video on the various visual ways financial information is presented.

To watch the QuickClip, use the camera on your mobile phone to scan the QR code or visit the link below.

 SCAN ME

www.quickclips.io/pm-11

 VISIT URL

Forecasting What Costs Will Come Next

As long as you keep your Gantt charts up to date and colored in, keep a running tally of what you are spending and what you are due to spend, and marry that with the numbers your accounting department supplies every week or month, you will always know what's really happening in your project day to day.

Watch a short video recap on why Gantt charts are so essential.

To watch the QuickClip, use the camera on your mobile phone to scan the QR code or visit the link below.

or

www.quickclips.io/pm-12

SCAN ME   VISIT URL

But what about the rest of the project? What about the future?

Regardless of which of the six scenarios you find yourself in, you need to use what's happened to help determine what will happen for the rest of the project. The "forecasted cost at completion" is the one number that everyone wants to know for your project.

There are two ways to calculate this cost—but first you need to determine if you are a glass-half-full or glass-half-empty type of project manager. When forecasting, it all depends on whether you are an optimist or a pessimist. Let me explain:

» **The Optimist:** If the project is running late or is overspent in the first half of the project, the optimist believes they can get back on track in the second half of the project.

» **The Pessimist:** If the project is running late or is overspent in the first half of the project, the pessimist believes that the same will happen in the second half of the project.

In my experience, most savvy project managers tend to be measured pessimists. They know from experience that it's so much easier for a project to be worse than the plan and difficult to recover. The truth is, the second half is probably not going to be better than the first half.

If the project has gone badly in the first half, by either being overspent or running late, then getting back to plan is clearly a good thing. Repeating what went before is bad. Conversely, if the plan is going well, because you underspent or completed the work ahead of schedule, then going back to the plan could be considered a bad thing, and repeating what you did in the first part would be really good (figure 113).

PLAN RECOVERY

fig. 113

	GET BACK TO PLAN	REPEAT THE FIRST PERFORMANCE
PROJECT *BAD* SO FAR	🙂	🙁
PROJECT *GOOD* SO FAR	🙁	🙂

Essentially, optimists predict more of the same if it's going well and change if it's going badly. Pessimists predict more of the same if it's going badly and change if it's going well!

Of course, it's not just about optimism or pessimism. Figuring out future costs also comes down to some assessment and a dash of common sense. If the first half was bad, and if you have the same team, and it was the same person who made both the first and second halves of the plan, then it's likely you'll have the same number of problems in the second half. But *will* the problems repeat? Maybe your problems are all behind you. You need to look at what went especially well or especially badly to assess how likely that is to occur in the future. For example, if something happened during the first part of the project that impacted supply of parts or labor and it was solved, or if a poor-performing supplier has now ended their involvement with the project, then you can confidently predict that that particular issue will not repeat. However, if something went wrong in the first part, then it's shrewd project management to assume that something else unexpected will arise in the second part.

It's always safest to assume the worst and expect what you've already experienced to continue. If you are running on time and on budget during the first half, you can reasonably and safely assume that the second half will run on time and on budget. If you are overspent or behind, you can reasonably assume that you will end up equally overspent or behind in the second half. But with enough evidence that the problems were one-offs, a "reasonable optimist" might be able to say, "The first half was bad, but the second half will go as planned." It would be a wild optimist who said, "The second half will be so good that we'll not only achieve the plan but we'll beat it. We will make up for the lateness/overspend in the first half, and the total project will come in on time and/or on budget." That is not going to happen unless you make significant changes to the specifications.

Be very careful about planning or promising to catch up on your first-half losses during the second half. Money overspent is as good as gone, and you'll always struggle to do the second half with less money than planned unless you reduce the quality or scope. Catching up on time is more doable, but usually only if you spend more money or, again, reduce the quality or scope. Never plan to recover both lost time and spent money in the second half. That's wishful thinking and will result in lots of unnecessary stress when you inevitably fail later.

If you are expecting to get back onto plan for the second half, then the calculations are very easy. Look at what you've spent so far and then add the planned cost or time for the second half. That's it. Alter your Gantt chart accordingly, and let the stakeholders know about the overspend or delay.

If you recognize that all your problems are *not* all behind you and whatever happened in the first half is likely to repeat in some form or another in the second half, then you need to forecast what that means for the project and share your new projections for time and cost with the key stakeholders. The calculations for this scenario are a little trickier but well worth the effort.

Cost Performance Index (CPI)

A *cost performance index* enables you to forecast any changes to the total spend based on the actual costs incurred in an earlier part of the project.

Say the first half of your project was supposed to cost $100,000 but ended up costing $120,000. The second half of your project is supposed to cost $200,000. What is the second half likely to cost based on the first?

CPI is calculated by dividing the actual cost by the planned cost.

$$\$120{,}000/\$100{,}000 = 1.2$$

Therefore, this project has a CPI of 1.2. All you need to do is apply the CPI of 1.2 to the budget in the second half of the project. In this example:

$$\$200{,}000 \times 1.2 = \$240{,}000$$

In total, the whole project was supposed to cost $300,000, but it's now expected to cost $360,000 based on the performance of the first half of the project.

All projects aim for a CPI of one, but that almost never happens. Projects very rarely come in on budget. You need to know what the CPI is for all your projects and measure it all the way through. You can use that figure to modify the plan if needed and get new sign-off for the revisions (more on that in chapter 13). It can and should be calculated at various intervals during the project and will give you as project manager a clear indication of whether the project is on track financially or slipping.

NOTE

Some people prefer to express the CPI as a percentage. A CPI of 1.2 would therefore be 120 percent. It's arguably more intuitive as a percentage, because every project is aiming for a CPI of 100 percent or lower—so any percentage over 100 is overspend. Either way, the resulting calculation is the same. "$200,000 x 1.2" or "$200,000 x 120%" gives the same $240,000 outcome.

To add to the confusion, the CPI can *also* be expressed as a percentage the other way up, by dividing planned cost by actual cost. In this example, $100,000/$120,000 x 100 = 83 percent, meaning the planned cost was 83 percent of what was actually spent. The key is to make sure that your project team decides on one way to calculate and express CPI and uses it consistently and exclusively. Don't mix the methods, or you will get a faulty picture of the project.

MY TAKE

Personally, when talking about money spent, I find it much more intuitive to have the CPI as a number where big is bad and small is good. It feels logical to me that an overspend should show as a number greater than 1, or greater than 100 percent.

Schedule Performance Index (SPI)

A *schedule performance index* allows you to forecast any changes to the expected finish date of the whole project, based on the actual time taken to complete an earlier part of the project, in a way similar to the cost calculations we have just been doing.

If you looked at any project management textbook, you would see an explanation of SPI as follows:

$$SPI = \text{Earned Value (EV)} / \text{Planned Value (PV)}$$

Let me explain what this famous formula means, before explaining why I think it can be improved as a forecasting method.

Here's a simple example: suppose you have a four-month project, and each month you are doing various tasks that cost $2,000, so the total project is going to cost $8,000 (figure 114).

SPI FOR LINEAR PROJECT

fig. 114

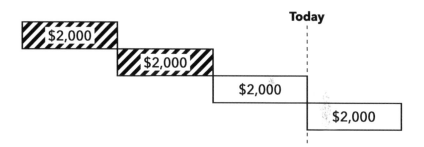

Suppose that after three months you are a month behind—you've only done the first two months of work on the project. Then your planned value is 3 x $2,000, which is $6,000, but your actual earned value is only 2 x $2,000, which is $4,000, and your schedule performance index is $4000/$6000 = 0.67, or 67 percent.

When will the project be finished, if you carry on at this rate?

An optimist would say that we are only one month behind, so if we get back onto plan, we can finish in two more months, taking five months in total.

But the pessimist would say that we are probably going to *continue* going a bit slower than planned, and with an SPI of only 67 percent, the original four months is going to stretch out to six months (4/0.67 = 6). That's the forecast.

We are using value as a measure of achievement, a measure of progress, which seems fine; most project managers are happy with this. But I'm not.

Let's have a look at why I don't like it, and you can decide who you agree with: me or most of the project management textbooks!

The problem with SPI based on value is that projects often have a *nonlinear spend rate*. We've already talked about this a lot. It's a key feature of projects compared to processes and payrolls. And if you measure progress by the value of tasks and then use that to forecast how long the whole project will take, you can get a hugely distorted forecast. In many cases the cost or the value of a task has nothing to do with its speed, its duration, or its lateness. Time and money aren't always connected in projects.

If we are trying to forecast when the project will be completed, it's better to look at how late the previous tasks have run and then think about whether the upcoming ones are also likely to run late by the same amount of time. Here is my preferred definition of SPI (schedule performance index):

$$SPI = \text{Expected Time Taken} / \text{Actual Time Taken}$$

In the previous example, we expected the first part of the project to take two months, but actually it took three months, so the SPI would be 2/3 = 67 percent—the same answer as before. And it's the same because we had a linear spend rate; we were spending the same each month. Figure 115 shows how the project looks when the spend rate is different each month.

The two methods now give very different answers, and you'll see shortly why my method is better. Let's say the third month involves a higher spend. Maybe we are using some expensive materials or we have some extra people working on the project, for a month only.

SPI FOR NONLINEAR PROJECT

fig. 115

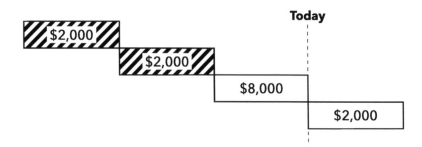

You can immediately see that although we're only a month behind, in spend terms we are way behind. We have only done $4,000 worth of "earned value" instead of the $12,000 that we should have done by now. The earned value formula for SPI tells us that this project is a disaster. Our SPI is $4000/$12000 = only 33 percent.

Therefore, the forecast for how long the project will take, at the current SPI, is four months divided by 0.33, or twelve months, which is clearly ridiculous. What on earth are we going to be doing for the next nine months? The calculation has been massively distorted by the high value of the work planned in the third month. When we're thinking about time and lateness, we really don't want to let the cost affect our calculations. Obviously, we need to keep an eye on cash flow, and if we were forecasting finished cost, we'd need to know that the months cost different amounts, but cost doesn't tell us much about duration. We already know that the answer is somewhere between five and six months, as we calculated earlier. Just because the third month is more expensive doesn't mean it is going to take any longer. After all, it was only originally planned to take a month.

I recommend using the simple and intuitively obvious definition of SPI, which is *how long it should have taken us* divided by *how long it actually took us*.

Here's another example: Suppose you are working on an eleven-month project, and the first few tasks were planned to take four months but have actually taken six. Your schedule performance, using my simple definition of SPI, is four divided by six. In fraction terms, that's 4/6; in decimal terms, 0.67. To calculate how long the supposedly eleven-month project will take at this rate, divide eleven months by 0.67, which gives you approximately 16.5 months in total (and, if you've already worked for six months, 10.5 months remaining).

However, you may find it more intuitive to arrive at an SPI figure you can multiply rather than divide. After all, the time you spend on the project is expanding; it makes sense to have a multiplier to use for an easy conversion. For this calculation, you would divide how long those tasks have taken (six months) by how long they should have taken (four months). Thus, 6/4 = 1.5, so you can multiply the remaining planned months by 1.5, assuming the rest of the project will carry on at a similar rate (and unless you have strong evidence to the contrary, that's a good assumption to make).

Whether you use the 4/6 or 6/4 formulation is up to you—as long as you know which method you're using and stick to it. There's a logic to using multiplication to calculate an expansion of time. But it also makes sense to use 4/6, because that way you'll be aiming for an SPI of one or greater, and you'll be using lower numbers to indicate slower progress and worse performance. The point is, decide whether "small is bad" or "big is bad."

MY TAKE

Personally, I think a high CPI should mean overspending and a low SPI should mean going slowly. That feels logical to me. I can also see the logic that you might want both numbers to be high. You could then have a nice simple rule: "High is good." But I still prefer to look for low CPI and high SPI because of what they mean: low cost and high speed. The main thing is to always check!

Monthly Monitoring Form

The final part of step 10 is to use a *monthly monitoring form*. If you've got a list of all your projects and it tells you the CPI and SPI of each one, that's everything you need to know. Those two metrics will tell you how your projects are doing financially and also how are they doing timewise.

If you are managing other project managers, get their CPI and SPI for each project, and also ask them each month if they are an optimist or a pessimist. This is not about badgering them to get back on plan, but rather about whether they believe the next part of the project is going to go like the last part, whether they are expecting more issues, and whether they expect improvements (and why).

If you are a senior leader, then you definitely want a forecast from all your project managers for every project, every month. If you're in charge of twenty projects and you have ten project managers looking after them, you need each project manager to give you a forecast for each project. What do they think the finished cost will be, and what will the completion date be? Over time you will have a stack of these monthly monitoring forms so you can look back and see whether those forecasts are gradually slipping. You will also be able to discern which project manager is most accurate.

And if one of your project managers says, "Oh, no, I can't do that, it's far too much work," you'll know they are not a very good project manager. Every project manager worth their salt should be able to *instantly* tell you the CPI and SPI of their project. They should already know if they are running 10 or 20 percent late, or spending over or under the plan.

A blank, printable template for a monthly monitoring form is available with your Digital Assets at go.quickstartguides.com/project. Use it as a simple guide to monitoring your projects and making sure you always know the crucial facts.

Chapter Recap

» Projects are, by far, the most dangerous financial investment for any business. Projects are rarely finished quicker than planned or cost less than expected. It's therefore critical that you monitor costs every month.

» To monitor costs, you need to get the numbers from the accounting department on a weekly or monthly basis. Make sure that costs have been allocated to your project correctly.

» There is always lag time in the figures from accounting. By the time they've sent the costs to you, the figures will be out of date because most projects are incurring more costs every day.

» You need to keep your own spreadsheet on spend so that you can monitor costs in real time and plan for known upcoming costs. By drawing on the accounting data and your own up-to-date spreadsheet on project costs, you can make sure the numbers tally.

» As long as you keep your Gantt charts up to date and colored in, keep a running tally of what you are spending and what you are due to spend, and marry that with the numbers your accounting department supplies you with every week or month, you will always know what's really happening in your project day to day.

» In measuring cost performance, there are six common scenarios. Regardless of which of the six you find yourself in, you need to use what's happened so far to help determine what will happen for the rest of the project.

» Forecasting costs for the total project depends on whether you are an optimist or a pessimist.

» Make sure you know the CPI and SPI for all your projects—and use an SPI that focuses on time, not costs.

» Complete a monthly monitoring form so you can prove you know what's going on with your projects.

| 13 |

Modify the Plan – Step 11

Chapter Overview

- » Most plans will need to be modified
- » The golden rules of plan modification
- » Running late and overspend options

Failure is simply the opportunity to begin again, this time more intelligently.
–HENRY FORD

In steps 9 and 10, you monitored progress and spend, so you should have a good handle on what's actually happening in the project compared to expectations and plans. You may, for example, know that you are running about a week behind, or that you've spent about 5 percent more than you anticipated.

But at what point do you admit that the resources you've agreed upon for the project, either a set time frame or a set budget, are not going to be enough? You may still have hope that you can somehow save the project. Maybe you'll get a run of amazing luck, or someone in the team will come up with a brilliant idea that will save time and money. But let's be honest: it's unlikely.

There will come a point where you have to take stock of what's happened so far, and how much time and money is remaining in the project, to assess whether the project plan needs to be modified. Most projects will need to be adjusted. It's not the adjusting that's the problem, it's how you adjust it. The aim for every project manager should be "no surprises." If you monitor cost and time, you will know what's happening with your project and you won't suddenly realize that you have exceeded the budget by 75 percent. You won't suddenly discover that you are going to be three months late finishing. Imagine you're running a marathon, you're in sight of the finish line, and then for the first time you check your watch and realize you're running way behind your target time. It's a bit late to start running faster! Steps 9 and 10 act like marathon time checks, allowing you to stay on track or at least know when you are off track early enough to do something positive about it.

You can't leave it till the last minute. Preferably at about the halfway point, you may need to go back to the stakeholders, tell them what's happened and why, modify the plan, and get approval for those modifications.

The Five Golden Rules

Step 11 is almost inevitable. Even with impeccable project management, there are so many moving parts in a project that it is almost impossible to deliver on time and within budget. Often, it's not your fault at all—the customer asks for changes, or the external environment changes, and this means the plan needs to be adjusted a bit. It's an unavoidable part of project management.

There are, however, five golden rules that will reduce the pain of step 11 for you and the stakeholders.

1. **Don't modify the plan too often**. Customers and stakeholders don't like it, and neither do the people executing the plan. Customers lose faith if you keep changing the plan, because they become unsure whether the latest changes will be the last. And it's annoying for the people working on the project; remember that your plan relies on other people doing certain tasks at certain points. They have already scheduled the work, so if the plan is running late, those people in the project need to know about it so they can modify their own plans.

2. **Modify your plan during the middle third of your project**. Don't modify too early or too late. You need to be far enough through the project to measure the schedule performance index (SPI) and the cost performance index (CPI) accurately. These metrics will tell you how much over the estimates your project is running in regard to time and cost. Seek to readjust the plan in the middle third of the project. If your project is nine weeks long, then you'll look to modify it in week four, five, or six. No later than week six. If you modify in the first third of the project, it looks like you are giving up too easily or that your planning was poor from the start. If you wait until the last third, you are cutting it too close to make the adjustments.

   It's best to make smaller adjustments over a longer period. Remember, there are usually other people involved, so they will need to reschedule, and you can't assume they will be available. Don't be tempted to put the conversation off past the middle third, hoping for a miracle. It'll just make it worse when you are forced to confess to the lateness or overspend later on. Plus, the customer is likely to be even more upset if you wait until the last minute to ask for more time or money. If you try to modify the plan suddenly at the end, the customer will always blame you for the changes, even if they, the customer, originally contributed to the problem.

It is generally better to know the truth as early as possible. It reduces the likelihood of piling wasted expense on top of wasted expense.

— GEOFF REISS

Golden rule number two only applies if *you* have changed the plan. If the customer or other stakeholders have changed the plan, even in week 1 or week 9, then you should figure out how those changes will impact the plan and ask for the necessary additional resources right away, regardless of what point you've reached.

3. **Ask for more than you need**. This sounds a bit greedy, or even dishonest, but it's not. Let me explain. Asking for more time or money twice is the biggest crime a project manager can commit, because it disrupts the customer (and all the people on the project) twice, and it can make you look incompetent or even untrustworthy. Bearing in mind that there are still unknown problems ahead, it's always better to ask for more than you think you'll need, either time or money. But do so only once.

Say you're halfway through your project and you're supposed to have spent $50,000 out of a total of $100,000. But it has actually cost $54,000 so far. How will you revise your budget forecast to complete the project? You could forecast a figure of $104,000, or $108,000, or something else …?

If you know for sure that the additional $4,000 in the first half was a definite one-off, then $104,000 may be manageable—but how do you know there won't be another surprise one-off cost to come? You could tell the stakeholders that it will be $108,000, because that assumes you will experience the same or similar deviation from the plan. But you don't really know the level of deviation. It could be more. Imagine if you opted for $108,000 thinking you were playing it safe with an overspend in the second half similar to the first, but it actually came in at $110,000. The stakeholder would not be happy because you would then need to ask for even more money to finish the project, after already offering a revised figure. It's always safer to add some extra. In this example, you should ask for $110,000 or even $112,000. You'll get the same amount of flak for forecasting $112,000 as you would for $108,000 and much less than you'd get for forecasting $108,000 and having to go back to make it $110,000. In fact, if you forecast $112,000 and then end up spending "only" $110,000, you'll be a hero for coming in under the new budget after the original budget will have been forgotten.

The same applies for time. If you are running two weeks behind in the first half of the project, you could assume that you will be running four weeks behind by the end, but it's always safer to ask for six weeks, a number you can definitely achieve. Asking for more time twice is the biggest crime, so make sure you won't need to.

4. **Use change request forms**. Change request forms document any modifications to the plan. These may be your modifications based on monitoring progress and spend, or they may be modifications that the customer or stakeholders request that will affect the plan. Often you will need to modify the plan because you are asked to by the stakeholders. They need to know what their change will mean to the project delivery, and they should sign off on any additional resources that the change will require. It is also easier to secure those resources at the moment when the customer is asking for the modification, because at that moment, you have the power. They are the one messing up your plan, and they can't go anywhere else because the project is being done by you and it's already well underway. Provided you can prove it with a revised Gantt chart, you can ask for plenty of extra time and money when the customer asks for a modification.

NOTE

Even if it's a small modification, always get it documented. This may feel a bit petty and bureaucratic, but they all add up. At the end of the project, when you are a million dollars over, you want to be able to wave a sheaf of signed change requests at the customer and say, "Here are all the changes you made, adding up to the million."

5. **Involve your team**. I've mentioned this before, but it's so important that it needs its own golden rule: involve your team regarding any modifications. You need to make sure that the people scheduled to do certain tasks can reschedule them in their current workload before you commit to the new plan. If you involve your team, you'll end up with a better plan and a more motivated group of people to carry it out.

Options If Your Project Is Running Late

It's pretty common for projects to run late, because things change. Plans, even excellent and thorough ones, rarely work out exactly as you hoped. We discussed this earlier in the book, but at that point in the steps it was largely hypothetical. In step 11, you need to modify the plan, so I've gathered up your options again in one place so you can quickly work out how best to do it. If you are behind schedule, you have five choices:

1. **Get more resources**. You can negotiate for more resources to speed up the project. This could mean more people working on the project, the inclusion of a night shift, additional contractors, or equipment or special machinery that can do the work of more people. Of course, more resources always cost more money.

2. **Reduce the quality/scope**. You could reduce the quality or scope of the project either with or without the customer knowing about it. Remember, the scope is how much the customer gets for their investment, and the quality is *how* what they get is done, although sometimes the two overlap or get blurred together. It's very risky to reduce the quality/scope of something without getting the change approved by the stakeholders, but sometimes they might not know the difference. And if it doesn't impact the finished project, then it may be an option. For example, you could reduce the quality of the paper that the marketing collaterals are printed on. Most people wouldn't know 90 gsm from 115 gsm, so maybe it wouldn't make any difference to the outcome. However, this is a risky move;

it's always better to have a discussion with the stakeholder about whether there is anything in the remainder of the project that could be reduced in quality or omitted from the scope to speed up the project without affecting the outcome too much.

3. **Overlap some of the remaining tasks.** This is a great option if it can be done, because it doesn't add any cost but does potentially speed up the project. Have a look at all the tasks that are still to be done. Is there any way to overlap any of them so that you start some of them earlier, while other preceding tasks are still being done? This option can add complication and risk, so make sure that the overlapping tasks are not dependent on each other.

4. **Let the project slip a little.** If time is not the key driver, then it may be OK that the project comes in a little late. You would need to have a discussion with the stakeholders to make sure they agreed, and you would also need to alert everyone involved in the plan so they could reschedule their tasks. This option is often easier to negotiate than you might imagine, especially if the stakeholders are even partially responsible for the project running late (perhaps they changed the specifications during the project). The idea of completing the main project on time and finishing off a few details afterward can often be a good solution.

5. **Abandon the project.** The final option is to abandon the project. This is not ideal because all the time and money that's already been spent will effectively be wasted. But if something has changed in the business and the outcome is no longer as important, then it may be better to abandon the project and cut your losses. It's rare, but it can happen.

There is one other option: "Do nothing and hope." Far too many project managers opt for this, and I do not recommend it! Assuming that some sort of last-minute miracle will present itself and save the project is madness. Don't keep postponing and hoping it will sort itself out. If you're in the middle third of your project, look at the facts now, and speak to the stakeholders right away to modify the plan. If you don't, you will just have to explain to very irate stakeholders in the final third what went wrong, and your credibility as a professional project manager will suffer.

Options If Your Project Is Over Budget

Running over on budget is also pretty common in project management. A supplier may go bust, forcing you to look elsewhere and have to pay more. Exchange rate fluctuations may make imported items more expensive. Commodity prices may have shot up, forgotten tasks may need to be added in, or sometimes a task has to be done twice. All sorts of things can happen to confound even the best-laid plans. If you find that your project is going over budget, you have only two options:

» **Reduce the quality or scope**. As mentioned, it may be possible to reduce the scope or quality of some of the remaining tasks to reduce cost.

» **Ask for more money**. The only other alternative is to ask for more money from the stakeholders. Maybe they held back a little in their own budget, or perhaps they are sympathetic about an exchange rate escalation, knowing there was nothing you could have done about that! Whether the stakeholders agree to more money will depend on the project and the key driver.

Of course, like the options for running late, a very popular option is to do nothing and hope. But as we've seen, hoping for a miracle isn't a good strategy. They don't usually happen, so in the end it becomes "not telling the customer until they find out." No one is going to be thrilled by a big fat overspend that they didn't know about until the project was finished. What if there is no more money but you spent it anyway? Never do nothing and hope! Be up-front and honest about the situation you're in. Work out the best solution for that project and get it signed off on by all the stakeholders. Make sure you ask for enough time or money so that you can definitely finish the project.

Chapter Recap

» Step 11 is the point where you take stock of what's happened so far and what time and money is remaining in the project, in order to assess whether the project plan needs to be modified.

» There will need to be some kind of adjustment during most projects—it's normal.

» If your project is running late, you can ask for more resources, reduce the quality, overlap some of the remaining tasks, let the project slip a little, or abandon the project.

» For projects that are overspending, you can ask for more money or reduce the quality or scope.

» Five golden rules apply to project modification: Don't modify the plan too often, modify your plan in the middle third of the project, ask for a bit more than you need, use change request forms, and involve your team.

» You must never "do nothing and hope"! While this option is popular with inexperienced project managers, it is not a good idea. Assuming or hoping that some sort of last-minute miracle will present itself and save the project is madness. Look at the facts and speak to the stakeholders, and then modify the plan.

| 14 |

Review – Step 12

Phew! The project is over. Hopefully it's been a roaring success—although even if it has been, there probably hasn't been any cake or celebration around the office. When you succeed, everyone thinks the project must have been easy.

So, is that it? Not quite. Every project management textbook discusses the importance of conducting a project review, and they are right. The idea is that the project team gets together and assesses the project objectively. What went well? What didn't work out quite as expected? And what could have been done better? The review also gives you a chance to celebrate with your team, marvel at what you've achieved together, take stock of the outcome, and thank everyone involved. There are no downsides to a review, and yet most project managers don't do one! There are a number of typical reasons.

7 Common Reasons for Avoiding Reviews

1. **"I haven't got time."** On the face of it, this reason makes sense. We are all busy. And, as a project manager, you are often working on more than one project at a time or moving immediately to another project as soon as one is finished. If project management is just one part of your job, you may have a ton of day-to-day work to get through; the idea of reviewing the project may seem like an unnecessary luxury. But then again, how long would a project review actually take? Even more important, how much time would it save in the long run?

2. **"I don't want to relive the pain."** If the project has been especially tough, this sentiment is understandable. It's too stressful. Getting through the project once was bad enough; why revisit the nightmare? The answer is that we don't want to have that pain again, so we *have* to think about why it happened. Hiding from it will allow it to repeat.

3. **"I don't want to admit my mistakes."** Sometimes the assumption about a project review is that everyone's errors will be paraded around for all to see. But this should not be the case. The review session needs to be open and honest, but there is no need to attach names to what went well or badly. It's all about capturing the learning points, not (tempting though it may be) pointing fingers.

4. **"I don't need the review, it's all in my head."** Even if that were true, which is unlikely, each person has only the memory of the part of the project they were involved in—and they will forget even that within a few weeks. Plus, if the takeaways from the project remain in the team members' heads, there is no opportunity for that knowledge to spread through the team or get passed on into the business for the benefit of future similar projects done by different people.

5. **"It went well, so we don't need a review."** Again, this avoidance tactic emerges from the assumption that the review is based on negativity. But a review is not only important when the project went badly. It should also be about what insight can be captured and passed along to the next project. And if the project did go really well, it presents an opportunity to assess how that success might be replicated and what might be done even better next time. If the project went well, there is even more reason to review it so the positive learning can be locked into the team.

6. **"We'll never do anything like that again."** If the project is unique or unusual, then the assumption is that the review is pointless because there will be no learning from the unique project that can be translated to any other project. But this is highly unlikely. Similar projects always come around again at some point. And even unique projects hold learning for other, different projects.

7. **"No one will read it."** True: if there is nothing to read, then no one will read it. But you have to start somewhere! Once you get into

the habit of project reviews and all the reviews are held in a central location, then other people *will* start to read them. At least the smart project managers will. There is no need to constantly reinvent the wheel. Learn from the past to fine-tune the future.

It's always a great idea to do a project review. And it might even be fun, or at the very least interesting to hear what everyone learned from the project.

How to Do a Review

First, the review doesn't need to be stuffy or boring. Make it fun. Book a meeting room and order pizzas, maybe get some beer or wine, or even book a local restaurant. That way you immediately signal that you are thanking everyone for their hard work and celebrating the fact that the project is finished. It also sets an informal and positive tone for the review. Make sure the review happens within about two weeks of the end of the project; otherwise, people start to forget the little details that could offer the greatest input.

Reviewing the project doesn't have to be complicated. Just ask three questions:

» What was good that we would do next time?
» What was bad that we would avoid next time?
» What could we do differently next time, for an even better outcome?

Record all the answers that the team provides. You can either designate a scribe or record the conversation and transcribe it later to mine all the gold. It doesn't have to be long—a bullet point list under each of the three questions could be enough.

The first two questions are about looking at the project and what happened and working out what was good and not so good about those actions or decisions. The third question is more about the things that *didn't* happen and what the good and the bad taught us for next time. The answers to question three may include things that were not tried on this project but which might solve a problem that was experienced or improve the next project in some way. Are there people we could have involved more, or sooner? Should we have subcontracted part of it, or brought part of it in-house? Should we have had one supplier only, or divided it among more suppliers? Should we have spent more time on the planning? Should we have had our meetings more often, or less often?

The key to a successful review is openness, a little fun, and absolutely no finger-pointing or blame. It's just an information-sharing exercise so that all the key learnings from the project can be recorded *and* so that the whole team becomes even better at project management planning and execution.

It might be wise to use the monthly meeting reports or even the various revisions of the Gantt chart to help jog everyone's memory about what actually happened in the project.

After the review meeting, write up the notes and store them in a file or folder, either physical or digital, for future reference. Maybe both, so there's a physical folder that people can flip through as well as a digital copy that can be searched for key words and so on. That's how these project reviews can start to feed back into steps 2 through 8 of future projects. It's particularly helpful for step 2, where people are listing the tasks (what did you include and what did you forget?) and step 8, where people are thinking about risk (what might go wrong with the project?).

Remember: every problem has happened before. By sharing the learning, the review process can help to stop those problems from repeating. Just imagine—you could eventually run out of problems!

Along with a Gantt chart, the review form at the end of the project is vital for embedding PM capability into the business. And if you are managing project managers, then the project is not finished until that review has been done. Be sure you make them do their reviews. The project is not finished, they are not off the hook, until you have received the write-up of their review.

Reviews are a great learning tool for you as a project manager—and also for everyone else on the team, including management. Creating a system where all projects are reviewed and those reviews are kept in a central folder allows you to embed the learning into the business long after the project is over and forgotten.

Post-Project Review

The *post-project review* is a review of the *outcome* of the project, rather than the delivery. This is rarer than the project review but possibly even more important.

The post-project review is conducted about two years after the project has ended. Often the people who were involved in delivering the project are not even around. They are certainly not necessary for this review. All that is being assessed in the post-project review is the validity of doing the project in the first place. This time the project *owner* is under the spotlight.

Every project is proposed by a manager or project owner or sponsor because they believe that it will improve something or deliver some sort of business benefit. That benefit may be more sales, greater efficiency, greater profit, increased reach, reduced costs, or some other advantage. If the project is accepted and acted on, this review looks back to determine if that assumption was correct. Did the project deliver what the project owner hoped it would?

In our example of setting up a business, a key stakeholder proposed that this new business be established. A business case for the endeavor was created that outlined why it was a good idea and the benefits that the parent company could expect from the new enterprise. The post-project review looks at those assumptions to establish whether the new business delivered on those expectations.

This can be a valuable source of learning for the business (should we do more projects like this in the future?). But it can also be uncomfortable for the project sponsor. Their responsibilities are being put under a microscope. They may well try to avoid this kind of review, and since they tend to be pretty senior people, they often succeed in putting it off until it gets forgotten. But this is a huge shame. If executed properly as a learning exercise, the post-project review can be invaluable in future project selection, making the business much better at yielding the intended reward—and limiting the projects that do not deliver those rewards.

Chapter Recap

» Every project management book discusses the importance of doing a project review after the project has been finished. And yet most project managers don't do one. There are seven often-cited reasons for avoiding a review, none of which is especially valid.

» The review gives you a chance to celebrate with your team, marvel at what you've achieved together, and take stock of what worked well and what might need improvement next time. It's also a great opportunity to thank everyone involved in the project. Make it fun.

» Make sure the review happens within about two weeks of the end of the project; otherwise, people start to forget the little details, which could offer the biggest insight.

» Keep it simple by asking just three questions: What was good that we would do next time? What was bad that we would avoid next time? What could we do differently next time for a better outcome?

» Record all the answers provided by the team using a bullet point list under each of the three questions.

» The key to a successful review is openness and absolutely no finger-pointing or blame.

» After the review meeting, write up the notes and store them in a searchable file or folder. That way these reviews can start to feed back into steps 2 through 8 of future projects.

» Along with a Gantt chart, the review form at the end of the project is vital for embedding PM capability into the business. If you are managing project managers, then the project is not finished until that review has been done.

» If you really want to squeeze all the learning you can from every project, make sure the business also does a post-project review two years after the project has ended. That way you can tell if the benefits that were expected as a result of the project were delivered.

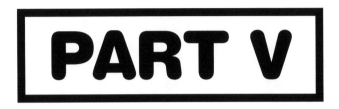

PART V

SUPERCHARGE YOUR PROJECT MANAGEMENT SKILLS

| 15 |
Planning of Larger Projects

Chapter Overview
» What to do when managing larger projects
» How to feel more comfortable with complex Gantt charts
» How to feel more confident managing the tasks

Not all the projects you will be involved in will consist of thirty tasks or less. In fact, it is almost inevitable that you will find yourself at the helm of a larger, more complex project sooner or later, especially as you get more proficient as a project manager. If this applies to you, then take it as a compliment or a badge of honor. You've obviously proven you have some skills in project management if project owners or your boss are asking you to take on larger projects.

But it can be daunting. Let's unpack how to make larger projects easier and less stressful right from the start.

Avoiding Overwhelm Around the Gantt

The process is the same for a big project or a small project. The only difference is the number of tasks. But this difference does mean that the plan gets harder to see as the project size increases. The human brain can really only understand twenty to thirty tasks when looking at a diagram. We can magnify this using subtasks. Thirty high-level tasks, each with thirty subtasks hidden inside it, would allow you to manage nine hundred tasks! And if you went to a third level, you could manage twenty-seven thousand tasks! The process is exactly the same as the process we've outlined so far. Of course, in reality you won't have every high-level task divided into twenty or thirty subtasks; some will contain only two or three subtasks, and some may not contain any. The important thing to remember is that it's always the same process. You can handle any size project with the process outlined in this book.

Once you have your Gantt chart, you have the central living document for the project. A single screen can tell you what's going on, what's been done, what's coming up soon, and who is responsible for what. You need a one-screen Gantt and then you have control.

Suppose, then, that the project to set up a new business suddenly gets more complicated, and you're asked to set up three new businesses at once, each in a different geographic territory. At first it may feel like your head is about to explode! But once you've had a short lie-down with a damp cloth on your forehead, the fog will start to clear a little. With your project management training, you will be able to see a way through.

The process from step 1 to step 4 is pretty much the same as usual: you agree on what's needed, get a list of tasks, and work out what depends on what. The project objective is to set up three new businesses, one each in New York, Sydney, and Edinburgh. These locations were chosen by market research. The project can naturally be broken down into three sub-projects based on the three locations. In fact, this is not only logical but preferable, because the task lists are likely to be only slightly different, depending on the location. Some of the tasks will certainly be on the task lists of all three sub-projects, but there will be specific tasks that arise because of the different jurisdictions of the new businesses.

Once you have created the project plan and the Gantt chart for one territory, you can save that worksheet and rename it as the second territory, making adjustments to the tasks. Repeat this process for the third territory. Now each new business has its own task list, its own running order with time/cost estimates, and its own Gantt chart. With all three feeding into a Gantt of Gantts, you can keep track of everything on one page. You can also make sure that you have enough resources if all the projects are going to peak at the same time.

If necessary, you could even go another level down to create sub-sub-projects! For example, in the case of these three new businesses, making a website for each geographic area could be a sub-project. In reality, it almost certainly will be anyway, because there are many tasks that need to be done in order to create a successful and functional website—research, domain registration, planning, copy writing, design, and launch. These tasks will probably all be done by the same group of people, so there is logic to making it a sub-project.

The key here is not to feed everything into Excel at once—you'll lose the will to live! Besides, even if you do that without melting your own brain, you still won't be able to see what's really going on, because you can't see how one sub-project relates to the others. As a result, you're much more likely to make incorrect assumptions, and therefore mistakes. Worse, you might not even know until it's too late. Remember, you can only really see twenty to thirty tasks at once.

Whatever your larger project is, you can break it down into smaller sub-projects, each with its own Post-it running order and estimations that are then fed into its own Gantt chart. This approach allows you to manage significantly more tasks without the overwhelm.

In chapter 8, I showed you how to create a basic Gantt chart and then save it and alter it to visualize either the hours or the money. The same principle applies here, where you have the high-level Gantt chart and then each sub-project. In this case, each new business has its own Gantt chart, and things like websites might have their own Gantt charts too. You can save each of them as a separate sheet in the Excel workbook and create hours and money Gantts for each sub-project. What you end up with is multiple Gantt charts that feed into one overall project Gantt. You can put the total cost and duration of "Make Website" into your high-level Gantt but still have enough detail to know where you are on any of the sub-projects. You can drill down into a particular Gantt whenever you need to.

Avoiding Overwhelm Around Project Planning

For larger projects, it may be the size and scope of what needs to get done that is most overwhelming, rather than the Gantt-making. Regardless of size, if you stand any chance of pulling off your projects successfully, you need to be organized. And that means getting really clear on what needs to be done for every part of the project. This is especially important for larger projects where it is easier for tasks to slip through the cracks.

The two best ways to manage this are to create work packages and to plan upward. Let's explore each of these practices.

Create Work Packages

Work package is a project management term for a sequence of activities that leads to a specific deliverable when using a work breakdown structure (WBS). In a sense, work packages are the subtasks of a larger task. In our example of setting up a new business, one of the tasks is "Make Website," but the work package for that high-level task will contain all the subtasks that need to happen to make the website.

Work packages are different from various activities that may be listed as tasks within a project. A work package is at a higher level in the WBS hierarchy than an activity. A work package supports a specific delivery, like "Make Website," as opposed to an activity contributing to that delivery, like "Register a Domain Address." Activities are one thing done by one person (or one type of person, such as a team of five people digging a hole). Work packages are a chunk of the work in the project, but a logical chunk, usually managed by one person, such as an HR, marketing, or IT manager.

Work packages are great for getting things done and assigning people to specific chunks of work that are required, without getting yourself bogged down in the multitude of tasks that go into the delivery of a larger project.

It makes the project much more manageable if you can assign the work package "Make Website" to Lulu in the graphics department, rather than taking it upon yourself to identify all the tasks and do all the work of estimation, especially if you don't have any experience in making websites. Far better to say to Lulu, "Hey, you are responsible for making the website." Right up front, you can speak to Lulu and get a commitment that she will build the website by a certain date and for a certain cost.

A work package is a small piece of a larger project that someone takes full responsibility for delivering. The work package is created/defined/selected by the project manager, who then gets a commitment from someone, like the department head of IT or HR or engineering, to carry out the work within particular dates.

Each work package will outline the type of work being done, such as marketing, designing, or programming, and detail the desired outcome. In our example, the website work package will list the design and building of the site, with the desired outcome being a fully functional, tested, gorgeous website that is search engine optimized and has e-commerce capability. In addition, it will include the following:

» **A budget**: How much can Lulu spend on making the website? (And does she agree that the budget you are giving her is realistic?)

» **Deadlines**: When does Lulu have to have the live website up and running? Does she agree that it's realistic to do it by then?

> » **Risks:** Are there any risks that will affect Lulu that she needs to be aware of? And are there any risks from within her work package that Lulu needs to tell you about? Can she mitigate those or simply monitor and flag if anything comes up?

> » **Task priority:** Lulu needs to be aware of the priority of the website. This is especially important if she is also working on other projects. You can't always have all your work packages as everyone else's top priorities!

How to Make Work Packages Work

1. Involve the person who will be assigned the work package as early as possible. They probably have a far better sense of what's possible than you do.

2. Get the person who is likely to be assigned the work package to help with cost and duration estimates. In our example, it makes sense to ask Lulu how much it will cost and how long it's likely to take to create a great website.

3. Make one person accountable for each work package. If you can't, then break the work packages down further until you can.

4. Create stand-alone chunks of work or activities.

Plan Upward

We discussed this briefly in chapter 4 when we were exploring how to list all the tasks. But it's worth revisiting here in the context of managing larger projects. Most projects come into being by downward planning. The senior members of the project, the project manager, and the owner put their own cost and timeline constraints into the high-level project plan and tell everyone involved that they need to come back with a plan to deliver within those constraints. This is quicker than asking everyone's opinion, which is why it's so often favored.

But it's always better to plan upward if you can. This happens when each person involved in the project individually works out how long each task or sub-project would take to complete, and how much it would cost, and feeds that information back into the larger project plan, giving you an accurate overview of time and cost.

Consider the making of the website, for example. The chances are that neither you as the project manager nor the project owner have ever built a website, so are your top-down planning estimates going to be accurate or wishful thinking? You'll get a more accurate estimate if you ask Lulu to come up with estimates for what's involved right from the start. This more realistic information up front can help you avoid wasting time and money trying to conform to estimates that don't have much basis in reality.

Imagine if you underestimated the work required and didn't give Lulu enough time. And in order to achieve your crazy estimate she had to spend loads of money on overtime or could only produce a really poor website for you. If only she'd asked for more time, you could have easily given it to her. Maybe the website was a floating task with time to spare, or maybe you could have extended the project, if necessary, in order to get a fantastic website.

Of course, there is a risk that Lulu is going to ask you for more time than is really necessary, because she likes to play it safe and is worried about delivering late. Or maybe she thinks she'll be getting more work coming in around that time, so she inflates the estimate. It certainly helps if you know enough to be able to gauge whether the estimate is realistic. If you don't have that knowledge, you can always ask someone who does for a second opinion. And you can ask to see Lulu's detailed plan in order to make sure it all checks out. Despite the risk of inflation of estimates, estimating upward is still going to be better, because if you can't judge *their* estimates, you certainly can't make the estimates to start with!

Chapter Recap

» One of the biggest mistakes project managers make is not making a Gantt chart in the first place (or making one and promptly ignoring it). Like everything else in life, a Gantt chart is only useful if you use it.

» Gantt charts can be daunting if they are allowed to get too big. To avoid feeling overwhelmed by Gantt charts for larger projects, don't put everything into Excel all at once. Instead, break the project down so that you have a main high-level project with sub-projects (and, if necessary, sub-sub-projects!) on separate Gantt charts. These multiple charts will feed into one overall Gantt while offering enough detail to tell you where you are on any aspect of the project.

» For larger projects with overwhelming size and scope, you need to be organized. The two best ways to manage them are to create work packages and to plan upward.

» "Work package" is a project management term for a sequence of activities that leads to a specific deliverable when using a work breakdown structure (WBS). In a sense, they are the subtasks of a larger task.

» Work packages are great for getting stuff done and assigning people to specific chunks of work that are required, without getting yourself bogged down in the multitude of tasks that go into the delivery of a larger project.

» Each work package should include details of the work to be delivered, the budget, the deadline, the risks, and the priority level. The person assigned the work package must agree on the timeline and commit to delivery.

» Planning upward usually takes longer, but it ensures that the people who have the most experience and insight about how long something will take and how much it will cost are making the estimations and are engaged in the planning.

| 16 |

Top Ten Mistakes You'll Now Avoid

Chapter Overview

» Project management is more than just getting things done
» Use the 12-step process
» Avoid ten common mistakes

For many people, project management is a fancy career-enhancing term for getting stuff done. But it's actually much more than that. It's about getting stuff done as quickly and efficiently as possible, with minimum disruption to the rest of the business. Anyone can get stuff done if there is an unlimited budget or an endless timeline, but it takes real skill and capability to get stuff done consistently within tight parameters. That's project management. And it is a game-changing capability for you, your career prospects, and the business that is lucky enough to employ you. Great project managers are surprisingly rare, largely because most of them don't have a process. Each project is viewed merely as more stuff to do and more problems to solve, so those involved often get stuck in with minimal planning, choosing instead (albeit unconsciously) to fire-fight and problem-solve their way through. But such an approach is littered with difficulty and condemns that project to some form of failure right from the start.

The great news is that you don't need to make those mistakes anymore. You have a proven process for managing any project. The process outlined in parts 1, 2, and 3 of this book is all you need to know to become an accomplished project manager or to take your existing project management skills to the next level.

For most people, project management is an addendum to their everyday job, something they are asked to do from time to time. This 12-step process is therefore perfect because it ensures consistent results without any onerous requirements to learn new software or become qualified in some specific project management methodology. (However, for those who do want to get really serious about project management, we will cover those qualifications in chapter 19.)

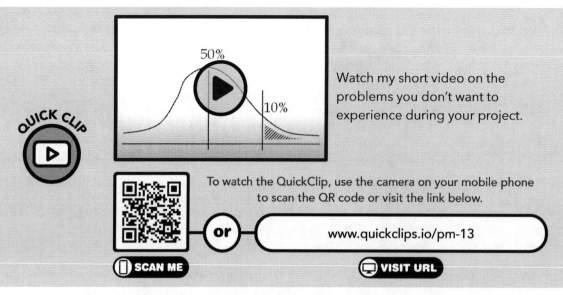

Watch my short video on the problems you don't want to experience during your project.

To watch the QuickClip, use the camera on your mobile phone to scan the QR code or visit the link below.

or www.quickclips.io/pm-13

SCAN ME VISIT URL

Using this process also makes it clear that most of the things that go wrong in projects originate from just ten common mistakes. If you avoid those ten potential pitfalls, your projects are going to be massively improved. Right now, let's recap those top ten mistakes, which the knowledge you've gained so far will enable you to avoid.

Mistake 1: Having the Plan in Your Head

The first time a fledgling project manager is asked to manage a project, it's usually a small one. Perhaps it only involves two or three tasks. It may be so small that it's not even called a project! Working out what needs to happen, when, and in what order is straightforward. They are able to do all the planning in their head, which leads them to the faulty assumption that planning in their head is generally a good idea and that project management is easy. Neither is true.

Of course, simple projects can be done without a great deal of planning, and that planning can possibly be done without writing anything down; but as soon as the projects start to become bigger, this approach invites trouble.

It's not possible to keep the project in your head. Once there are multiple tasks and the project involves other people, then it's too hard. It also makes the plan very hard to share with others. The project team is kept in the dark, which invites even more problems.

Having the plan in your head is also stressful. It's too much to remember, especially if you also have your normal day-to-day duties to consider. It's far too easy for things to slip through the cracks, making the project run late or blow the budget.

Using the 12-step process avoids those issues, because the project is laid out for all to see. You can show the project owner or your boss the plan and you can share it with your team. That way everyone knows their respective responsibilities, without relying on your memory and your assumptions.

Mistake 2: Saying "Maybe" or "I'll Try"

Everyone makes this mistake at least once in their project management career. Perhaps it's the first time someone has been asked to manage a project and they want to show their boss that they have a positive attitude. Perhaps the boss or project owner is particularly forceful or persuasive. Either way, saying "OK, maybe we can finish the project by then," or "I'll try" or "I'll do my best" are all fraught with danger.

First, the boss or owner doesn't hear "maybe." They hear "yes." That may make you a hero in the short term, but it will almost always make you the villain when you fail.

Great project managers hold firm. You will almost never hear a skilled project manager say "maybe" or "I'll try." Instead, they listen to what the stakeholders want in the first kick-off meeting. They tell the stakeholders that they need to go and work out if what the stakeholders want is possible in the given time frame or budget. No promises are made in that first meeting. Only once they have done that assessment and planning will they come back to the stakeholders with a definitive "Yes, this can be done" or "No, this can't be done—but it can be done if we have a little more time or resources, or if we modify the scope." And the project manager can prove it by showing the stakeholders the Gantt chart.

The process allows you to be definitive and to prove that you either can or can't do the project as requested.

Mistake 3: Answering the Question, "What's the Best You Can Do If It All Goes Really Well?"

Stakeholders are impatient. There is always a boss, customer, or project owner that is going to push for a best-case scenario. It's inevitable. It's also natural. They want the project done as soon as possible and as well and as cheaply as possible. Most projects are designed to deliver something new, something that may change the fortunes of the business. They want good news so they can pass that good news along to their boss. (If you are a boss reading this, do everyone a favor and don't ask this question!)

Inexperienced project managers are often tempted to play along with this question and either make a guess or err toward their most optimistic planning predictions. If you promise the best you might achieve, you'll have a 99 percent probability of failure. Project management is challenging work. So many things have to come together as expected to deliver the whole project successfully, and life rarely works like that. There are always unforeseen issues that nudge the plan off course.

Stick to your guns. Tell the stakeholder that you need to do the planning, and then stick to what your plan tells you. If you answer this question by giving your most optimistic timeline, even if that timeline is based on a thorough plan, the project owner will hold you to that duration. They will completely forget that you said it was unlikely or that everything would have to go perfectly. All they will say is, "But you said it would be finished in X weeks!"

This process allows you to navigate this question without sounding evasive or negative. Instead, you can be definitive about when the project can be delivered, and you can demonstrate why.

Mistake 4: Not Involving the Team Enough

As the title suggests, the project manager is the manager of the project. The implication, especially for the inexperienced, is that the buck stops with them. This is true, but the project manager is not omnipotent. They can't be everywhere at once. They can't know everything they need to know. And yet the temptation is to try. The project manager gets the brief and hides away in a quiet room and starts to figure out what's possible. What they don't know, they estimate or guess. Perhaps there is pressure from above to come back with a plan quickly, or perhaps the project manager just wants to be the hero and is going it alone for the glory. Either way, it's a huge mistake.

As a project manager, you will always get a better plan if you involve others. That may be by using your team or seeking out expert opinion or finding people in the business who have done similar projects. This is smart not because of the obvious mix of input and that two heads (or more) are always better than one, but because of buy-in.

Even an outstanding project manager won't get a project finished alone. They need other people to execute the plan, and that execution will always be better if you involve the team right from the start. Presumably you are going to assign individuals to tasks that they have experience in. So why wouldn't you lean on that experience in the planning stage to ensure that the plan for those tasks is doable? Involving the team will always produce a more accurate plan with fewer missed tasks or issues—and a better eventual execution.

There are countless opportunities for team involvement in this process: listing the tasks (step 2), creating the running order (step 3), estimating the time and cost (step 4), coming up with ideas for crashing the plan (step 5), resource planning (step 7), assessing risk (step 8), assessing progress (steps 9 and 10), modifying the plan (step 11), and reviewing the project (step 12). Basically everything!

Mistake 5: Having a List of Tasks and Dates

When I ask to see someone's project plan, about half the time they proudly show me a list of tasks with dates attached. Making a list of tasks and putting dates next to them can work, especially if the project is very small and simple. It's certainly better than nothing, and better than keeping the plan in your head. But, like planning in your head, early success using lists on small projects can be misinterpreted as a workable solution for all projects.

It's not. Projects rarely stay small or simple for long. What happens when that person is asked to manage something much larger? Lists with dates attached won't cut it. To begin with, *where do they get the dates?* Usually, they are made up or guessed. In theory, you could get the dates from a Gantt chart, but if you had a Gantt chart, you'd be using that instead of the list. The list of start and end dates is usually guesswork.

It's also impossible to see what's critical and what isn't, and whether tasks might overlap or whether there are dependencies where one task can't be started until another is finished. When are you going to be particularly busy? What about speeding up the project? A list won't show what tasks can be done alongside each other. Each task is an entry in the list, but it is almost impossible to tell if that task is big or small, whether it's a critical task or a floating task, how much float there is for it, or whether it can run late and by how much. And a list of tasks will certainly not help the project manager to identify the critical path.

You may start with a list of tasks (step 2), but by the time you've reached step 6 you've added so much more information and created a Gantt chart that will solve every one of the issues that lists have, and more.

Mistake 6: Not Planning Resources for All Projects

This mistake is possibly the most common of all. Every business has limits on what they can do in terms of projects—although it's not always clear that the higher-ups realize this. There are always managers in various departments cooking up new projects to make their part of the business better, but it's rare that anyone is looking at the big picture of the total wish list and measuring it against resources.

Most often forgotten in this project fever is the people. People are often the biggest constraint to a business's project aspirations. Inevitably there are not enough people in the business to manage the day-to-day operations and also be involved in executing all the projects that we'd like to do.

Even if a project manager is using the 12-step process and making great plans for their department, what are all the other project managers doing at the same time? And even when there is project management proficiency in the business, the various projects are very rarely consolidated so that all of them are properly resourced and planned. As a result, either the business comes up with loads of projects that are never acted on, or the wrong ones are acted on, or projects are started and quickly forgotten about. Not only is this a huge waste of time and money, it's bad for staff morale, not to mention the opportunity costs of so many failed projects.

If you're using the 12-step process, it will automatically lead you to step 6, the creation of your project Gantt chart. Once it's created, there is only a small additional step to create a Gantt of Gantts at step 7, which allows you and all the other project managers and senior leaders to know exactly which projects are happening at what time in the business. Not only does the Gantt of Gantts allow you to look at what's already been done, but it alerts everyone to which projects will start in the future. It also helps everyone to see clashes and to prioritize those projects properly rather than throwing a bunch of projects at the wall and hoping one or two of them will stick.

Mistake 7: Stories Rather Than a Colored-in Gantt Chart

Projects involve creating or bringing about something new. That brings a touch of jeopardy to the mix, and jeopardy is great fodder for stories. In meetings, it is very easy for project managers to tell a good story about how the supplier pulled out at the last minute or went bust and how the project team worked into the night to find a solution, and so on. It's all very exciting, and stories can be great at relaying what's already happened in the project. Tales of woe and tales of heroism and all that. But these stories are also useful in obfuscating what *should* have happened in the project. Stories tell you (selectively) what *has* happened, but they don't compare what *has* been done with what *should* have been done.

There is nowhere to hide in a project. The colored-in Gantt chart of step 9 negates the need for stories because it is obvious from the colored-in parts what has happened in the past, what is happening right now, and what should have happened by now but hasn't. The stories can still be told if you like, but the process of getting everyone up to speed on what is actually happening in the project is much faster with a quick look at the Gantt chart. This form of update may not be as exciting or entertaining, but it is significantly more accurate. You'll also see the whole picture, not just the part that the story is about. To sum up: if someone is telling you a story about their project, *be suspicious!*

Mistake 8: Thinking Underspend Is OK

In business there is always a focus on profit, or the bottom line. This is essential, as the business must know and manage all of its ins and outs. When it comes to projects, the cost is always critical. But the people who are measuring these things are often looking at different sets of information.

In the accounting department, they are only concerned with costs—how much a project has cost so far and what it will cost by the end. But estimating the cost at completion is almost impossible for them because they don't have any idea about the *progress* of the project. Conversely, the project manager may know the progress but may not be very interested in the costs, or may not have accurate data, because even if they are sent monthly figures, those figures are probably already out of date, or in a format that is hard to understand. Cost information is pretty useless on its own, as is progress information. To know the real situation regarding any project, you need both. If you don't pay attention to both cost and progress, then you could be heading for a nasty surprise.

As we've discussed in this book, a project that looks underspent is not automatically doing well. It may be that they have spent 90 percent of the planned budget so far but have only done 80 percent of the planned work. In fact, "underspent" halfway through is usually "overspent" at the end, because it's usually a sign that the project is behind schedule. And behind schedule means you have had a problem, which often also translates to overspend. And if you are already overspent when you are halfway through, then you are probably overspent.

You are always looking at progress and cost at the same time so you won't be caught out. This is especially true if you also keep your own cost spreadsheet on the project. Keeping a close eye on your resources Gantt chart (for seeing nonlinear spends) and your time Gantt chart (for seeing lateness) allows you to get a far more accurate picture of your project in real time and keep it on track.

Mistake 9: Rescheduling Too Late

This mistake, also far too common, is born out of an overreliance on hope and wishful thinking. This is understandable, especially for an inexperienced project manager. They want the project to go well. But unexpected problems are inevitable. The project may start to slip because they missed (and then had to add) an important task, or perhaps a task had to be done twice. Sometimes the plan starts to slip because of something completely unexpected and unavoidable, like a supplier going bust or new legislation.

The temptation is to believe something good will happen that will allow the project to get back on track. Perhaps one of the team will find a useful workaround or an innovative solution to something. Maybe the stars will align and everything will magically resolve. Maybe there is a team-wide belief that the project has had so much bad luck that the tide is bound to turn soon. "We are owed some luck!" It. Never. Happens.

The worst thing you can ever do as a project manager is to know that a project is off course and do nothing or say nothing about it until you reach the end, or very nearly the end, when you are forced to finally, suddenly confess. Bosses and customers don't like surprises.

It's really hard to stick your head in the sand about progress and expectations, because your colored-in Gantt charts will show you very clearly if you are off plan, either spending too much money or not making enough progress. In turn, this information allows you to look at the plan at the midway point so that you know if you need to modify it. Most plans need to be modified at some point. The key is to modify in the middle third of the project and to only do it once.

Mistake 10: Not Reviewing

I get it! The project is over. It was a nightmare—or maybe it was great—but everyone involved has a ton of other stuff to get on with now. They either jump straight back into their day-to-day workload or are brought into a new project. The last thing they want to do is dissect what did or did not go well during the last one.

But avoiding a review is still a mistake, and the way to avoid this mistake is to reframe it. Reviewing the project is not really about you or what each project member did or did not do; it's about building up a knowledge bank for the business to draw on so that every new project gets better and easier for everyone involved. An organization should never have to reinvent the wheel or repeat mistakes over and over again. If one person has learned that lesson, share the insight and allow everyone in the business to learn it.

The project is not finished until the review has been done. It can even be fun, a way to celebrate together. And it doesn't take much time to record in a one- or two-page bullet point list the key takeaways and learnings. If those reviews are all kept in a central file, they can become an invaluable resource for the project manager, the project team, and the business.

Chapter Recap

» For many people, project management is a fancy career-enhancing term for getting stuff done. But it's actually much more than that. It's about getting stuff done as quickly and efficiently as possible, with a minimum of disruption to the rest of the business.

» Great project managers are surprisingly rare, largely because most of them don't have a process.

» Using the 12-step process in this book will help you to avoid the ten most common mistakes.

| 17 |

Remember the People Side
of Project Management

Chapter Overview
» The biggest cause of problems in projects
» Keeping communication lines open
» Taking the lead and staying positive

The P in PM is as much about "people" management as it is about "project" management.

– CORNELIUS FICHTNER

Leadership and management are specialist areas in themselves, and the primary focus of this book is the planning and control of projects. However, there are certain people-related activities that project managers need to know about, because people are usually the biggest cause of problems in projects. Projects always involve change, and people don't naturally love change, because it involves loss. There is often resistance. In addition, project teams are often temporary, which brings an extra set of problems. Team members who don't know each other well or have experience working together may have personality conflicts. Or it may be that certain people on the team don't like each other. It takes time to develop highly functional teams, and time is often the one thing that a project team doesn't have.

This chapter will explore project management activities that can minimize resistance and maximize engagement, while making sure the project gets done. What makes a good project *manager* into a great project *leader* is the ability to work well with others and get the best out of everyone on the team.

Communication

The person who communicates leads (and vice versa). One of the key roles of the project manager is to be a great communicator, telling everyone what's going on, all the time. At the very least, there should be weekly or monthly progress meetings and a communications plan that outlines when the stakeholders will be updated, how often, and by what method. Maybe they get an email once a week or a written report once a month or a phone call every day. As mentioned in chapter 11, the communications plan may be done in step 1 so that all the stakeholders know what to expect in terms of updates and so on, but it is more often formalized in step 9, when the project is underway and is being monitored for progress. It is usually at this stage that the stakeholders will most appreciate the communications plan. It may be written and agreed on, or it may remain more informal. It will depend on your project and stakeholder preferences.

The single biggest problem in communication is the illusion that it has taken place.

– GEORGE BERNARD SHAW

On top of progress reports, every change, every significant event or achievement, every new risk or new question, should be communicated to all the stakeholders who need to know or who might need to know. If you're great with numbers and graphs but don't feel totally comfortable with chatting with people at all levels, then you'll need to work on this. The best project managers are communicators as well as planners and estimators.

Listening is also an important project management skill. An effective project manager has a natural tendency to ask people how they are getting on. Do they understand the plan? How are they feeling about the plan? Do they have any issues? And what they are planning to do next?

Think of project management as a process that goes from incoming information through decisions to results. The incoming information is usually in the form of things being done or not done, problems being detected and questions being asked. Decisions are then made either by the project manager or with the project team. And finally, the results of this planning are communicated to everyone who needs to know. Communication is therefore a huge part of successful project management.

The following are the two main ways that a PM communicates with other team members:

» **Diagrams**: Network diagrams are a great way to plan the relationships between the various parts of the project, and the Gantt chart is the best way to show a project plan and, later, the progress made on the plan. A diagram is always preferable to words because it is almost always easier to understand and a faster way to communicate key points.

» **Meetings:** There are four types of meetings, and they should not be mixed together (figure 116). Once you understand which type of meeting you are having, it becomes much easier to ensure that the meeting is productive.

FOUR TYPES OF MEETINGS

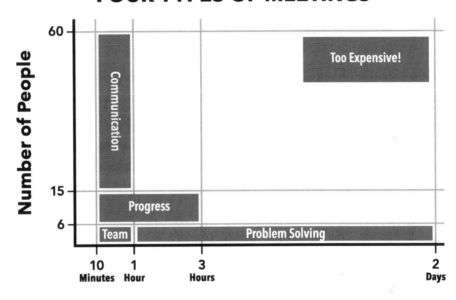

fig. 116

You may notice from figure 116 that the meetings have been categorized by type, how long they will last, and how many people will attend. These meetings can be conducted face-to-face or remotely using Zoom or a similar platform.

Team Meetings

The shortest and smallest meeting is the weekly team meeting. It may even be held daily for short and fast-moving projects. This is an informal meeting where each person gets to do the following:

» Briefly summarize how they're doing
» Explain what they're planning for that day or week
» Talk about anything that is worrying them
» Mention anything the others need to know about

Don't get bogged down in solving problems at this meeting. Any problems that come up should be parked or added to the agenda for a problem-solving meeting. Keep it moving, otherwise people will start to make excuses as to why they can't attend next time. This is not a progress-checking meeting, either; there is no pressure or criticism. It should be entirely positive and motivational. You as the leader are also a contributor—it's important that you give a quick summary of what you're working on that week.

Watch a short video on the four types of meetings.

QUICKCLIP

To watch the QuickClip, use the camera on your mobile phone to scan the QR code or visit the link below.

or

www.quickclips.io/pm-14

SCAN ME

VISIT URL

Progress Meetings

Every project will need regular progress meetings. Monthly meetings will usually be enough, but if your project is very large or complex—or short overall—then these meetings may need to be biweekly or even weekly. This is a fast-moving fact-based meeting, preferably based on the Gantt chart, where the group looks at whether all the required tasks have been done. If not, why not, and what can be done to get back on track?

It's not about blame, but there should be some pressure for people to come with good news, certainly to have kept any promises they made at the last meeting. Maybe people will work extra hard for the day or two leading up to the meeting! Your job is to set the tone—tough but positive—and keep it moving along. There might be up to fifteen people at the progress meeting, but only those involved in execution, not the stakeholders. Sometimes there will be people who only attend the first or second half. It's important not to get dragged into solving problems.

Highlight them, add them to the problem-solving agenda, and move on.

Problem-Solving Meetings

Spinning off from the previous two types of meetings will be the occasional problem-solving meeting, where you will have a small group of attendees—six at the most. The meeting takes as long as necessary; maybe a few hours, maybe an away day, or even a retreat for a couple of days. It should be open-ended and creative; your job as the leader is to make sure that everyone contributes and feels safe suggesting ideas and commenting on each other's ideas and solutions.

Communication Meetings

The communication style of a team meeting is reporting all-to-all; progress reporting is all-to-you, and problem solving has no reporting. Communication meetings are you-to-all. You are there to update everyone on the project's progress. Maybe the people at the meeting are not the ones doing the work, but the ones waiting for the results, like the users, or the general public, or other stakeholders who are affected by it. Maybe they are excited by it, maybe they are dead against it, or maybe it's a mix. Your job is to tell them clearly what's happening. You may show them the Gantt chart or share financial information, but whatever you do, it needs to be concise. They are allowed to ask questions for clarification, but the purpose is not to get into a debate about the validity of the project or to do any problem solving. It's just about communicating to the stakeholders what's happening.

QUICKCLIP

Watch a short video on the top three skills of a project manager: listening, delegating, and thanking.

To watch the QuickClip, use the camera on your mobile phone to scan the QR code or visit the link below.

SCAN ME

or

www.quickclips.io/pm-15

VISIT URL

The most important thing in communication is hearing what isn't said.
– PETER DRUCKER

Control

Control is one of the key things to think about when you're in a position of leadership, including as a project manager. If you try to keep too much control, it'll take too much of your time and potentially demotivate your team, resulting in a poorer outcome. Generally speaking, the more you can delegate, and the more freedom you can give your team, the better—within the bounds of competence and trust.

But there is a refinement on control: how you divide the control/freedom between the planning and the doing. Maybe can you let them plan it, but you monitor them carefully when they carry it out. Or maybe you do most of the planning, but then, knowing the plan is good, you can leave them to carry it out. Neither aspect has to be all or nothing; you can share in the planning, for example, or give them freedom in implementation while still having them report on progress. In terms of control, you need to decide:

» How much involvement to give your team in the planning
» How much freedom to give your team in the implementation

Figure 117 provides a quick guide to the delegation and control options you may explore, depending on the situation and the project.

Options 1 and 4 are not recommended, for obvious reasons. If you choose these, you are becoming too much of a control freak. If you do most of the planning (never ideal, but maybe you are the only one who can), then you don't need your team to check with you before they do each part! And if you share the planning with your team (perhaps because you have lots of expertise to contribute), then again, they don't need to check each part of the plan with you before they do it. You already know what the plan is because it was agreed on collectively. You want them to tell you *after* they have done each part of the plan (options 2 and 5).

The only time you'll probably want the team to check with you *before* they do a task, perhaps before they spend money or talk to a customer, is when you have completely delegated the planning to them (option 7). Option 7 is useful when you appear to have a capable team but you don't know them very well yet. Perhaps you'll ask them to do the planning themselves but to look at their Gantt chart before they go ahead with the project—or to check each task with you before they execute it.

DELEGATION OPTIONS

		HOW MUCH FREEDOM IN THE IMPLEMENTATION?		
		"Check before" Your team has to check with you before they do anything	**"Report after"** Your team keeps you informed every time they do something, or with a weekly summary	**"Free to act"** Your team just gets on with it
HOW MUCH INVOLVEMENT IN THE PLANNING?	**"Consult"** You do the planning, but you show it to your team	**OPTION 1** Not Recommended	**OPTION 2**	**OPTION 3** Not Recommended
	"Share" You plan the project together	**OPTION 4** Not Recommended	**OPTION 5**	**OPTION 6**
	"Delegate" You let the team do the planning	**OPTION 7**	**OPTION 8**	**OPTION 9** Not Recommended

GRAPHIC

fig. 117

Personally, I prefer the first option, where they see the whole plan before they start, because a Gantt chart shows everything at the beginning, so you can all view it once and then move them up to option 8 where they let you know after they have done each task by coloring in the Gantt chart. You can have a monthly meeting at which you all compare notes. But if you get at all anxious during the month, between meetings, you can go online and have a look at the shared colored-in Gantt chart for an instant update.

Option 8 is great when you have a team that is tried and trusted; you can give them the job to plan, and then they can report to you as they go along. They usually feel more empowered, and you aren't taking much of a risk because they can only go wrong by one task. If the tasks are quite small, then if anything does go wrong you are not far off track, and you can revert to option 7 if you need to keep a tighter grip on control. When you have no idea how to do the job yourself, option 7 or 8 is essential. As a manager, you might often be in charge of a team that knows much more than you do, so it makes sense to let them do the planning.

Options 2 and 5 are for situations where you have as much expertise (or more) as your team.

If you're doing the planning yourself, then you're looking at option 2. This is best for plans where you are the brains and the project team is the hands that will execute the plan. You have a trusted team of implementers, but you are the designer. Maybe you are an architect and they are builders, or you are the marketing strategist and they are the website builders. You should certainly consult with them to check that nothing is missing from your plan, but then they can execute and report on progress as they go along by coloring in the Gantt chart.

Sharing the planning will give you the best quality of outcome, even though it'll take more of your time and may be less motivational for the team than options 7 or 8. You might want to share the planning as a coaching opportunity or if the job is especially large or important. The only other question is about control: having shared the plan, do you want them to report after each task (option 5), or just get on with it, free to act (option 6)? Remember, you can still look at the Gantt chart every now and then if you need a quick update.

Can you tell what's wrong with option 3? It is not recommended because if you can trust your team to the extent that you don't even need to check on them during implementation, why are you not sharing the planning with them, or delegating it altogether? To be excessively controlling over the planning but have no control over the implementation seems an odd mixture. However, I have seen people do it, for all the wrong reasons. They do all the planning because they don't believe that anyone else has any good ideas, and then they abdicate the implementation because they can't bear to watch—they know that if they monitor, they will end up interfering, so they walk away and leave the team to it. These are not the reasons you should be choosing these management styles!

Finally, there is option 9, which has so little control it's worrying. Personally, I like to have *some* control, over either the planning or the implementation. If the project is virtually a rote process, you've done lots of similar ones before, maybe you can set them free to get on with it. Or perhaps you would want to delegate the planning and then let the team get on with it. But even then, it takes so little time to check on a colored-in Gantt chart each week, why would you not do option 8 instead of 9? After all, the team needs to keep a colored-in Gantt for their own communication anyway, so all you would be doing is looking at it for your own peace of mind.

To sum up, you don't need to memorize all nine options, or even the six recommended ones. You just need to consciously decide, for every project and every team, which level of involvement you're going to have in the planning and which level of freedom you are going to give them for the implementation.

Understanding these options also involves digging further into two important aspects of control: delegating tasks to others and monitoring the team's work.

Delegation

This is easily one of the most important skills for a project manager to master. Poor delegation leads to micromanagement, which can negatively impact the morale of the team. It can also create a bottleneck around the manager as they insist that everything be run past them first. Poor delegators often do stuff they find easier or more fun than their day-to-day job, rather than what's necessary for the success of the project. Of course, sometimes a task can't be delegated because you're the only one who knows how to do it. But you probably can delegate more than you think.

The advantages of delegating:

» Frees up more time for the project manager to manage
» Improves team morale and motivation as the team feels trusted
» Allows the team to learn and develop
» Increases job satisfaction for the manager and the team
» Reduces risk, as now there is more than one person who can do that task, not just the PM
» Increases project management capability, which can lead to promotion
» Increases project efficiency

Almost every step of the project management process can be delegated, or at least shared:

1. **Define the project**: Involve your team in agreeing on the specifications and thinking about what's in scope and what isn't, and what the key driver might be. Sometimes this will involve only the key stakeholders, but the more fully you can bring team members into this process the better. Everyone buys in to the project from the start.

2. **List the tasks**: Bring your team into the brainstorming process and the creation of the work breakdown structure. And ask the experts you have working with you.

3. **Create the running order:** Involve your team in making the Post-it note diagram. It's more fun, and you get more buy-in and a better plan. You yourself don't need to know all the tasks that will need to be completed. Involving your team ensures that you capture as many of the expected tasks as possible.

4. **Estimate the tasks:** Involve your team in the estimating of the tasks. The people who do those tasks or have done them before are most likely to make accurate estimates. Also get input from the team on contingency. Ask your team what might go wrong.

5. **Crash the plan:** Discuss with your team whether it's better to put the costs up, put the quality down, or overlap some tasks.

6. **Create the Gantt chart:** This is the one exception to involvement; only one person can draw it. However, you could delegate it to one of your team members! It's a mechanical task based on the Post-its, so anyone should be able to do it. Get a different team member to create the Gantt chart each time so everyone knows how to do it and has experienced how easy it is to do.

7. **Plan for resources:** Work with the team to decide who is best suited to do each task. Consider not only who could do them the fastest, but also who would enjoy doing them or could learn from them.

8. **Do risk planning:** Definitely involve the team in thinking about what might go wrong and what you could do about it.

9. **Monitor progress:** The team must be involved in a weekly or monthly meeting.

10. **Monitor cost:** The team should understand the cost side of things as well, so they have a greater appreciation of the costs and know how to keep an eye on them.

11. **Modify the plan:** The team has a key role to play in working out how best to modify the plan.

12. **Review:** The team needs to be involved in the review; otherwise, you will miss key learnings. Make it fun, maybe doing the review over pizza and beer or organic smoothies.

Delegating small things is easy; it's delegating important things that's more difficult. The challenge is to keep increasing the size of what you delegate. If there are some tasks that only you can do, you're not a good enough boss! What if you are away or busy? You need to get someone trained for every task. At the very least, break the tasks down into small parts that you can delegate. We discussed this granularity in chapter 4.

The project manager should be like the captain of a ship, standing on the bridge and checking that everything is OK. Are there systems for everything? Are all the people trained and motivated? It's the captain's job to ensure that the people and systems are fine, that the "machine of people" is running smoothly, and nothing else. The captain should not be making the occasional bed or serving soup in the dining room! Similarly, the project manager should not be justifying their existence by writing code or visiting customers. They should be making sure that all those things are getting done, to the right level of quality, at the right time, by means of great systems and great people.

Tips for successfully delegating tasks to others:

1. Tell them the outcome you need but not how to deliver that outcome, even if you know. Let them do the task their own way. Remember, they are competent—that's why you've chosen them to do it.

2. Explain the importance of the job in relation to the project, or even to the organization.

3. Tell them why you have chosen them to do the task. This might be because you consider them the best person for that task, or you think they will enjoy it, or you want them to learn about it and you're going to help them with it.

4. Make clear the resources and parameters of the delegated task. How much money can they spend? What level of decisions can they make? What people can they pull in to help? And by when does it need to be done?

5. Make clear the kind of reporting you want. How often should they report back to you? Before or after they do parts of the task? By email or face-to-face? And so forth.

6. Check that they are happy. Have they understood what you expect from them? Do they feel they can do it? Will they enjoy it?

7. Make it clear that you will always be there for support. It's OK if they get stuck or have difficulties, but they need to alert you so that you can figure it out together.

Monitoring

Monitoring is what reduces the risk of delegation.

Delegation is not abdication, where you walk away and leave them to it. That is *always* risky.

The level of monitoring on a project is also known as "grip." How tight a grip do you keep on the people you have delegated to? We've already seen that you have several grip choices: "Check with me before you do it," "Report to me after you do it," and "No need to report, just carry on." These actually form a sliding scale, as follows, from least control to most control:

FREEDOM

fig. 118

- No reporting or measuring.

- No reporting, but there's a budget you can monitor.

- Report to me if you fall behind or come across a problem.

- Report to me at the end of the current part of the project. (Could be several months)

- Report to me once a week. (If the person is fairly new but the project is easy, or if the work is difficult but the person is experienced)

- Report to me every day. (This would be for short or risky projects, perhaps if the person was relatively new and the work was difficult.)

- Show me your daily task "to-do list" to make sure that I'm happy with what you're working on.

CONTROL

You can see that by the time you get to the bottom of this list, the level of control is high—almost insultingly high! I personally wouldn't want my boss asking me every day what I'm going to work on that day. But if someone has let you down, or is very new and is effectively being coached, then it might be appropriate. The key is to consciously choose the level of control you are going to take with each person and each project, so you might have different levels of grip with the same person if they are on a more difficult or unfamiliar project. And remember that you can delegate *anything* if you keep a tight enough grip on what they are doing. Grip helps you delegate effectively.

Other People Skills for Optimal Team Performance

Projects can be challenging, and often it's keeping the people working hard but staying happy that adds to the pressure. This section runs through a few of the most important considerations when creating and then managing outstanding project teams.

Motivation

Projects tend to be more motivational than processes, because they are new and different and because there's a feeling of progress, of moving toward completion, as opposed to processes, many of which never end. But still, sometimes at the beginning of a project it can feel as if there is a mountain to climb.

Motivation is therefore important, because motivated and engaged people work harder. Gallup research has consistently shown the correlation between employee engagement and team performance. Engaged, motivated team members care more about quality and about the customer. They tend to be more creative and are better at problem solving. How do you create a motivated team?

1. **Explain everything**. Specifically, explain the importance of the whole project and of each of the tasks (and therefore of every person). Usually, the whole project fails if even a single task isn't done, so it's relatively easy to show that everyone is important.

2. **Introduce the customer to the team**. The closer the project team can be to the external customer, the better. You don't need to bring the team in on the initial negotiations, but if they can hear "from the horse's mouth" why quality is important or why the delivery date is critical, you won't have to keep pushing them; they'll naturally understand and want to do a great job.

3. **Give team members ownership**. Make sure everyone has something, however small, that is owned by them. And make sure all tasks are owned by someone; otherwise, they can drift. This is quick and easy to do when you put names against tasks on the Gantt chart. Every task has a name, and every name appears at least once on the Gantt chart.

4. **Involve the team**. When people feel part of the planning process, they are much more likely to be motivated to execute that plan. It's much more motivational than being told, "Here's the plan, go make it happen." Involvement is not just competence based. Everyone on a team has something to offer, and there will always be more buy-in the more you involve others at every stage. If someone on the team is new to the work and not yet fully competent, involvement may be "information in," meaning you bring them into the meetings as a way to coach them, to feed information and skills into them. You show them what you're doing and why, you ask them what they think and what they would do, but always with the safety net of your being there to make the final decision. And this learning process will motivate them. But if they are experienced and competent, you are involving them for "information out," where you really are getting information from them, and, even if you have strong opinions yourself, you deliberately go with their ideas and their plan, because you know it's more likely to be done, and done well.

5. **Make the team feel safe**. Projects can be scary, a journey into the unknown where people might get in trouble—or even get fired if they don't deliver the desired outcome. You need to make people feel safe in that environment. Your project should have a supportive atmosphere, where your door is always open and everyone knows they can always ask for help. Demonstrate that when problems arise, they are met with a constructive "OK, let's see how we can fix this together" rather than irritation, anger, or blame. That way people won't feel the need to hide things from you.

6. **Thank people**. This is such an underrated and underused part of management! Projects may be stressful at times, but at least they have a finish line, so everyone is usually thanked at the end. And there are definite tasks throughout the project, so people can be

thanked when each task is completed. Never miss the chance to show your gratitude and appreciation for other people's efforts and contributions. Never take the glory for someone else's wins. Broadcast the win to the rest of the team. Be as specific as possible in your praise. "Thank you for getting the branding work done" is always more meaningful than "Thank you for your hard work." (Conversely, if you need to pull someone up on performance, do it privately and in a spirit of coaching and support.) Giving thanks is really powerful—and free!

Rewards and motivation are an oil change for project engines. Do it regularly and often.

– WOODY WILLIAMS

A final thought on motivation: Rather than focusing entirely on the tasks to be done, stand back once a month and do a motivation review. On your commute or over your morning coffee, flick through each person on the project team in your mind and ask, "Are they motivated? Do they have enough challenge in their work? Are they still learning? Do they have ownership of their tasks? Are they happy?" The last thing you want is a sudden surprise when someone you've neglected starts to become a disruptive influence on the team—or suddenly leaves.

Watch a short video on how best to influence different types of people.

To watch the QuickClip, use the camera on your mobile phone to scan the QR code or visit the link below.

or — www.quickclips.io/pm-16

SCAN ME   VISIT URL

A Vision of the Future

Projects are all about change, so managing a project inevitably involves managing change. The project manager needs to motivate the project team to do the work and also convince those on the receiving end of the project to accept and continue to use the new way of working, whatever the project is delivering. Some project managers take the attitude that once the project is delivered, their work is done. What the department or business does with that delivery has nothing to do with them. But it's not enough to say, "There, your new computer system's installed" or "That's your new strategy" and then walk away. A successful project is not just about delivery, it's about whether the project sticks or not. Is the new computer system used by everyone? Is the strategy implemented?

We naturally tend to resist change, because change often means loss—loss of knowledge, loss of resources, loss of security, loss of power, or loss of collegial relationships. And this resistance will make the project take longer and cost more to get completed. How can a project manager reduce this entirely natural and understandable fear of loss?

The answer is to provide a clear vision. When there is a clear vision of the improved situation after the change—why it's necessary and why it's going to be better for everyone—then those affected tend to be more accepting. When a reassuringly high level of communication is implemented regarding the process of the change, then most people will feel better about it. They may still not like it, but they are more likely to embrace it.

There's a famous model known as the Kübler-Ross Change Curve (figure 119), which shows a dip in morale when everyone has to let go of their old safe ways. Clearly the best way to get through this dip is to keep everyone's sights on the promised land on the other side of the change where it's all going to be worth it! A project manager who says, "Don't worry about that, just do what I say" is going to meet a lot more resistance.

Interestingly, this model was first developed to help people understand their reactions to *death*. It may seem surprising that reactions to a new computer system or an office move might be similar, but it all comes down to loss: the loss of something as a result of change. And, at least with projects, there really is a better world for everyone at the far end. That's why we're doing the project, after all!

THE KÜBLER-ROSS CHANGE CURVE

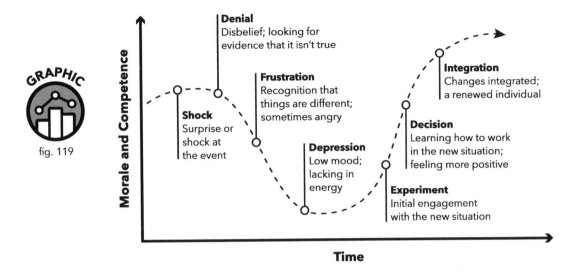

GRAPHIC

fig. 119

Morale and Competence (vertical axis)

Time (horizontal axis)

Denial
Disbelief; looking for evidence that it isn't true

Frustration
Recognition that things are different; sometimes angry

Shock
Surprise or shock at the event

Depression
Low mood; lacking in energy

Experiment
Initial engagement with the new situation

Decision
Learning how to work in the new situation; feeling more positive

Integration
Changes integrated; a renewed individual

The project manager needs to paint the picture of this better world and show that there is a great plan for getting there. No one is going to end up stranded down at the bottom of the dip! Luckily, this is easy to show people, because you will always have your plan and your Gantt chart. And if they are involved in the making of the plan, that's even better.

Positivity

Your team will take their cue from you. If the project is starting to wear you down, you need to keep that under wraps. In the middle of the project, when those involved may be down in the dip of the change curve, it's vital for you to stay positive. This is also likely to be when the project is at its busiest, so there are bound to be all sorts of problems cropping up. Maintaining a can-do, problem-solving, positive focus is essential so the team will stay upbeat too.

This doesn't mean you can't acknowledge problems. People are not oblivious to challenges and it's important to be honest; the key is facing those challenges together with positivity and resilience. By staying positive, you send a clear message to the team. They'll also enjoy the project more and deliver better results.

It's especially important to stay positive when someone has made a mistake or has fallen behind. If you respond negatively, they may not come to you next time; they'll plow on without asking for help, and things will get worse and worse before you discover the issue. Your team member might even hide things from you for fear of your reaction, perhaps hoping that somehow they'll be able to put it all right before you find out. Always aim to be supportive, even if you are tired and busy and what they have done seems utterly stupid.

There is a style of management known as "seagull management," where the manager essentially flaps in making lots of noise, poops on everybody, and then goes flapping off again. This has been illustrated and popularized in the TV show *The Apprentice*, where the boss monitors the teams, usually with a couple of observers who make notes throughout, and then at the end in the boardroom the teams are told they are useless and one of them gets fired. It may make entertaining TV, but it's terrible management!

Instead of practicing seagull management, make a point of actively coaching the people on your team in areas where their skills are a little light. You could argue that as a project manager this isn't your job, particularly if you are just borrowing people for a short period for your project. You don't have the time or money to train people within the project; that's the job of their line manager. But if their job is a series of projects, then they have to learn on *every* project, including yours. And there might be some things that they can only learn on your project. Training people by giving them jobs that they find difficult and then spending time helping them and teaching them is, ultimately, part of your job. I know it may sound like a pain, but it's actually one of the most rewarding parts of being a project manager. You are helping to develop project managers of the future.

There are managers who think that the best way to develop people is to give them maximum feedback, both positive and negative. This is a tempting idea, but negative feedback given as criticism doesn't improve performance; more often, it demotivates the person receiving it. They'll sidestep anything resembling that task in the future in order to avoid more criticism, and they'll avoid contact with the person who gave it to them. Any negative feedback needs to be couched in very positive terms: "X didn't work out, but it's not a big deal, we can fix it, and it's not your fault, it's mine for not explaining/teaching/preparing you for it." This is not management BS; it's true! You then coach the person so they learn from their experience, why it didn't work and what they might try next time. That's the positive way to give negative feedback.

Accountability

Project managers function as bandleaders who pull together their players, each a specialist with individual score and internal rhythm. Under the leader's direction, they all respond to the same beat.

— L. R. SAYLES

Everything is the project manager's fault. It really is! If you delegate something and it goes wrong, it's your fault, because you chose who to delegate to. You made the judgment that they could do it, you failed to monitor their progress, or you failed to support or coach them.

Maybe it wasn't a people problem, maybe it was a system problem—something fell between the cracks, some information was incorrect, or the system didn't communicate well enough and a misunderstanding occurred. Still your fault. The project manager's job is to build a machine of people that will carry out the project—to work *on* the machine, not *in* the machine. That gives you a lot of ownership.

Maybe the project was impossible from the start. *Still* your fault—for agreeing to do it!

Are you depressed by the thought that everything is your fault, even though you can't know every detail and can't control everything that every person does? Don't be. If you have a good team and good monitoring systems, you'll be alerted to problems in plenty of time. If the team is reporting to you every week, then the plan can only go wrong by a week. If the Gantt chart is granulated down to tasks for that week, then you'll know what's not been done. The great thing about a robust project plan shown on a Gantt chart is that you don't get any surprises near the end of your project. As soon as you get behind, you are alerted and have enough time to get back on track. And then it's not about blame; it's about what everyone on the team can do to get things sorted out.

You will find that sometimes there are people on your project team who deliberately try to take advantage of the fact that the buck stops with you. They may say to you, "I don't know what to do about this," "I can't make any progress on this," "Boss, I've got a problem." They may be hoping that you'll say, "OK, leave it with me," but if you do step in and take over, even if it would be easier and quicker to do so, you are effectively rewarding bad behavior. It's a cop-out for both of you.

This is sometimes called "taking the monkey," where the task they brought into your office is like an invisible monkey on their back that has now jumped across onto *your* back. If you have five people who each give you two monkeys every week, that's forty potentially difficult monkeys in a month that you are taking on, in addition to running the project! The people who passed you the monkeys are now asking you for updates as to whether the monkeys are solved, so in a way, you've switched roles: you now have five new bosses as well as your real one, all giving you work!

Be very selective about what tasks you take over from your team. It is an absolute last resort. Before you get to that point, speak to the person who is struggling:

1. Ask them what they have already tried or considered.

2. Ask them what their options are.

3. If they don't know, ask them how long it will take to generate some options. Or suggest you both work through some options.

4. Ask them which option they prefer.

5. If they don't know, ask them how long it will take to assess the options, or work through the assessment together.

6. Ask them to choose the option they believe is most likely to work.

7. Ask them to come back and tell you how it went.

By coaching them in the moment, or even adding the issue to a meeting agenda for the team to discuss, you leave the monkey on their back where it belongs.

The buck stops with you to make sure a good decision is made—but not to make all the decisions or do all the work. Your job is to support others to make good decisions too, and ensure that all the tasks, including the unpleasant or gnarly ones, are done. The buck stops with you to make sure that the buck stops with them.

System Thinking

A lot of this chapter could be called "system thinking," a term coined by Peter Senge in his fantastic book *The Fifth Discipline*. A good project manager doesn't make decisions in reaction to problems; they are always looking ahead, standing back and thinking about the system of project management. Is the process the best one? Are the systems employed the right ones? How are the people interacting as a team? Could team members be moved around so that they support each other better and interact in a more effective way? This is the "machine of people" that you are constantly working on so that the machine will carry out your project successfully for you.

GRAPHIC

fig. 120

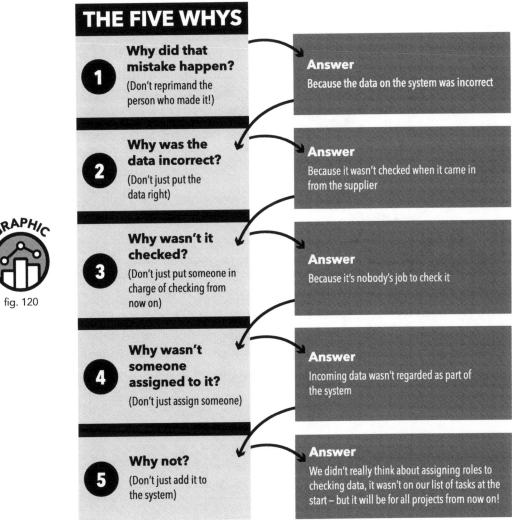

THE FIVE WHYS

1 **Why did that mistake happen?**
(Don't reprimand the person who made it!)

Answer
Because the data on the system was incorrect

2 **Why was the data incorrect?**
(Don't just put the data right)

Answer
Because it wasn't checked when it came in from the supplier

3 **Why wasn't it checked?**
(Don't just put someone in charge of checking from now on)

Answer
Because it's nobody's job to check it

4 **Why wasn't someone assigned to it?**
(Don't just assign someone)

Answer
Incoming data wasn't regarded as part of the system

5 **Why not?**
(Don't just add it to the system)

Answer
We didn't really think about assigning roles to checking data, it wasn't on our list of tasks at the start – but it will be for all projects from now on!

As you gain experience, you'll get better at spotting bad projects and be able to compare them with good ones and see the difference. But it starts with standing back, observing, and thinking, rather than jumping in, reacting, and fixing problems. As a great project manager, you will always be thinking:

a. Who can fix this problem for me, so they can learn from the experience and I can have time to think about why it happened? Fixing a problem yourself is working "in" the machine rather than "on" it.

b. Ask *why* five times—approximately. The idea of the Five Whys is to keep asking why until you get to the root of the problem, which is invariably going to be a system fault (figure 120). By drilling into each response and actively engaging with what is being said, it's possible to get to a clearer idea of what's really causing the problem.

If you can get to the root cause, you fix the problem permanently, for all areas of this project. And you also fix it for projects to come in the future. Managers often don't like to ask why more than once, because inevitably the chain circles back and points to them. But this is the only way to fix root causes, to improve the machine of people.

Teams

> *Get the right people. Then no matter what all else you might do wrong after that, the people will save you. That's what management is all about.*
> — TOM DEMARCO

Teams are always challenging to run, and project teams are the most challenging, because they are often temporary. In many cases, you do not choose your team members; instead, you're at the mercy of whoever is available. And you don't have control over their pay; their line manager has that control. As a result, the team members often regard their line manager as their "real" boss and consider you temporary. Project management is therefore very much about influencing, rather than seeking to exert power.

You have this random group of people with different skills, many of whom you don't know that well, and you have to make them feel like a team and work like a team. At least you can be united around a common goal. That's an advantage of projects: there is usually an exciting end point or outcome, as opposed to teams that carry out *processes*, which never end. A team kick-off meeting can be a great way to foster a sense of unity. This is distinct from the project kick-off meeting; the team kick-off meeting occurs later, once the project has been given the green light.

The ideal team has a mixture of personalities: creative people, people who can spot flaws in plans, detail people, big-picture people, task people, caring people. But different types of people often clash. The biggest challenge in managing in teams is the mix of different personalities.

Here's a list of every personality needed on the ideal team. One person might be able to cover two or three traits or skills (will *have* to if your team has fewer than ten people), but they all need to be covered. If any skill set or personality is missing, it can negatively impact the outcome. You really need one of every type, and *only* one. If you have several of one type, they might clash (figure 121).

IDEAL TEAM MIX

fig. 121

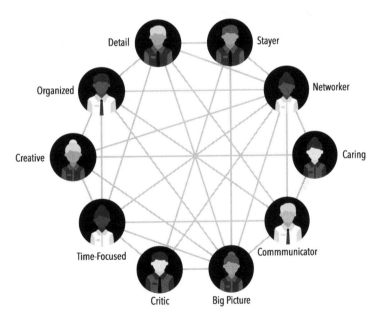

1. A creative ideas person
2. A critic to spot what's wrong with a plan, or what might go wrong
3. A big-picture person with long-term vision, unencumbered by details and short-term barriers
4. A detail person
5. A caring person to make sure everyone on the team is happy.

6. A time-focused, pushy person to get the job done on time
7. An organized, systems-focused person
8. A communicator, both to the team and the outside world
9. A networker, someone who collects people and ideas from the outside world
10. A stayer, someone with grit to plod though repetitive tasks until they are done

What can the project manager do about the inevitable problem of gaps, overlaps, and different personality types with different views and priorities and temperaments?

1. Recognize the problem and think about the mix of personalities that you have. What's missing?
2. If you do get a chance to recruit one more person to your project, obviously get the technical skill you need, but also think about their temperament. Which of the ten roles are you short of, and can you get this as part of the package?
3. As the project manager, make sure you get along well with all the types. Understand their different perspectives. Adapt your communication style so that you relate to each type. Value the strengths of each person even though you may be more apt to notice their weaknesses.
4. Encourage everyone on the team to do the same. When everyone appreciates each other's strengths and weaknesses, it's easier to distribute tasks according to strength and to plug any gaps.
5. Make sure everyone is aware of their strengths and is encouraged to use them. Sometimes people can't see their own strengths!
6. You might need to encourage team members to use their second or third choice of strengths as well as their top capability, if you have nobody with that as their number one choice.
7. Research has shown that the best size for a team is four. So if your project is employing ten people or forty people, it'll work best if you divide it into sub-teams of about four, maybe three or five. Come up with the mix that is most relevant to the tasks of that sub-team.
8. Watch for conflict and defuse it right away. This can come about between people who are too similar or too different. Get the issues on the table and push through to a resolution. Often the conflict is little more than a miscommunication or misunderstanding.

No one can whistle a symphony. It takes a whole orchestra to play it.
— H. E. LUCCOCK

Stretching Others

A key part of your role as a project manager is to stretch the people on your team so that every project is a learning and development opportunity for them. Consequently, you may not always want to give a task to the person most suited for it. Depending on the importance of the task, you may instead assign it to the person on the team who will benefit most from doing it.

Besides, if you constantly assign tasks to the person who can do them easily, it's likely that person will get bored and leave the company. What a waste! The best people want to be stretched too. If you have really strong team members, delegate parts of *your* job to them, so they can keep learning and developing. As you assign them bigger and harder tasks, they won't be quite as good at them as they were on the easy stuff, but that's OK. It's all part of their development, and they'll enjoy it. And it's freeing up more of your time, which is also beneficial.

Stretching others also includes preparing team members to be proficient project managers who have a good grasp of the 12-step process. Not only will this mean you have people ready to step in and manage projects, but you're helping with their career development.

Finally, when possible, let people set their own targets. They'll be more motivated if it's something they have set rather than been given arbitrarily. For instance, ask, "How long do you think this will take?" or "How good can you make this in the three weeks and for the two thousand dollars that we've been allocated?" An added benefit is that they will often aim higher than you would have asked them to!

Your job is to build a team of people who are better than you. Do that over and over again, and you're sure to be promoted.

Chapter Recap

» One of the key roles of the project manager is to be a great communicator, telling everyone what's going on, all the time. A communications plan outlines when the stakeholders will be updated, how often, and by what method.

» The two main ways that a PM communicates with others are diagrams and meetings. There are four types of meetings: team, progress, problem-solving, and communication meetings. They should not be mixed.

» Control is one of the key things to consider when you're leading anything, including projects. Generally speaking, the more you can delegate within the bounds of competence and trust, the better.

» Delegation is the single biggest way to save time, and the lack of delegation is the single biggest reason why project managers fail. Delegation is a key skill for project managers.

» The level of monitoring on a project is also known as "grip." How tight a grip do you keep on the people you have delegated to? More grip equals less risk, but also less motivation.

» Great project managers motivate the team, stay positive in the face of challenge, and create a compelling vision of the future that everyone can get behind.

» Everything is the project manager's fault. Get used to it.

» Coach and help others by asking five whys to get to the root cause of issues and resolve them. This is known as systems thinking.

» Recognize that great teams need a mix of personalities and skill sets, and that those differences may be the cause of angst and conflict. Always nip any conflict in the bud.

» Don't always assign tasks to the best people. Seek to stretch everyone on the team so they learn and develop while doing the project.

| 18 |

Managing a Project Manager

Chapter Overview

» Eventually, you'll be asked to manage other project managers
» Always ask your project managers to show you their plan
» Know what to ask for in your project plan based on size of project and experience

The focus of the book has been helping already busy employees and managers to understand and use a really simple, proven 12-step project management process without the time and stress of learning a complex software system. This process works. And it works regardless of the size or complexity of the project.

Once you use it, your project management success rate will skyrocket and your stress levels will plummet. The outcome may include your eventually being asked to manage other project managers. When this happens, the first thing you should do is give all your project team members this book and ask them to read it. The next thing you should do is reread this particular chapter.

For the ability to answer three simple questions: 'what to change?', 'what to change to?', and 'how to cause the change?' Basically, what we are asking for is the most fundamental abilities one would expect from a manager.
— ELIYAHU M. GOLDRATT

Show Me Your Plan

As a manager of those in charge of projects, the four most important words you can utter are "Show me your plan!" In business, too many people are embarking on projects without a plan, maybe not even recognizing that their project is a project. Years ago when I was an operations manager, I remember being asked to undertake various big challenging projects by my scary boss and mumbling, "OK, boss, leave it to me," and walking out of their office thinking, "Gosh, I hope I can do this!" I had no idea whether I could, and my boss had no idea that I had no idea. Sometimes I succeeded and sometimes I didn't. Maybe some of the jobs were impossible, or maybe my plan wasn't good enough. But certainly my boss was out of the loop, discovering at the end—too late, really—that I had either succeeded or failed. There should therefore be a quick and easy way to check that a project is going to be done well. This is just commercial common sense.

The starting point of that process is the request for a plan. If you ask the project manager for a plan, then one of five outcomes will occur:

1. **The project manager brings you a *great* plan.** You are able to see the plan in the context of all the other work in the department and possibly all the other plans in the company. You know you've got enough resources, and the time estimates all look viable. You can sleep soundly at night knowing it's a great plan. All you need to do is check in occasionally to make sure the project is on schedule according to the plan.

2. **The project manager brings you a plan that is pretty good but not perfect.** As a seasoned project manager yourself, you spot a few errors. Perhaps a task has been missed or the plan could cope with more concurrent tasks—or not so many. The plan gets amended and improved, and you can sleep soundly at night knowing it's now a great plan. All you need to do is check in occasionally to make sure the project is on schedule according to the plan.

3. **The project manager brings you a *terrible* plan.** It's full of holes, forgotten tasks, and estimates that are way too optimistic. There's no critical path and no Gantt chart. Maybe it's not a plan at all, but rather a list of tasks with some estimates attached. You pull this book off your shelf and go into coaching mode. Time to break out the Post-its. You revise the plan into something great. Phew! That was a close call; imagine what would have happened if you hadn't asked for the plan. You can sleep soundly at night knowing it's now a great plan. All you need to do is check in occasionally to make sure the project is on schedule according to the plan.

4. **The project manager reports back to say that they tried making a plan and realized that it's impossible to do the job in the timescale required with the resources available.** This is a great result, because now you know. Whether they're right or wrong, you can have a look at what they've got and see for yourself. Maybe you can help them

tweak the plan and make it possible within the time frame, using task overlapping, crashing the plan, or sliding the floating tasks. Maybe you'll confirm it can't be done. Maybe they really do need more time and/or more money. Either way, you can sleep soundly at night knowing that either the project has been shelved or the plan has been amended to make it work. Or a new plan has been created, with additional resources to make it possible. All you need to do is check in occasionally to make sure the project is on schedule according to the plan. Again, good thing you asked for that plan.

5. **The project manager says, "A plan? I don't know how to make a plan."** You say, "Great! Let me show you a really effective, simple way to create a plan." You grab some Post-its and get started. Again, you pull this book off your shelf and dive into coaching mode. They leave your office with a great plan, and you can sleep soundly at night knowing it's a great plan. All you need to do is check in occasionally to make sure the project is on schedule according to the plan.

Good Questions to Ask a Project Manager

Once you've seen the project manager's plan for the project and, if necessary, worked with them to tighten it up, you can rest easier that the project is in good hands and that it will be simple for the project manager and you to monitor.

But your role is not over. You need to keep in touch with your project manager and stay connected to progress. Below are some additional questions that you could ask as the project progresses. You don't have to go through this whole list, but these are the kinds of questions that can help you to get a clearer picture of what's going on while also making sure that your project manager is on top of these issues and knows the answers.

Of course, if your project manager is really experienced and brought you a great plan right off the bat, then you probably don't need to ask any of these questions. It will only annoy them if you do. Don't micromanage proven project managers. But if this is your project manager's first project, or if they seem a little wobbly or unsure, or if their plan wasn't great to start with, then ask all these questions. Your job is to support and coach less experienced project managers so they can gain experience and improve their project management capability with each project. It will also help you and the project manager to get a greater sense of what's really going on and alert them to any issues they may have missed.

1. What's the key driver in this project, do you think?
2. How did you list all your tasks? Can I see your work breakdown structure (WBS)?
3. How much contingency have you allowed for the whole job?
4. What are the best- and worst-case scenarios for time and cost? (If they know their stuff, they won't tell you outright the answer to questions 3 and 4 but instead will be a little cagey about revealing all their contingency publicly. If so, you can relax; they know what they're doing!)
5. Which are the critical tasks?
6. Have you planned the resources?
7. How many people will you need at the peak of the project?
8. Who do you need when, and have their bosses agreed to this?
9. What are the risks in this project?
10. How likely and serious is each one, and what have you done to reduce it?
11. Can I see your Gantt chart before the project kicks off?
12. Can I see your colored-in Gantt chart during the project? Are you coloring in when complete or proportionally?
13. How often do you have a progress meeting?
14. How much time are you allowing per week for managing this project?
15. (If running late) Are you going to slip the project or crash something? If so, what?
16. How are you monitoring the cost? And what's your estimate for the final cost at completion (or EAC, estimated cost at completion)?
17. (Once the project is over) Have you done a review? If so, what did you learn? If not, why not?
18. Where will you keep the review write-up?

What's in a Project Plan?

As a savvy manager of other project managers, you will already have asked to see the plan. But what should you expect to see when they hand it over? Obviously, this depends on the size and complexity of the project and the experience of the project manager. There are three options, so you and your project manager need to decide which is right for each project. Let's take a look at those three major options; much of this will be review for you, but it's helpful to see it organized into three categories.

Bare Minimum

Regardless of the size or complexity of the project or the experience of the project manager, the project plan should include the following as a bare minimum:

» **Project brief**: This outlines the purpose of the project and communicates that purpose and the agreed-upon approach, so that everyone on the project team is on the same page.

» **Gantt chart at the start**: This is absolutely essential. You should never start a project without a Gantt chart. It is a great tool for visualizing the whole project on one page.

» **Colored-in Gantt chart throughout the project**: This is also essential; otherwise, the plan gets shoved in a drawer and forgotten about. The colored-in Gantt chart ensures that the plan stays live and you can immediately see progress at a glance.

» **Project review**: This will ensure that learning is gained from the project for next time.

Ideal

The ideal project plan (especially if the project is becoming more complex or the project manager is less experienced) should include the following:

» **Bare minimum as above, plus ...**

» **Project initiation document (PID)**: This is a detailed plan of how the project will be executed. The PID is actually a whole collection of forms and agreements that add more rigor to the project. It goes into much more depth:
  • **Project justification**: Why are we doing this project, and why now?

  • **Options appraisal**: What are the other choices apart from doing this project? And why was this particular project chosen?

- **Exclusions**: What is *not* in the plan? For example, if the project is to build a hospital, maybe the plan does not include a parking lot or the recruiting of staff. Outlining what is not in the plan can often help to clarify the deliverables. Exclusions are definitely the project manager's friend!

- **Assumptions and deal-breakers**: This outlines assumptions or issues that will cause the project to stop. For example, the project may assume that the business is going to secure planning permission or that legislation affecting the project won't change.

- **Costs and sources of money**: How much is the project going to cost and where is the money coming from? Are there stage payments? If so, when will the money be released?

- **Spend over time**: This outlines the cost of the project over time so that everyone who needs to know that information does know it and has agreed to the budget.

- **Resources required**: This mainly applies to people but can also consist of equipment. This document shows where those people are coming from and that the department heads who "own" them have signed off on those people (or equipment) at that time for that period.

- **Risks**: What are the risks to the project and the company as a result of this project, and how are those risks being mitigated? What risks remain after mitigation?

» **Monthly reports**: These are excellent for keeping everyone informed, but they are also really useful long after the project is finished, allowing you to review the project and read exactly what was happening when.

» **Change request forms**: These documents are used to sign off on any changes to the project made by the stakeholders. If anyone wants you to make a change to the project, they have to sign for the extra time and money, or for any reductions to the scope in other areas in exchange. These forms are also the project manager's friend because they ensure that you have the right resources to finish the project and that stakeholders fully realize the implications of their changes and agree to those implications.

» **Rough Gantt of Gantts:** It doesn't have to be perfect or particularly pretty, but it can give senior leaders a better overview of all the projects and how those aspirations impact resources. It also helps to trigger proper prioritization conversations regarding which projects will be done and in what order.

» **Post-project review:** About two years after the project is finished, the post-project review looks at whether the expected benefits of the project were actually delivered.

» **Project control form:** This allows you to look at all the projects on one page and see which ones are running late or overspending.

Blank, printable templates for many of the above documents are available with your Digital Assets at go.quickstartguides.com/project.

Cover All Bases

If the project is especially large, important, or complex, then you may want to consider adding additional elements to the project plan to make sure you cover all the bases and gain even greater control over the project, thus making it more secure. You may want to add the following to the above "ideal" list:

» **Communications plan:** This is a one-page document that outlines who the project manager needs to keep informed of progress, whether they need to be consulted before action is taken or informed afterward, how often they should be kept informed, and by what method (meeting, email, etc.). This is sometimes done in step 1, or (better late than never) step 9, or not at all. It depends on the project. A blank template of a communications plan is available with your Digital Assets at go.quickstartguides.com/project.

» **Approval route:** This is a laid-down and agreed-upon process for who has to approve projects of a certain size. For example, if the project is larger than $1 million, it has to be signed off on by the finance director.

» **Escalation rules**: These outline what will happen if there is an issue, before there is an issue. For example, it may be agreed up front that if the project overspends by 5 percent or $10,000, whichever happens first, then it must be reported to the finance director. Escalation rules set simple trigger points for additional reporting.

» **"What is a project?" rules**: This defines what a project is, so that your project managers can't plead ignorance about not putting together a plan. In chapter 1, I said that a project is anything that has a start and an end point, involves more than ten tasks or more than two people, or takes longer than three weeks. A definition like this makes it clear to everyone when a project is a project. And it can help you decide whether you need the "bare minimum," the "ideal," or the "cover all bases" project plan.

» **Size of project**: This may include assigning levels to projects. For example, a business may have bronze, silver, and gold projects. Gold projects may be any project over, say, $20 million that takes more than a year to complete. If your project is a gold project, then all the bases need to be covered, whereas there may be more wiggle room in bronze or silver projects.

» **Progress visibility**: This is rare but it's a great idea: make all projects available for all to see. By using some cloud-based program like SharePoint or Google Docs, you can make the progress of all projects visible to everyone in the business.

Chapter Recap

» Once you use the proven 12-step process in this book and increase your project management success rate, it is almost inevitable that you will be asked to manage other project managers.

» This 12-step process not only gives your project managers a simple methodology to follow, but when they follow it, it gives *you* an excellent overview of the project and how it's progressing.

» As a manager of those in charge of projects, the four most important words you can utter are "Show me your plan!"

» There are five possible outcomes when you ask a project manager for their plan. But the request will illuminate the capability of your project manager and will allow you to feel safer or to recognize their need for further assistance. With any of the five outcomes, you will end up with a great plan.

» Consider asking your project managers additional questions. Exactly what you ask and how often will depend on the size and complexity of the project as well as the experience of the project manager. Don't micromanage proven project managers. Make sure you support and coach less experienced project managers.

» A savvy manager knows what to expect in the project plans. There are three major options: bare minimum, ideal, and cover all bases. Choose what is right for each project depending on its size and complexity.

| 19 |
Careers in Project Management

Chapter Overview
- » A great career path with huge demand
- » Pros and cons of project management
- » The best qualifications and what to avoid

Project managers rarely lack organizational visibility, enjoy considerable variety in their day-to-day duties, and often have the prestige associated with working on the enterprise's high-priority objectives.

—JACK MEREDITH AND SAMUEL MANTEL

In this final chapter, we are going to explore life after your first couple of projects. Most project managers don't have "project manager" in their job title. Instead, their title refers to some sort of management role, such as operations manager or head of engineering. Perhaps they are a publishing assistant, graphic designer, or in some other more junior role. Project management may not have even been in the job description, but the duties of that job include project management nonetheless. As I've said before, at its simplest, project management is getting stuff done as quickly and efficiently as possible. If that stuff is endless, then it's a process; if that stuff has a start and a finish line, then it's a project, and you are engaged in project management. So many jobs across all sectors and all levels involve some aspect of project management. And there is a huge demand for project management capability.

As soon as you have proven project management capability, your employability skyrockets. That is a fact. Most companies, even those that don't need to hire full-time specific project management professionals, look favorably on project management experience in all roles. Business is about getting things done, and project managers can get things done.

Project Management as a Job/Career

What are the possibilities for your career when you have some project management experience under your belt? What are your options if you don't yet have the experience but recognize the career potential of focusing on project management?

Advantages of Project Management as a Career

» It's enjoyable if you like variety. In project management there is rarely a dull moment. Each project is different and provides a new learning opportunity. Although the process of project management and how to pull it off is the same, the content of each project is always different.

» Project management is a transferable skill. Once you understand Gantt charts, you can run any project in any company of any size. You'll need a good team to handle the detail and help execute, but the skill set is the same.

» Project management will stay in demand, because companies are always growing and changing and creating new products.

» Employers pay well for proven project management skills. If you're not being well paid, look around for an employer who will appreciate you more.

» Projects always come to an end, and it feels good to get regular closure. Even if a project is especially tough, you know that it will eventually come to an end. If your everyday work is challenging, that might *never* end until you leave the company!

» It's great experience for other parts of your life. We all need project management in our lives, whether to manage our finances, take care of home and family demands, or plan a party or a vacation. Life is project management!

Disadvantages of Project Management as a Career

» Projects can be difficult because they are one-offs, which often means going into the unknown with tight constraints. But depending on your personality, this can be a positive.

» It's usually impossible to keep everyone happy. You can't do an excellent job really quickly for hardly any money, and yet that's what the customers always want, and often what the salespeople have already promised them!

» Projects rarely work out exactly according to plan. This can be frustrating, but as soon as you realize it's the nature of the beast, it's fine.

» Project management can be stressful. When the buck stops with you, then you are accountable, and any failures will be clearly visible. Often you don't fully control the people on your project, you're juggling a lot of things, and there is always a crunch point at the end.

» You are only visible if it goes badly. If it goes well, it was "easy," and you probably won't even be noticed.

Nevertheless, when it all comes together or a crisis is averted or the team solves a problem, there is no better job in the world. But hey, I'm biased.

QUICKCLIP

Watch my short video for more thoughts on career strategies.

To watch the QuickClip, use the camera on your mobile phone to scan the QR code or visit the link below.

or — www.quickclips.io/pm-17

SCAN ME   VISIT URL

Starting Out in Project Management

I strongly believe that experience is more important than qualifications. Of course it's best to have both, but what do you do if you recognize the opportunity of project management as a career but you are a newbie? The chances are, if you're reading this book, you are a newbie. But as long as you know what to do and how to document your experience as it grows, you will be able to demonstrate capability and secure that new role.

If you are just starting out:

1. Volunteer to help on as many projects as you can.

2. When helping, offer to do some, most, or all of the planning. You have a proven system now, so grab those Post-its and get planning.

3. Volunteer to run a small project to start with.

4. If there's nothing to volunteer for at work, try out your project management skills on something outside work. Maybe something at home, like renovating a kitchen or building a shed in the garden or organizing an amateur dramatic performance. You'll get some practice and build up your confidence.

5. Once you have a little more confidence, volunteer to help with larger projects. Pay attention to what works and what doesn't work, especially when you are not yet leading the project.

6. Find a project management mentor in your company to whom you can go for advice.

7. Document your roles in these projects, along with the plans and the results.

8. When going for interviews for project management roles, or roles that involve project management, take along your documentation. Show the interviewer your network diagrams, Gantt charts, and figures on performance. There's nothing as powerful as seeing real evidence. Even if a project is small, it shows that you understand the process.

9. When applying for an interview, remember that you can call and ask questions. Often the job advertisement will list a particular project management qualification. But this may only be their hoped-for scenario, or maybe the writer of the job ad doesn't really

understand project management. If you can demonstrate project management capability, you may still get an interview. Ask. The request for a qualification is often just an HR shortcut for demonstrating experience.

Qualifications in Project Management

Before we launch into the various qualifications and certifications, you should know that I don't have any certified project management qualifications. But I've managed a ton of projects and have spent my life wading through all the complexity of project management to simplify it down to a super-simple 12-step process. That's what I teach—project management for busy people.

I've considered the Project Management Institute's Project Management Professional (PMP) certification, the gold standard in project management qualifications (more on that in a moment). But I have never needed it. I've been doing projects as part of operations management positions, so it's not a prime requirement. But if you see your future in full-time project management and want to start making the big bucks, then you might want to add some qualifications to your experience for maximum impact and earning power.

There are two things to consider when you are looking at qualifications such as a project management certificate or degree: the qualification itself and who is providing it. Although there are countless options, I'm only going to focus on the really good and the really bad. Let's start with the really good.

Project Management Professional (PMP)

Project Management Professional (PMP) is the gold standard in project management qualifications and is issued by the Project Management Institute (PMI). The PMI is seen as the global governing body of project management, and PMP is globally recognized. In my opinion, PMP is the only PM qualification worth getting.

The reason I feel so strongly about PMP is that it is the only qualification that demands project management experience. If someone has the PMP certification, they have proven that they have project management experience and they have passed a pretty rigorous exam.

According to the PMI website, at time of writing (2021), to get PMP you need the following:

» A college degree
» 36 months of leading projects

» 35 hours of project management education/training or CAPM®️ Certification (see more on this in a moment)

OR

» A high school diploma or an associate degree (or global equivalent)
» 60 months of leading projects
» 35 hours of project management education/training or CAPM®️ Certification

Although the official wording states "leading projects," you just need to demonstrate experience on projects across five process groups:

1. Initiating planning
2. Executing
3. Controlling
4. Managing
5. Closing

If you are serious about doing PMP, then join the PMI first, because the exam is cheaper for members, and membership comes with a whole host of additional benefits. As of 2021, the cost of the exam was $405 for PMI members and $555 for nonmembers. Considering that membership is $129 per year, it's a no-brainer. Check with the PMI at the time for up-to-date figures and requirements.

In order to pass the exam, you need to do exam preparation. PMP is a little like a driving test. You might have plenty of driving experience and skill, but you can still fail the written test if you haven't studied the specific rules of the road in your country. There will be terminology and specific processes that you can't guess based only on your ability to drive. The same is true of PMP. The exam is tough, and rightly so. Otherwise, what's the point of having the qualification? It's why PMP is globally recognized as the best project management qualification, because it can only be passed by people who have proven experience and have done the work necessary to pass the exam.

Certified Associate in Project Management (CAPM)

Certified Associate in Project Management (CAPM) is also from PMI. As such, it is probably the next best option. The main difference is that you can get your CAPM without project management experience. If you're looking for a qualification that has meaning and can differentiate you from other candidates, then CAPM can enhance your credibility regarding managing projects. Having CAPM demonstrates that you understand the fundamentals and terminology of project management as well as the processes for effective project management. It is valid for five years.

To apply, you need the following:

» A secondary degree (high school diploma, associate degree, or the global equivalent)

» 23 hours of project management education completed by the time you sit for the exam. The PMI runs a Project Management Basics online course that fulfills this educational prerequisite.

At the time of writing, CAPM costs $225 for PMI members and $300 for nonmembers. But in my opinion, you would do better to focus on gaining project management experience, documenting that experience, and then, once you have the right amount, applying for the PMP and taking the exam.

There are other similar qualifications. For example, the UK version of PMI, the Association for Project Management (APM), offers some options such as the Project Fundamentals Qualification (PFQ), the Project Management Qualification (PMQ), and the Project Professional Qualification (PPQ). But again, experience is likely to trump all three. PMP and CAPM are also far more widely recognized.

Now for the bad …

PRINCE2 Foundation and PRINCE2 Practitioner

Don't go there! PRINCE2 is on the way out, so *PRINCE2 Foundation* and *PRINCE2 Practitioner* are on their way out too. They are also incredibly boring and not especially helpful, in my opinion.

They are too complex for most projects, you have to reregister every five years by retaking the exam, and they don't tell you *how* to do the many parts of project management. But the worst part of the PRINCE2 qualifications is that they are not based on practical experience. The foundation course is essentially learning the PRINCE2 method and passing an exam. There is no experience, proven or otherwise, baked into the qualification. Someone could therefore have PRINCE2 certification after a week of study but have limited or no experience. Whereas if someone has the PMP, you know they know what they're talking about.

There are also Agile qualifications, and many different providers issue them. It's a bit of a jungle. Agile is perhaps best suited to fast-moving environments such as IT, where the methodology uses short development cycles called sprints to focus on continuous improvement in the development of a product. If you're working in non-IT, for example with physical or construction projects, then Agile won't be for you anyway. Also, the world of Agile is less qualification-focused than traditional project management, so a qualification is less valuable. But if you do think an Agile qualification may be of interest, then check out the PMI offering called Agile Certified Practitioner (ACP).

Other Learning Options

If you don't yet have the experience but want to know more, and maybe want to pick and choose specific courses on Gantt charts or project management basics, I have loads of courses on LinkedIn Learning. There are also some great courses there from other authors, like Bonnie Biafore and Doug Rose.

Check out Udemy too, for lots of good project management courses, from me and others. Most of all, learn from your experience as a project manager, document your projects, and if and when you feel the time is right, get your PMP. It is the only qualification, in my opinion, worth having.

If you want to get into project management at a very senior level and want to be a full-time project manager, then I would definitely recommend PMP. If project management is something you enjoy as part of your main role and you want a way to be successful in project management, then follow the 12-step process outlined in this book. Document your experience as you go so that if you ever change your mind and want to go for PMP, you will have all the evidence to demonstrate that you qualify to take the exam.

Chapter Recap

>> Many jobs exist across all sectors and all levels that involve some aspect of project management. There is a huge demand for project management capability.

>> Proven experience is always more valuable than qualifications. Volunteer to get involved with projects, and document them so you can prove your involvement. Learn from the experience and get better with each project.

>> If you want to go into project management full time and you want the best of the best in terms of qualifications, then PMI's PMP is the only option.

>> Don't waste your time with Agile or PRINCE2 qualifications— proven expertise is not required to gain certification.

>> Focus on gaining more experience and, once you have enough, go for PMP.

Conclusion

Congratulations! You've made it through this rather epic book, and I hope you now understand—and maybe even like—my 12-step process. I hope you're motivated to try it out on your actual projects, as soon as you put this book down. You'll be amazed how well it will work. I have used the exact same process countless times throughout my career, on projects as small as creating a garden shed right up to multimillion-dollar public works projects spanning years, and it works every time. As you now know, it's composed of these 12 steps:

» Step 1: Define the Project
» Step 2: List the Tasks
» Step 3: Set the Running Order
» Step 4: Put Estimates on the Tasks
» Step 5: Crash the Plan
» Step 6: Use Gantt Charts

» Step 7: Resource Planning
» Step 8: Risk Planning
» Step 9: Monitor Progress
» Step 10: Monitor Costs
» Step 11: Modify the Plan
» Step 12: Review

Watch this video walk-through of the 12-step process.

To watch the QuickClip, use the camera on your mobile phone to scan the QR code or visit the link below.

or

www.quickclips.io/pm-18

📱 SCAN ME

🖥 VISIT URL

You can also watch my 12-step project management process explained with a dash of humor in a showstopping five-minute rap song! (clydebankmedia.com/PM-19)

I have been fortunate enough to spend my career in project management. It has taken me around the world many times, and the work has always been so varied and challenging. No two projects are ever the same. The teams on each project are always different, as are the objectives and the parameters. There is always scope for deeper learning. But the process outlined in this book has been consistent and has gotten me out of trouble more times than I can remember. Think of it as the skeleton of every project. It keeps things upright and everything in the right place.

Writing this book has been a project in itself, and I've used the 12 steps for this too. It works!

In many ways, project management is about life. All of us are project managing most of the time. At home, with our family, organizing the annual vacation, or pulling off the impossible at work. Most of us don't get shown a proven system, so we lurch from one close shave or near miss to the next. Putting out fires is the main activity of each day. But there is a better way, and now you know what it is.

I wish you all the very best using the 12-step process and would love to hear how you get on with it. Connect with me on LinkedIn, and let me know!

REMEMBER TO DOWNLOAD YOUR FREE DIGITAL ASSETS!

 **Project Brief Template**

 Monthly Monitoring Form

 Six Cost Performance Scenarios

 Risk Assessment Template

TWO WAYS TO ACCESS YOUR FREE DIGITAL ASSETS

Use the camera app on your mobile phone to scan the QR code or visit the link below and instantly access your digital assets.

or go.quickstartguides.com/project

 SCAN ME

 VISIT URL

About the Author

CHRIS CROFT

Chris Croft comes from an operations background, having started with an engineering degree from Cambridge, qualifying as a chartered engineer, and working as a senior manager in manufacturing for ten years. He gained an MBA and worked as a university lecturer for four years before starting his own training company in 1998.

He has written numerous books and also writes a regular blog at ChrisCroft.com on subjects ranging from project management to time management and happiness.

He is one of the world's most-viewed authors on Udemy.com and on LinkedIn Learning (previously Lynda.com), with 36 courses, 22,000 views a day, and 18 million students in total. His course Project Management Simplified is one of the most-viewed project management courses in the world, with 3,000 people a day watching it on LinkedIn Learning.

About QuickStart Guides

QuickStart Guides are books for beginners, written by experts.

QuickStart Guides® are comprehensive learning companions tailored for the beginner experience. Our books are written by experts, subject matter authorities, and thought leaders within their respective areas of study.

For nearly a decade more than 850,000 readers have trusted QuickStart Guides® to help them get a handle on their finances, start their own business, invest in the stock market, find a new hobby, get a new job—the list is virtually endless.

The QuickStart Guides® series of books is published by ClydeBank Media, an independent publisher based in Albany, NY.

Connect with QuickStart Guides online at www.quickstartguides.com or follow us on Facebook, Instagram, and LinkedIn.

Follow us @quickstartguides

Glossary

Accrual Accounting
A system of accounting that includes not only money that has been received and spent, but also what is due to come in and scheduled to go out. It offers a more accurate picture of the likely longer-term financial situation than does cash accounting, which does not include scheduled payments and receipts. (See also Cash Accounting.)

Agile
A collection of principles used in project management, focusing on small, workable, incremental delivery. The requirements, plans, and results are evaluated and reevaluated continuously. This helps the Agile team to respond quickly to changes either inside or outside the project.

Agile Manifesto
A set of principles and values embodying the Agile process, created in 2001 by a group of software developers.

Arrow Diagramming Method (ADM)
A schedule network diagramming technique where scheduled activities in a project are represented by the use of arrows. ADM is essentially another name for project evaluation and review technique (PERT).

Association for Project Management (APM)
The UK equivalent of the US-based Project Management Institute. It is the only chartered body for the project profession, with over 35,000 individual members and more than 500 organizations participating in its Corporate Partnership Programme.

Basecamp
An online project management platform that allows for sharing of updates and progress with team members.

Business Case
The justification for a proposed project or undertaking on the basis of its expected commercial benefit.

Cash Accounting
A system of accounting that includes money that has been received or spent, giving a definite picture of an organization's finances at any given moment—but not including scheduled or committed spend, or monies due to be received at a later date. (See also Accrual Accounting.)

Certified Associate in Project Management (CAPM)
A project management qualification, one step down from Project Management Professional (PMP). Both are issued by the Project Management Institute (PMI) but achievement of CAPM does not require proven project management experience.

Change Request Form
A piece of paperwork that officially indicates a change being made to the parameters of a project. Whenever a stakeholder makes this kind of change, the project manager should insist on a signed-off change request form so that everyone knows and understands the ramifications of the change (more cost or time) before they occur.

Communications Plan

A plan that clarifies how and when stakeholders are to be kept updated on the progress or problems of a project. It is always wise to agree on a communications plan at the start of each project or once a project has been approved.

Contingency

Extra time or money that is deliberately added to tasks, especially those on the critical path, to allow for a margin of error in the estimates and therefore to help keep the project on track.

Cost Performance Index (CPI)

A method that allows one to forecast changes to cost based on the actual costs incurred in an earlier part of the project. CPI is calculated by dividing the actual cost by the planned cost.

Crash the Plan

The process of reducing time or cost in a plan to better meet stakeholder aspirations.

Critical Path Analysis (CPA)

See Critical Path Method.

Critical Path Method (CPM)

Also known as critical path analysis (CPA). A project management methodology that allows one to identify the amount of time necessary to finish each task and therefore identify the critical path through the project. The critical path is the shortest time or most realistic time in which the project can be completed.

Dependency Chart

A visual illustration of the chain of dependencies that must occur for a project to be delivered—essentially another name for a network diagram.

Dynamic Systems Development Method (DSDM)

A technique using eight principles to direct a team and create a mindset of delivering on time and within budget. Principles include focusing on the business need, delivering on time by timeboxing work, and emphasizing collaboration with end users, team members, business representatives, and other stakeholders.

Earned Value Analysis (EVA)

A calculation that reveals whether a project is within budget and on schedule at a given moment. It takes into consideration the work that has been accomplished and the costs incurred so far with respect to the original budget and schedule.

Endowment Effect

A concept from behavioral economics referring to the emotional bias that causes individuals to value an object they own more highly than its market value. Human beings like and are more engaged with things they had a hand in coming up with or creating.

Excel

An easy-to-use spreadsheet program that can make fabulous Gantt charts too. Part of the Microsoft Office suite of products.

Extreme Programming (XP)

A software development methodology whose goal is to deliver software as needed, when it is needed. It has short development cycles, focusing on the needs of today rather than those of the future, sometimes called the "You aren't gonna need it!" or YAGNI approach.

Feature-Driven Development (FDD)

An Agile methodology consisting of five activities: the development of an overall model, the building of a feature list, the planning by feature, the designing by feature, and the building by feature. FDD is scalable even to large teams due to the concept of "just enough design initially" (JEDI).

First Kick-Off Meeting

The initial meeting between the stakeholders and the project manager in which the stakeholders outline the desired outcome of the project. The project manager must then determine whether it's possible to deliver the project within the parameters that the stakeholders have asked for.

Flow Diagram

A specific type of activity diagram (also known as a flowchart) that communicates a sequence of actions or movements within a complex system. Similar to a network diagram, but network diagrams can't have branches or loops.

Gantt Chart

A horizontal bar chart showing the start, finish, and duration of each task in a project; can also show the dependencies between tasks. Popularized by American engineer Henry Gantt in 1910. Gantt charts take project visualization up a notch from the network diagram.

Gantt of Gantts

A Gantt chart that shows, on one page, the resource profile of all the projects a business or department is undertaking. It allows the boss to see at a glance where each project is against expectations.

Granularity

Fine detail. In projects, it relates to how far each task needs to be broken down in the planning process. Each identified task should be able to be broken down enough so that either one person or one team can be responsible for that task.

Iron Triangle

The combination of the three major constraints on any project: time, money, and quality. It is impossible to deliver a project quickly, well, and cheaply; there is always a trade-off. Two of the three are possible, but something has to give.

Kanban

A workflow management method for defining, managing, and improving services that deliver knowledge work. It aims to help one visualize their work, maximize efficiency, and minimize work in progress and therefore throughput times.

Key Driver

The factor in a project's iron triangle of money, time, and quality that outweighs or is considered more important than the others by the project owner. It is the criterion which, if not met, will cause the project owner to consider the project a failure.

Lean

A way of thinking about a project that is focused on creating added value with fewer resources and less waste. Also, a practice consisting of continuous experimentation to achieve perfect value with zero waste.

Managing Successful Programmes (MSP)

A best-practice program management framework. When an organization undertakes a large, complex transformational change program, it uses MSP to break down the overall change into smaller, more manageable interrelated projects.

Microsoft Project

Project management software that must be purchased in addition to the usual Microsoft Office suite of Word, Excel, and PowerPoint.

Minimum Viable Product (MVP)

The minimum workable offering of a new product or service that can be tested in the market and fine-tuned. If customers buy and like the MVP, then the business knows it's onto a winner.

Monday.com

A cloud-based work operating system where teams create workflow apps to run and share their processes, projects, and everyday work.

Monthly Monitoring Form

A management tool in the form of a one-page summary of all the projects going on in a business at any one time. Outlines the name of each project, the progress, and the spend to date.

Network Diagram

The visual representation of a project showing what needs to be done in what order by when. The term originates in computing, where a network diagram would visualize a computer network, but its use has extended to other areas, including project management.

PMBOK

An acronym for Project Management Body of Knowledge, also sometimes called the PMI recommended process. First published by the Project Management Institute (PMI) in 1987. PMBOK is the collective accumulation of proven knowledge about project management over the last 100 years.

PMBOK Lite

The author's slimmed-down version of PMBOK. It is the 12-step process outlined in this book, all one really needs to know about project management to deliver any project.

Post-Project Review

A review that takes place a couple of years after the delivery of a project to assess whether or not the project delivered its expected or promised benefits. Doesn't usually involve the project manager but rather senior management and the project owner.

Precedence Diagram

An illustration where activities or tasks in a project are displayed graphically as boxes (which can also be referred to as nodes). The activities are then linked together via a line or arrow that represents the logical relationships between tasks.

PRINCE2

A highly structured project management methodology originating in IT projects in 1989. Designed to cover all types of projects, although it still has a distinct IT flavor.

PRINCE2 Foundation

An organization that assesses whether a candidate can recall and understand the PRINCE2 project management method.

PRINCE2 Practitioner

A certification that confirms one's ability to apply understanding of the PRINCE2 project management method in context.

Product Breakdown Structure (PBS)

A hierarchy like a work breakdown structure (WBS), only instead of activities it shows outcomes or deliverables. The final product is at the top, with all that's needed to make that product outlined underneath.

Project Brief

An outline of the purpose of a project; it communicates that purpose and the agreed-upon approach so that everyone on the project team is on the same page.

Project Evaluation and Review Technique (PERT)

Another way to create a network diagram, only instead of focusing on tasks and activities as CPM does, it focuses on events and deliverables. Also known as "activity on arrow" and occasionally as arrow diagramming method (ADM).

Project Initiation Document (PID)

A detailed plan for how a project will be executed. The PID outlines what, why, how, who, when, and how much, but in much greater detail than a project brief or business case.

Project Management Process

A term for project management that defines what to do when in a project. It outlines all the activities from initiation through closure of a project, in sequential order.

Project Management Professional (PMP)

The gold standard in project management qualifications, issued by the Project Management Institute (PMI). The PMI is seen as the global governing body of project management, and PMP is globally recognized.

Risk Exposure

The assessment of potential loss or damage that may be caused by a project or to a project. All efforts need to be made to identify risks in a project and to mitigate those risks, if possible.

Running Order

The assessment of all the tasks that need to be done, what must happen first and what order the rest of the tasks should be completed in, to determine how long the whole project will take.

Schedule Performance Index (SPI)

A method of forecasting any changes to the expected finish date of an entire project, based on the actual time taken to complete an earlier part of the project.

Scrum

A process framework used to manage product development and other knowledge projects. It provides a way for teams to establish a hypothesis of how they think something works, try it out, reflect on the experience, and make the appropriate adjustments.

Scrumban

A versatile approach to workflow management that combines the structure of the Scrum technique with the flexibility and visualization of the Kanban technique. Both Scrum and Kanban live under the Agile banner.

Second Kick-Off Meeting

A meeting at which the project manager comes back to the stakeholder group and explains whether what they want can be done within the parameters set out in the first kick-off meeting.

Sprint

A term used in Scrum that relates to a short period of time, often two weeks, in which the team must finish a specific task, milestone, or deliverable.

Stakeholder

Anyone who has a stake in a project, whether doing it or affected by it. This includes team members, the project manager, the project owner, the sponsor, and the end customer.

Standard Deviation

A statistical term that relates to the amount of variation or dispersion across a data set.

TeamGantt

A project management platform that gives users the ability to execute tasks without losing sight of the big picture.

Trello

A visual collaboration tool that creates a shared perspective for a team on any project in a fun, flexible, and rewarding way, using drag-and-drop within and between columns.

Wrike

A comprehensive collaboration and project management tool that helps users manage projects from start to finish, providing full visibility and control over tasks.

Work Breakdown Structure (WBS)

A systematic way to show all the work that will be needed in a project. Essentially a tree diagram that lists all the tasks and shows the relationship between those tasks, like a company organizational chart or a family tree.

XP (Extreme Programming)

A software development methodology whose goal is to deliver software as needed, when it is needed. It has short development cycles, focusing on the needs of today rather than those of the future, sometimes called the "You aren't gonna need it!" or YAGNI approach.

References

CHAPTER 2

Agile Manifesto. Accessed September 22, 2021. http://agilemanifesto.org/.

Association for Project Management. Accessed September 21, 2021. https://www.apm.org.uk/about-us/.

Axelos. n.d. What is PRINCE2. Accessed September 22, 2021. https://www.axelos.com/best-practice-solutions/prince2/what-is-prince2/.

Conrad, Andrew. 2019. "What Exactly Is Agile? A Definition of Agile Project Management." Capterra. November 18. Accessed September 22, 2021. https://blog.capterra.com/definition-of-agile-project-management/.

Higgs, Malcolm, and Deborah Rowland. 2000. "Building change leadership capability: 'the quest for change competence'." *Journal of Change Management*, 1:2, 116–131. DOI: 10.1080/714042459

Higgs, Malcolm, and Deborah Rowland. 2005. "All changes great and small: Exploring approaches to change and its leadership." *Journal of Change Management*, 5:2, 121–151. DOI: 10.1080/14697010500082902

Isern, Joseph, and Caroline Pung. 2006. "Organizing for successful change management: A McKinsey global survey." The McKinsey Quarterly.

Kotter, John P. 1990. *A Force for Change: How Leadership Differs from Management*. New York: Simon & Schuster.

Project Management Institute. Accessed September 21, 2021. https://www.pmi.org/about/learn-about-pmi/.

Visual Paradigm. n.d. "What is PMBOK in Project Management?" Accessed September 22, 2021. https://www.visual-paradigm.com/guide/pmbok/what-is-pmbok/.

What Is PRINCE2. n.d. PRINCE2 Benefits. Accessed September 28, 2021. https://www.whatisprince2.net/prince2-certification/prince2-benefits.

CHAPTER 3

Goldratt, Eliyahu M. 2016. *The Goal: A Process of Ongoing Improvement*. London: Routledge.

Kahneman, Daniel. 2011. *Thinking, Fast and Slow*. New York: Penguin.

Reiss, Geoff. 2007. *Project Management Demystified*, 3rd Edition. London: Routledge.

CHAPTER 4

Schilpp, Paul A. 1970. *Albert Einstein, Philosopher-Scientist*. Carbondale: Library of Living Philosophers.

CHAPTER 13

Reiss, Geoff. 2007. *Project Management Demystified*, 3rd Edition. London: Routledge.

CHAPTER 18

Goldratt, Eliyahu M. 2016. *The Goal: A Process of Ongoing Improvement*. London: Routledge.

Senge, Peter M. 1990. *The Fifth Discipline: The Art and Practice of the Learning Organization*. New York: Doubleday.

Index

MVP. *See* Minimum viable product

client time minimization benefits of, 27
confusions regarding, 25–26
contingency, 29
customer involvement, 39
dependencies accounted for by, 27
disadvantages of, 28–29
editions of, 24
history of, 24
inflexibility of, 28, 35
PRINCE2 versus, 34, 40*f*–41*f*
task lists and, 28–29
as time-consuming, 28
tools included in, 22*f*
PMBOK Lite
advantages of, 26–27
Agile versus, 36
definition of, 26
indications for, 41*f*–42*f*
planning in, 34
when to use, 41*f*–42*f*
PMI. *See* Project Management Institute
PMO. *See* Project management office
PMP. *See* Project Management Professional
Positivity, 293–294
Post-its
critical path created using, 114–115
Gantt chart created using, 149, 156, 169–170
network diagram created from, 83–88, 139
running order created using, 83–88, 150, 151*f*, 170, 179
team participation with, 87, 150
Post-project review, 253–254, 309
PPQ. *See* Project Professional Qualification
Precedence diagram, 91
Precedence diagram method, 94
Premises, 135
PRINCE, 29
PRINCE2
advantages of, 32–33
Agile versus, 35, 40*f*–41*f*
bureaucratic nature of, 34
characteristics of, 40*f*–41*f*
components of, 30*f*, 30–32
definition of, 29–30
disadvantages of, 33–35
expensiveness of, 34
indications for, 41*f*–42*f*
inflexibility of, 34–35
ownership of, 30
PMBOK versus, 34, 40*f*–41*f*
popularity of, 30
principles of, 30–31
processes of, 31–32
project managers and, 35
for public-sector projects, 33
roles and responsibilities in, 33
themes of, 31
three-level approval technique of, 56–62, 57*f*

time requirements for, 34
when to use, 41*f*–42*f*
PRINCE2 Foundation, 319–320
PRINCE2 Practitioner, 319–320
Problem-solving meeting, 280–281
Process(es)
in businesses, 16
continuum of, 15*f*
definition of, 15
moving as, 15
in PMBOK, 36
in PMBOK Lite, 36
of PRINCE2, 31–32
project versus, 12*f*, 13, 15–16
Product breakdown structure, 97
Progress meetings, 280–281
Progress monitoring
communicating to stakeholders as, 217–218
cost monitoring and, 223–224, 273
delegation of, 286
Gantt chart for, 144–146, 145*f*, 213–217, 224, 232
PMBOK's benefit for, 27
Progress visibility, 310
Project(s)
abandoning of, 248
agreements and outcomes in writing, 55–56
assessment of, 52–53
behind-schedule, 247–248, 273
benefit delivered by, 16, 255
in businesses, 16
change from, 16, 21, 292
characteristics of, 12–16
continuum of, 15*f*
deadline for, 13
defining/definition of, 14, 18, 45–64, 135, 285, 310
details of, 59
duration of. *See* Project duration
ending of, 13
everyday examples of, 11, 14
finish line for, 13
justification for, 307
large. *See* Large projects
life span of, 13
linear. *See* Linear projects
for making something new, 14, 67
multiple. *See* Multiple projects
new house as, 14
novelty of, 16
objectives for, 48–49, 59, 67, 260
as one-offs, 314
overbudget, 226*f*, 226–227, 249
parallel, 85*f*, 85–87, 149, 174
prioritizing of, 191
process versus, 12*f*, 13, 15–16
quality of, 47
resource-limited, 188
running late, 247–248, 273

WHAT DID YOU THINK?

We rely on reviews and reader feedback to help our authors reach more people, improve our books, and grow our business. We would really appreciate it if you took the time to help us out by providing feedback on your recent purchase.

It's really easy, it only takes a second, and it's a tremendous help!

NOT SURE WHAT TO SHARE?

Here are some ideas to get your review started…

- *What did you learn?*
- *Have you been able to put anything you learned into action?*
- *Would you recommend the book to other readers?*
- *Is the author clear and easy to understand?*

TWO WAYS TO LEAVE AN AMAZON REVIEW

Use the camera app on your mobile phone to scan the QR code or visit the link below to record your testimonial and get your free book.

SCAN ME

or

www.quickstartguides.review/projects

VISIT URL

GET YOUR NEXT
QuickStart Guide®
FOR FREE

Leave us a quick video testimonial on our website and we will give you a **FREE *QuickStart Guide*** of your choice!

RECORD TESTIMONIAL

SUBMIT TO OUR WEBSITE

GET A FREE BOOK

TWO WAYS TO LEAVE A VIDEO TESTIMONIAL

Use the camera app on your mobile phone to scan the QR code or visit the link below to record your testimonial and get your free book.

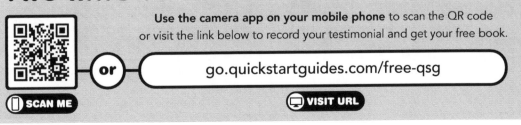

SCAN ME

or

go.quickstartguides.com/free-qsg

VISIT URL

SAVE 10% ON YOUR NEXT
QuickStart Guide®

USE CODE: QSG10

www.quickstartguides.shop/business

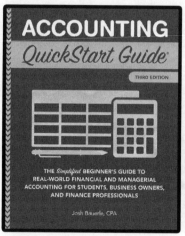

www.quickstartguides.shop/accounting

www.quickstartguides.shop/investing

www.quickstartguides.shop/html-css

CLYDEBANK MEDIA

QuickStart Guides®

PROUDLY SUPPORT ONE TREE PLANTED

One Tree Planted is a 501(c)(3) nonprofit organization focused on global reforestation, with millions of trees planted every year. ClydeBank Media is proud to support One Tree Planted as a reforestation partner.

Every dollar donated plants one tree and every tree makes a difference!

Learn more at www.clydebankmedia.com/charitable-giving or make a contribution at onetreeplanted.org.

Made in the USA
Las Vegas, NV
28 March 2024

87891131R00201